MASCULINITY AND ITS CHALLENGES IN INDIA

MASCULINITY AND ITS CHALLENGES IN INDIA

Essays on Changing Perceptions

Edited by Rohit K. Dasgupta and
K. Moti Gokulsing

Foreword by Ruth Vanita

McFarland & Company, Inc., Publishers

Jefferson, North Carolina

LIBRARY OF CONGRESS CATALOGUING-IN-PUBLICATION DATA

Masculinity and its challenges in India : essays on changing
  perceptions / edited by Rohit K. Dasgupta and K. Moti
  Gokulsing ; foreword by Ruth Vanita.
      p.   cm.
  Includes bibliographical references and index.

  ISBN 978-0-7864-7224-6
  softcover : acid free paper

    1. Masculinity—Social aspects—India.   2. Men—India—
Social conditions.   3. Men—Sexual behavior—India.   4. Power
(Social sciences)—India.   5. Man-woman relationships—India.
6. India—Social conditions—1947–   7. Social change—India.
I. Dasgupta, Rohit K.   II. Gokulsing, K. Moti.
HQ1090.7.I4M36 2014
305.310954—dc23   2013041591

BRITISH LIBRARY CATALOGUING DATA ARE AVAILABLE

Front cover: film still from *My Brother Nikhil,*
2005 (© Anticlock Films)

Manufactured in the United States of America

McFarland & Company, Inc., Publishers
  Box 611, Jefferson, North Carolina 28640
  www.mcfarlandpub.com

Acknowledgments

This book would not exist without the hard work of the contributors. We have been extremely lucky to work with a group of very generous and exciting academics. Our main acknowledgement is to them.

Some of the ideas that have helped conceive this book were presented in conferences at the University of Sussex, University of Leeds, University of the Arts London and at an invited lecture at Jadavpur University organized by Sayantan Dasgupta and the Department of Comparative Literature.

The editors are indebted to Sanjay Srivastava and Ruth Vanita for their enthusiasm and help. We would also like to acknowledge the help and support of the various people who read parts of the manuscript and offered significant feedback and suggestions: Lord Meghnad Desai of the London School of Economics, Professor Ashis Nandy of the Centre for the Study of Developing Societies, Richard Allen of New York University, Wimal Dissanayake of the University of Hawaii, Steven Baker of the British Council, Lipi Begum of the London College of Fashion, and Gurmit Singh of the University of Leeds. We would also like to thank Onir and Anticlock Films for granting us permission to use the cover image.

Rohit would also like to thank the following people for their encouragement and support: Sara Davidmann of the London College of Communication, Sharif Mowlabocus of the University of Sussex, William Raban of the London College of Communication and Sunil Gupta. On a more personal note Rohit would like to thank his parents and family for their encouragement and Tim for his patience and constant support. He would also like to thank his friends in India and London.

Table of Contents

Foreword

RUTH VANITA

Over the last decade, Women's Studies departments worldwide have been changing their names to incorporate words like "gender" and "sexuality." This is in part a response to the recognition that if, as de Beauvoir famously put it, one is not born but becomes a woman then men too are not born but are made. This book explores the different ways men are made in modern Indian cultures.

When I show icons, both medieval and modern, in my classes on Hindu texts and traditions, American students often react with surprise to what they perceive as the feminine appearance of the Gods, whom they have difficulty distinguishing from the Goddesses. This may partly be put down to their preconceptions of what constitutes manliness, but is also partly due to the androgyny of both male and female ideals as represented in icons of the divine. While demons almost always sport large moustaches, Gods are usually smooth-skinned and without facial hair, a tribute to their eternal youth, but also to an androgynous ideal of beauty. Furthermore, both Gods and Goddesses generally wear bright-colored decorative clothing and jewelry.

Enquiry into Indian nationalist internalization of Victorian ideals of manhood began with the seminal work of Ashis Nandy and has been carried forward by numerous scholars. This book is part of the new wave of scholarship that more fully incorporates self-chosen or ascribed sexual identities into the enquiry. As Nandy pointed out and scholars in the present volume confirm, the nineteenth century constitutes a turning-point of sorts, especially the period after 1857 when the self-view of both Hindu and Muslim men took a severe battering.

In my recent work on Urdu poetry and on what I term the poetics of play, from the late eighteenth century to the late nineteenth, I found that perhaps the most important indicator of the shift in perception and practice of masculinity is urban Indian men's transformed relationship to dress. In pre-1857 north Indian urban cultures, many men routinely wore jewelry and brightly colored clothing, footwear and headgear. On special occasions, they also wore clothes richly decorated with gold borders, embroidery, spangles and beads. Such attire was not read by Indians as signaling effeminacy or any particular sexual predilection, although it is relevant that attraction to a beautiful young person of either sex was considered par for the course and had no bearing on a man's masculinity. Noticing and commenting positively on another man's looks and dress was common in both poetry and prose at this time.

Bright, shining clothing was not confined to young men. In 1803, the poet Qatil described his friend, the poet Insha Allah Khan, pen-name "Insha" (Elegant Style), preparing for Holi at the court of the Nawab of Awadh: "Insha Allah Khan Insha ... in a robe specially gifted to him as an honour, the yellow saffron color of which put Kashmir to shame, and the fringe of which shone like shimmering water in a garden of marigolds, set out for the festivities."[1]

Insha had served as a soldier and was renowned for his pugnacity. He was also known for his beauty, and his own writings, prose as well as verse, reveal his delight in dress. This interest was not at all unique to him. His intimate friend, Sa'adat Yar Khan, pen-name "Rangin" (Colorful), a professional soldier, was equally interested in sartorial matters, and describes himself as wearing a sparkling scarf on his head. Many Urdu poets of the period, in Lucknow, in Delhi and in Hyderabad, show a detailed and wide-ranging knowledge of the provenance of different types of fabric, men's as well as women's outfits, jewelry, make-up and shoes. When I read this poetry to modern audiences, both in India and in the U.S. or U.K., many people can hardly believe that men could be so knowledgeable about the nuances of female attire.

When urban upper and middle-class Indian men switched to Western dress over the course of the century following 1857, followed by upwardly mobile lower-middle class and even some working-class men in cities, the switch was accompanied by shedding color and jewelry. With this shift, we lost a whole way of being and a whole way of seeing. The Gandhi-led nationalist movement countered the switch to Western dress with *khadi*, but significantly the *khadi* worn by men was usually white or drab colored. In Indian villages, although the switch to Western dress is making rapid inroads, poorer men who have not made the switch continue to incorporate color into their attire in the form of such items as turbans, or *tahmats*, and often continue to wear these when they migrate to cities; also, in cities, Sikh men's turbans constitute, as it were, a bright spot.

I can testify from experience that working in a women's college in Delhi, where one is routinely immersed in a sea of rainbow colors, is vastly different from working on a campus in the U.S., where an occasional spot of brightness is all one sees in an expanse of gray, black, white and dull blue. Over time, I suspect, the difference in exposure to color affects one's emotional state and one's orientation towards work and play.

That attitudes to pleasure, play and sexuality in India underwent a major change in the colonial period proper is now well established. What is less researched and perhaps less measurable is the effect on the individual mind and being of losing a direct sensual (tactile as well as visual) relationship with color and glitter. Equally important are the emotional effects for everyone of losing about half the color visible in any Indian city on any given day.

It is often assumed, partly due to the influence of English Romanticism, reinforced by anti-consumerist thought, that emotions are properly directed only to living beings and to nature. I would venture to suggest, though, that emotional well-being may also be connected to a happy relationship with beautiful and sensually pleasurable material objects, such as clothing and jewelry. In the modern West, the importance of this category of emotions for men in particular has been kept alive largely by men who do not see themselves as exclusively heterosexual, beginning with Oscar Wilde (whom Nandy rightly characterized as an internal resister of the norms of Victorian masculinity).

In twentieth-century India, cinema has been perhaps the most important nationwide transmitter of past traditions of masculinity imbricated with emotion, *rang*, *rasa*, and play. Over the last few decades, designers, both female and male (many of them gay male), have reintroduced color into male festive wear, so that middle-class men who, earlier in the century, would have worn only dark-hued Western suits to weddings and celebrations are now equally likely to wear bright-colored *kurta-pajamas*, *sherwanis* and shawls. This perhaps signals a new self-confidence displayed also by many Indian women today whose wardrobes even-handedly incorporate Indian and Western clothing.

Masculinity studies is now working in tandem with gender and sexuality studies and sexuality rights movements to change perceptions of gender both on and off Indian campuses. The explorations in this volume move in many directions, from cinema, fiction and comic books to sexual identities and terminologies. Continuing earlier discussions and also opening up new avenues of enquiry, these essays signal the rapidly expanding focus of gender and sexuality studies in the Indian context.

Note

1. Quoted in *Kulliyat-e Insha*, ed., Khalil-ur Rahman Da'udi (Lahore: Lahore Majlis-i Taraqqi-yi Adab,1969), 51. Translation mine.

Ruth Vanita is a professor of liberal studies and women's studies at the University of Montana. She is the author of Gender, Sex and the City: Urdu Rekhti Poetry in India *(2012),* Gandhi's Tiger and Sita's Smile: Essays on Gender, Sexuality and Culture *(2006), and* Love's Rite: Same-Sex Marriage in India and the West *(2005).*

Introduction: Perceptions of Masculinity and Challenges to the Indian Male

ROHIT K. DASGUPTA *and*
K. MOTI GOKULSING

"The physical organisation of the Bengali is feeble even to effeminacy. He lives in a constant vapour bath. His pursuits are sedentary, his limbs delicate, his movements languid."— Thomas Babington Macaulay, 1880:566

"A boy trying to pursue girls is common but boys pursuing boys has become a fashion. Gay culture in Hyderabad is increasing drastically. All the gay men in Hyderabad go to clubs or pubs once every week or ten days to celebrate. They drink and dance with whomever they want."— TV9's homophobic story: Gay Culture Rampant in Hyderabad, 2011

"Gender inequality is a problem in this country."— Manmohan Singh, Prime Minister of India, NDTV: 28 December, 2012

The quotes above are indicative of the changes that are taking place in Indian society with regard to the bipolar world of distinctive masculine and feminine attributes. Following in the footsteps of the feminist movement of the 1960s and 1970s, the new emerging field of masculinities and men has made some significant progress in recent years. R. W. Connell's publications since the late 1980s and in particular, her landmark book *Masculinities: The Science of Masculinity* published in 1995 have provided a useful theoretical account of gender and can be used as a starting point for the discussion of masculinities. One of its central points is that there is not one model of masculinity but rather multiple masculinities. As far as Indian masculinities are concerned, the available literature which includes some interesting work by Nandy (1983), Srivastava (2004), Osella and Osella (2006) is rather limited. The interdisciplinary essays in the current volume are aimed at helping to close this gap.

5

The subtitle of Connell's book *Masculinities* is *Science of Masculinity* and while some aspects of science such as, for example, clinical psychology, contributes to our understanding of masculinities, the main focus of the essays in the current volume is on how masculinities are socially, culturally and historically shaped. But a prime question we are confronted with is: how are masculinities formed and what contributions can they make to our understanding of the shaping of Indian men today?

One of the significant outcomes of the feminist movement since the 1960s has been to argue successfully that there is a distinction between sex and gender and that sex does not determine gender. This has led to a substantial literature exploring gender differences and their origins. Early feminist writers were mainly concerned with women's subordination in society and concepts of femininity. There has been limited attention focused on men and masculinity has been regarded as straightforward and unproblematic. But gender and sex have an ever-evolving meaning and recent feminist writers have criticized the idea that there is some essential female experience that divides all women from all men. Of the limits of the 1970s gender theory, Lynne Segal (1999:42) observed:

> Many men have little or no purchase on the power that is supposed to be the prerogative of their sex while a significant minority of women have access to considerable power and privilege. Gender binaries never exist in the contexts of race, class, age, sexual orientation and multiple other belongings — each with their deeply entrenched connections to power and authority, or the lack of it [quoted in Elliott 2009:190].

It is useful to remember that social movements in, for example, education, media, sports, religion, family and work helped the feminist movement of the 1960s and 1970s. That period also saw the rise of gay liberation in many western countries. It was, however, Queer Theory that emerged in the USA during the 1980s which opposed the idea that heterosexuality was the only normal and natural sexuality and homosexuality was rejected as a distinct category of people and behavior (Fulcher and Scott 2003:170).

However, just as there is a great diversity in the feminist movement so that we speak of "feminisms," so too is there diversity in the field of masculinity, enabling us to speak of masculinities as they are influenced by such variables as class, caste, age, nationality and identity.

This volume draws together thirteen scholars concerned with exploring masculinity in an Indian context. A very large part of the thinking and writing about Indian men is confined to a narrow stratum with an urban, middle class bias. In the last few years there have been a few book length studies on various aspects of Indian masculinity which have used interdisciplinary approaches to the subject (Srivastava, 2004, 2007; Osella and Osella, 2006,

Alterno and Mittapalli, 2009). Theorizing Indian masculinity is a challenging experience. In a common sensical sense masculinity refers to characteristics or qualities which are considered typical or appropriate to a man. But how does an Indian man differ from others? Is it indeed even possible to make a distinction between the experiences of men in diverse societies that comprise our world or is there one hegemonic male authority that we try to problematize? These are some of the questions that the contributors to this volume had to grapple with when trying to understand Indian masculinity.

Masculinity, unlike femininity, is most often unseen or unnoticed owing to the normativity of its nature. It is unmarked because it is taken to be the norm and not thought about unless in opposition to something else. It is precisely because of this "significant absence" (Barthes, 1967: 77) that its silence speaks. Over the years and across numerous contexts, men's bodies have become important sites where masculinity has been played out. Connell presents a new framework in order to provide a more convincing and nuanced explanation for the construction of masculinity. In her essay "Teaching the Boys: New Research on Masculinity" in 1996 she explained how masculinity is constructed from a very early age within the aegis of an education structure where practices such as curriculum division, sports and disciplining systems reinforced a gender dichotomy. Another striking feature of her essay was the recognition of the different forms of masculinity, which "do not sit side by side" (1996: 209) and she flatly rejected the idea of men being a homogenous group of oppressors. Masculinity can therefore be seen both as hegemonic and marginalized. Some masculinities are more honored than others, while others such as homosexuality and queerness flatly stigmatized and marginalized. Hegemonic masculinity refers to a position of authority and dominance. This hegemony is not just in terms of other masculinities but in relation to "the gendered order as a whole" (ibid). One manifestation of this aspect of masculinity is patriarchy. Walby (1990) calls it a system of social structures and practices, in which men dominate, oppress and exploit women. Patriarchy in India as in the rest of the world has seen a shift from its private nature, where women have been oppressed by their husbands, fathers and other male members of their family, to public patriarchy where they are collectively subordinated by a society led by men. Ancient Indian texts such as the *Manusmriti* contain numerous references of prejudice, hatred and subjugation of women under a patriarchal system:

> Men may be lacking virtue, be sexual perverts, immoral and devoid of any good qualities, and yet women must constantly worship and serve their husbands [5/156].

However the theory of patriarchy is not without problems as Bradley (2013: 207) has argued, the difficulty of using a "totalistic theory based on only one dynamic is that it presents a distorted view of all women as victims" and all men as perpetrators. What we want to argue is that men carry the burden of victimhood as well. The patriarchy that systematically subjugates women also subjugates men who do not conform to the class/caste and sexual subjectivity of the mainstream.

Indeed despite the fragmentary efforts made during the last few years, there exists a vast difference that distinguishes the lives of men in different parts of India which is impacted by caste, class, religion and sexual orientation. It is therefore very difficult to put together comprehensive descriptions of the vast and complex realities of Indian men in one volume.

Colonial Masculinities

One of the most important areas of research in gender and postcolonial studies is the analysis of indigenous masculinities within colonial contexts. This contour of exploration foregrounds the gendered, race and class dynamics of colonialism and nationalism and also provides opportunities for alternative gender practices that challenge hegemonic structures of white, middle-class patriarchy. In theorizing the production of masculinities in postcolonial systems, it is useful to remember that an interplay between power and structure creates hegemonies which in turn transform indigenous ideologies of gender and power.

Questions around representations are central to an understanding of postcolonial masculinities. Masculinities in the colonies were created and perpetuated as a contrast to the colonizers' own masculinity. For instance, native African and Indian men were seen as hypersexual whose sexuality was a threat to the virtuous white woman in imminent danger from such unchecked sexuality, thus creating a justification for colonizers to check and discipline other cultures. The predatory nature of men was reviled and violently subdued through colonial practices. Practices such as polygamy, sati, and burkhas were seen as a part of the widespread patriarchy existing in the colonies and providing the pretext for the "white man saving the brown men from brown men" (Spivak, 1988:297). The argument was that if Indian men could be so patriarchal and violent within the confines of their family, how could they be fair in their dealings with the British government (Sinha, 1995). This imaginary essentializing of colonial masculinities serves to both obscure and appropriate an unsettling difference.

Colonialism itself was a highly gendered process which was driven by a gendered force of subordination. According to Mclintock (1995), to understand colonialism and postcolonialism one must recognize that race, gender and class are not distinct but rather come into existence in conflicting ways. Post-colonialism itself is an unsettling development and recent work by Rumina Sethi questions its scope and existence (2011). The masculinity of the post-colonial male then needs to be interrogated within contradictory sites of complex interaction between racial ideologies and the state. The postcolonial male has been represented as one with no agency whose subordinate presence in the colonial lexicon renders him powerless. However this assumption is based on a false universal and generalized colonial condition.

Much of the current scholarship about the nation and gender has fixated itself on the role of women who are constructed as symbols of the nation and "mother" land. Thus as the literary critic Sangeeta Ray (2000) points out, more than often the women's bodies become sites of contesting culture, tradition and the nation. However in recent years questioning this gendered version of nationalism has thrown up new questions on the role of masculinity and the male body. Kavita Daiya proposes that while violence by men against women has gained ascendancy in recent academic discussions, there needs to be a more deliberate focus on the violence suffered by male bodies in the public sphere (2006, 2008). John and Nair in their seminal work *A Question of Silence* point out that "questions of male sexuality have rarely been a focus of scholarly analysis except for celebrated instances of celibacy" (1998:15) in India. In fact the Gandhian gloss of the "necessity of overcoming desire as the irrevocable truth of the Indian male milieu" (Srivastava, 2004:15) has been commented upon by scholars such as Srivastava (2004, 2007) and Kakar (2007). This desexualization, de-eroticization of the Indian male sexuality is important in postcolonial India as it can be seen as a reaction to the imaginary essentializing of the hypersexual native male in the colonial era.

Queer Masculinities

The expansion of the British Empire in the eighteenth century also dictated colonial policies of sexual regulation, which were driven by a Victorian "fanatical purity campaign" (Bhaskaran, 2002:16). The British anti-sodomy law was introduced in Britain in 1860, which reduced the punishment of sodomy from execution to imprisonment; however when enacted in colonial states like India as in Section 377 of the Indian Penal Code, it was seen as a retrogressive move. The law states:

> Whoever voluntarily has carnal intercourse against the order of nature with any man, woman or animal, shall be punished with imprisonment for life, or with imprisonment of either description for a term, which may extend to ten years, and shall be liable to fine.

Explanation: Penetration is sufficient to constitute the carnal intercourse necessary
to the offence described in this section [Arondekar, 2009: 76; Bhaskaran, 2002: 15].

Prior to the enactment of this law queer sexuality was accommodated if not
approved. As Vanita and Kidwai point out "at most times and places in pre-
nineteenth century India, love between women and between men, even when
disapproved of, was not actively persecuted. As far as we know, no one has
ever been executed for homosexuality in India" (2000:xviii). However with
the passing of this law, homosexuality was officially condemned by the state
and framed as a criminal activity. This is not to say that colonialism entirely
drove queer sexuality underground but rather it can be argued that colonialism acted as a device to obscure the queer identity, an unwillingness to "come
out" to the public. It signified ambivalence about revelation of queer identities. In colonial India the minoritization of queer sexualities was a political
agenda of purporting queer sexuality as a "special oriental vice" (Ballhatchet,
1980; Bhaskaran, 2002). Ballhatchet (1980) suggests that sexual energy was
another reason for imperial expansion, he mentions British men with "tastes
which could not be satisfied in England ... agreeably satiated overseas" (1).
However there was anxiety by the British administrators about the sexual
freedom India posed for its people, and homosexuality was blamed on Indian
customs. Lord Curzon once remarked: "I attribute it largely to early marriage.
A boy gets tired of his wife, or of women at an early age and wants the stimu-
lus of some more novel or exciting sensation" (cited in Ballhatchet, 1980:
120).

Ballhatchet describes the various debates in the Parliament at the possibility of sexual relations taking place between the white elite and the native
subordinate groups. There was a need for sexual regulation and one major
point of concern was the presence of prostitutes in the army cantonments,
however, "the prospect of homosexuality was revealed in guarded terms by
the authorities whenever there was a talk of excluding prostitutes from the
cantonments" (1980: 162). This might seem contradictory to the Victorian
morals of that time but it would appear that the fundamental concern was
for the preservation of power by the authorities to regulate the lives of those
under their command. Attitudes to sexual conduct are likewise correlated to
the safeguarding of vested interests and constitution of power.

Robert Aldrich argues that "colonialism ... encouraged sexual irregular-
ity, heterosexual and homosexual" (2003:4). The colonial aspects of homosexuality suggest sexual ambivalence which produced both physical and emotional
desire and also illustrate a variety of homosexual relationships. Aldrich also
notes that "the colonies provided many possibilities of homoeroticism, homosociality and homosexuality" (ibid: 3). Thus there was a multiplicity of pos-

sibilities and perspectives in which queer bonding and queer desire could take place in the colony.

Homosexuality was also seen as a threat to masculinity. Ashis Nandy (1983) situates the homosexual criminalization of Oscar Wilde in a colonial context — for the valorization of masculinity. Mrinalini Sinha points out the colonial imagination's contradictory tendency to assign hyper virile masculinity and thus degenerate sexuality to some colonized males (often associated with the non-intellectual class) and hyper effeminacy (often paradoxically associated with the colonized elite who were the intellectual non-laboring class) to others (1995:19). Nandy, however, uses queer effeminacy and the anti-masculine image of Gandhi to critique colonialism. He writes, "It was colonial India ... still preserving something of its androgynous cosmology and style, which ultimately produced a transcultural protest against the hyper masculine world view of colonialism in the form of Gandhi" (1983:45).

Drawing on Vanita (2000, 2002, 2005), one can state that modern homophobia in India is deeply intertwined with modern nationalism. In its attempt to revise and reconstruct nationalism for Independent India, masculinity becomes a foundation stone equating it to rationality, chivalry and moral superiority and sexuality and effeminacy (a form of non-masculinity) had no place in this new rhetoric.

Queer Pride March in India, 2009 (photograph by Daniele Lazaretto).

Masculinity in Crisis?

Of late there has been a wave of media coverage about the crisis of masculinity. Anthony Clare in his book *On Men: Masculinity in Crisis* says:

> At the beginning of the twenty first century it is difficult to avoid the conclusion that men are in serious trouble. Throughout the world, developed and developing, antisocial behaviour is essentially male [2001:3].

He goes on further to state that men who at one point knew of their role as providers for the family have found this role diminished in recent years and this set of changing circumstances of having to renegotiate their place within the social structure has exacerbated this "crisis." While Clare's choice of the term "crisis" may seem a little farfetched in this situation, it cannot be denied that the very form of masculinity is shifting and giving rise to new forms of masculinity(ies).

According to commentators in the field of masculinity studies such as Brittan (1989), women's demands for freedom and equality have left men confused about their role. The dependent housewife model of the family is in decline and one of the questions that come to haunt men is how can they prove their masculinity and superiority in these changing circumstances. Furthermore sociologists such as Bradley (2013) suggest that the rise of feminism together with new models of masculinity has emerged in response to economic and cultural changes. Thus the New Man (a softer caring creature), sometimes labeled feminized man, replacing Connell's hegemonic masculinity has led to a moral panic about what it means to be a man at the beginning of the 21st century.

Indian men growing up in the eighties and nineties have grown up seeing a particular form of patriarchal masculinity which is being challenged in contemporary times. So is masculinity in crisis? Most certainly it would appear that masculinity is in a period of flux, with the definition of what a man is and how he is to behave being uncertain. What is more certainly true is that masculinity as it was played out in the last few hundred years is definitely being challenged.

In an interesting article, Pradhan and Ram (2010) asked young males in India, what a "real" man is like and received answers such as "[being able to] earn and maintain a family, to take decision, to physically satisfy spouse/partner, and to procreate besides having a well built body" (546).

What these responses demonstrate is the unease men are having in recent years in adapting to the changing geographies within which their masculinity is based. Primary self defined characteristics such as maintaining a family and earning wages are now being taken over by many women and this has led to confusion over the nature of masculine performance itself. Interestingly the article also notes that the young men see aggressiveness and sexual domination as a form of masculinity, not just to prove their masculinity but to also stamp their superiority over the other gender (Pradhan and Ram, 2010).

In Popular Culture

Masculine representations in popular culture are both varied and at the same time also allowed for several masculinitie(s) to be represented. O'Sullivan et al. (2001:231) have defined popular culture as "of people in general; well liked by people in general ... usually synonymous with good in ordinary conversation." While this definition of popular culture as a site for the production of meanings that is "well liked" and "of people" in general might show a bias in favor of popular culture, the mainstream view of popular culture is slightly more skewed as Gokulsing and Dissanayake have noted. "Popular culture is also synonymous with what is gross, vulgar and cheap — unworthy of study" (2009:2). Therefore the transgressive potential of such a medium in perpetuating and representing masculinities is quite rich.

One of the prime examples of this is Indian cinema. The role of Indian cinema in the Indian public imagination is unparalleled and therefore it is no surprise that this medium plays such an important role in the construction of public consciousness regarding social and political issues. Gokulsing and Dissanayake, writing about Indian popular cinema, contend that "the discourse of Indian Popular Cinema has been evolving steadily over a century in response to newer social developments and historical conjunctures" (2012: 17). Cinema in India participates in the continual reconstruction of the social imaginary. In addition to being a "dominant form of entertainment" (2012:15) Indian cinema also represents the interplay of the global and local. While popular Indian cinema has a long history of featuring cross dressing male stars in comic or song sequences — who can forget Amitabh Bachchan in "Mere Angane Mein" (In my Compound) from *Laawaris* (Abandoned, 1981), or Aamir Khan's cabaret dance in *Baazi* (Gamble, 1995) — representations of men and masculinity have changed over time. The effeminacy of Dev Anand characterized through his innumerable films which Kavi (2000: 308) calls "a strange effeminacy that bordered on the child like" and "had an innocuous sensuality about him that conspired to make his heroine into an oedipal figure" has largely been replaced. Desai (2004) critically notes how actors such as Dilip Kumar, Dev Anand and Raj Kapoor spawned a generation of Indian youth who modeled themselves on them. However the sensitive lover-boy hero was soon replaced by the masculinity championed by stars such as Dharmendra (also known as the "He Man" of Indian Cinema). This trend has continued even today, when hypermasculinized actors such as John Abraham and Salman Khan have given actors such as Shah Rukh Khan a reason to prove their masculinity and virility to their female audiences by undergoing a complete makeover through adopting a muscular gym-toned body ("Dard e Disco" in *Om Shanti Om*, 2007).

While homosexuality is rarely addressed explicitly, many of these earlier films bear "the markers of queer suggestions" (Ghosh, 2009:59). Ghosh (2002) maintains that this fascination of Bollywood for a queer subculture can be traced back to Indian cinema's fascination with romantic love as an exalted emotion. This connotative homoeroticism can be traced through the same sex masculine friendship plots that drive several of these films. *Sholay* (Embers, 1975) and the recent hits *Dil Chahta Hain* (What the Heart Wants, 2001) and *Student of the Year* (2012) are testimonies of the passionate male friendship that exists within Indian cinema.

Other instances of masculine representations can also be found in Indian television, which since 1992 has been one of the fastest growing television industries in the world. While shows such as *Kyunki Saas Bhi Kabhi Bahu Thi* (Because the Mother-in-Law Was Also Daughter-in-Law Once) and *Kahaani Ghar Ghar Ki* (Story of Every Family) have dominated the Indian soap opera viewing public for years with its brand of Indian-ness espoused through women in traditional wear, stay at home wives, with limited or no sexual agency and men as breadwinners; what needs to be further interrogated is what reaction do these characters effect in public consciousness. An article in *Hindustan Times* (22 July 2012) argued that men were being presented with a dichotomy — while Indian cinema has been instrumental in its representation of female actors as strong characters with an agency,

John Abraham in *Dostana*, 2008.

television continues to portray women in need of male validation. The Indian man in "crisis" therefore turns to the mother-sister ideal of the traditional Indian women portrayed on television to reinforce his masculinity and also reject the women with agency who threaten to imbalance this power equation. Scholars such as Rebecca Feasey (2008) have critically noted that television studies have produced a profusion of literature theorizing the representation of gender on the small screen; however most of this work has focused only on constructions of femininity in television. She observes that feminist research on representations of femininity and women's roles on television has provided significant insights but have left masculinity untouched. Leaving masculinity untheorized, further notes Feasey, allows it to be understood as unwavering and permanent, and therefore not worthy of critique or questioning.

In line with Feasey's arguments, both areas — the male viewership of Indian soap operas as well as (the few) masculine representations in Indian television — would merit further study. Of course Shah Rukh Khan's famous Lux soap advertisement, where he is shown bathing in a tub with rose petals and surrounded by a bevy of women is a testament to some of the inroads that have been made in the last few years in the representation of masculinity on Indian television.

Representation/Regulation/Exclusion: Overview of the Essays in This Volume

In the opening essay, "'Sane Sex,' the Five-Year Plan Hero and Men on Footpaths and in Gated Communities: On the Cultures of Twentieth-Century Masculinity," Sanjay Srivastava provides an overview of the modern culture of masculinity in India. According to him, masculinity in South Asia exists within different contexts. In the context of the twentieth century, he identifies a "new" masculine type whom he refers to as "The Five Year Plan (FYP) Hero." The FYP hero's manliness did not stem from "bodily representations or aggressive behaviour" but rather through a science based masculinity. This was represented in the films from the 1950s and 1960s through both the spatial habitat of the hero (highways and metropolitan places) as well as through profession (engineer, doctor, scientist). Nehruvian politics was ambitiously aimed at advancing India's technological and scientific objectives and India's postcolonial elite made their way to Silicon Valley and other "nodes" of information and technological revolution which characterized the new Indian modernity (and by extension the formulation of a new Indian masculinity). Srivastava's essay ventures on further to look at the demise of this form of masculinity (the FYP Hero) and the rise of Amitabh Bachchan, the "angry young man" of Indian cinema. Srivastava notes that Bachchan's masculinity was based on his representation of the provincial male body relating to skin color, language and expression of homoerotic aura in several of his films. In the final part of this essay he focuses on "footpath pornography," by which he refers to Hindi language booklets available in North India characterizing a subaltern masculine culture. Thus, Srivastava, not only tries to make sense of the changing role of masculinity within Indian modernity but endeavors to provide a context for understanding its social potential.

In the second essay, "Critical Masculinity Studies in India," Mangesh Kulkarni critically surveys debates on indigenous masculinities and gives an outline of the emerging agendas for future research and teaching in the area. Critical masculinity studies has in the last few decades focused on examining how men and masculinities are gendered, and how those gendering processes intersect with other social relations and social divisions. This approach calls for studies on men that are critical, interdisciplinary, relational, materialist, deconstructive and anti-essentialist. Kulkarni argues that while critical masculine studies is yet to find an academic foothold within the Indian academe, it is needed for two very important reasons:

> For one masculinities are deeply implicated in a whole host of problems looming over the country, ranging from an abysmally low sex-ratio to communal violence. Besides, during the last two decades, the country has witnessed the emergence of men's groups, as also the publication of a significant body of writings examining various dimensions of men's lives [Kulkarni, this volume].

His overview of the current literature on CMS and agenda for future research and intervention makes a strong case for studies in Indian masculinity.

The notion of intersectionality, a sociological theory favored by feminist scholars was first put forward by Kimberle Crenshaw (1989) to address issues of race and gender within a composite framework. Intersectionality acknowledges the power overlaps and the complexity of layered identities. By layered identities, we want to propose the various scopes within which our identities reside ranging from class, caste, racial, sexual and national identities. Gender identities cannot be studied without this intersectional focus where all these different trajectories are addressed. Writing about intersectionality and gender, Sussane V. Knudsen says, "ethnicity is combined with gender to reflect the complexity of intersectionality between national, new national background and womanhood/manhood" (2006:61). Roshan das Nair's essay takes on this intersectional dimension focusing on intersectional gender, i.e., gender in interplay with other social categorizations and power differentials such as ethnicity, class, nationality, sexuality, age, etc. In this essay, "If Singularity Is the Problem, Could Intersectionality Be the Solution? Exploring the Mediation of Sexuality on Masculinity," he explores how processes of social and cultural change can be initiated or sustained by integrating a critical understanding of intersectional gender, by counteracting multiple inequalities and processes of discrimination, and by other kinds of transformative work.

Simon (2003) calls identity a seductive concept and a multifaceted phenomenon. One of the attributes of identity studies in recent years has been to address body politics and the emergent field of Fat Studies has evolved in similar ways to Women's Studies and Queer Studies to resist discrimination and promote body acceptance. Pranta Pratik Patnaik in his essay, "Bearly Indian: 'Fat' Gay Men's Negotiation of Embodiment, Culture and Masculinity," explores the intersections of identity that emerge for fat Indian men focusing on their experiences and perspectives. Through detailed study of a gay website and interviews, Patnaik contends that while the internet and queer dating websites such as Pink promote tolerance and acceptance for an oppressed class of men — gay men in this instance, at the same time it also systematically denies certain men representation because of their bodily attributes. Patnaik is right in observing that the media has played a very important role in promoting an "ideal typical male body" which has been detrimental to men who do not "fit" this mainstream image. He further contends that fat men are trapped in such hegemonic images of masculinity. Fat gay masculinity thus produces a collection of attitudes and assumptions which open up newer arenas for us to grapple with.

Kama Maureemootoo's essay adds a further dimension to the transformations currently taking place in Indian society with regard to how male same-sex relationships are viewed, investigating how levels of societal and individual acceptance continue to span a wide spectrum in spite of the 2009 decriminalization of Section 377 of the Indian Penal Code. Incidents such as TV9 Telugu outing gay men using the dating/networking website Planet Romeo in 2011 in a news report titled "Gay Culture Rampant in Hyderabad" (quoted in this essay), are evidence that tolerance (let alone acceptance) of same-sex relationships is still fragmented. In "The Nation as Mimicry: The (Mis)reading of Colonial Masculinities in India," Maureemootoo examines the polarized debate ensuing from the death of Dr. Srinivas Ramachandra Siras, Reader and Chair of modern languages at Aligarh Muslim University in Uttar Pradesh, India. Maureemootoo looks at his suspension from teaching duties and subsequent death in "mysterious circumstances" following a surreptitiously filmed sexual encounter between Siras and a male sex partner. The essay initially considers notions of tradition versus modernity, privacy versus infringement of rights, before examining how the concerns raised by the Siras case "are, in effect, postcolonial residues that haunt India's contemporary cultural and political scapes," formerly also occupying the thoughts of Indian nationalists in the late nineteenth and early twentieth century.

Moving forward, David A. Ansari in his ethnographic research conducted with South Asian queer men in London addresses the complex relationship which exists between culture, race and sexuality. In "Mobilizing for Sexual Health: The Experience of Queer Indian Men in London," Ansari examines how Indian queer men living in London challenge the stigma of non-heterosexual behavior and desires while collectively mobilizing for improved sexual health. Ansari conducted nineteen interviews with participants from a sexual health charity which provides sexual health and HIV prevention and support services to Black and Minority Ethnic (BME) communities in London. The findings illustrate that the men (interviewed in this study) face unique challenges to their sexual expression arising from cultural stereotypes of same sex activities, family and societal expectations of young men and religious proscriptions. Respondents described shared identities, spaces for dialogue, collective access to resources, mutual learning and long term connections formed with each other and with outside groups. Ansari's essay also highlights the factors affecting service uptake amongst these men and the strategies developed to address stigma and improve sexual health. These findings expand our current understanding of sexuality within ethnic minority communities in a multicultural society in the context of gender-based sexual and mental health programs.

Queer theory has historically engaged in a sustained critique of the normative standards of heterosexual masculinity; however our focus in this volume has been on a critique of the cultural readings of how masculinity is played out. Aniruddha Dutta, in his essay "Masculinities of Desire, Derision and Defiance: Global Gay Femmephobia and *Kothi-Hijra*-Trans Heterosexualities," offers an analysis of normative, counter-normative and politically ambivalent evocations of masculinity within spaces and milieus of gender/sexual variance such as *kothi*, transgender and gay networks in eastern India. Beginning with the question of what sorts of masculinities are valorized as objects of desire or ideals for subject-formation, Dutta interrogates the construction of a liberated and urbane gay identity framed around "good" masculinities as opposed to "backward" *kothis* and transgenders who supposedly desire the "bad" patriarchal masculinities and thus remain trapped in a victimized femininity. On one hand, he interrogates the notion of gender fluidity within urbane community networks as implicitly "good" and "progressive" and examines how it may conceal non-deconstructed masculine privilege, and on the other, he examines the evocation of "patriarchal" gender roles within non-metropolitan subcultures as being both potentially conservative and counter-normative. Dutta contends that recognizing how evocations and usages of masculinity might occur in such politically unexpected and unstable ways can help us imagine social change beyond tired binaries such as patriarchy and sexual progress or rural conservatism and urban liberation.

In "Corporal Punishment: English and Homosocial Tactility in Post-colonial Bengal," Niladri R. Chatterjee argues that there is an intriguing relationship between language/culture and the body. In this provoking essay Chatterjee writes:

> Men or boys who do not speak English hold hands in public, embrace each other a lot more, even kiss each other on the cheek far more frequently than those who can speak English. In fact, in my own English-speaking circle of friends I have noticed a particular horror of physical contact among male friends, and an inversely proportional lack of corporeal self-consciousness among those who do not speak English [this volume].

Chatterjee states that the pathologization of the male body gets underway in England at the same time when English becomes a public policy for the British government in Bengal and thus homosocial tactility should be studied in a way that takes into account the site of its performance and the class of subjects performing — an intersectional focus which like the other contributors to this volume, Chatterjee agrees needs to be engaged with. Chatterjee's essay asks the reader to problematize and read how "englishing" of the male body in Bengal have produced anxieties around tactility that did not exist earlier.

The final essays of this collection focus on literary and cinematic representations of masculinity in India. In "Of Girmitiyas and Mimic Men: Alternative Masculinity in V.S. Naipaul's *A House for Mr. Biswas*," Vishnupriya Sengupta argues that in the course of depicting the tensions of an individual trapped in a claustrophobic ghettoized society and family ruled by a matriarch, the novel deals with the subversion of masculinity, evinced forcefully through the underlining concepts of the Girmitiya and "Mimic" man as they surface in the novel. Focusing on Naipaul's male protagonists, Sengupta has argued that the complex intersections between gender performance, nationalism, race and class destabilize Indo-Caribbean masculinities and aggravate the already unstable power balance at a personal and cultural level. As we have argued in this introduction, colonial masculinities in India have undergone emasculation as well as a level of anxiogenic hypermasculinity stemming from the colonized male's (supposed) unchecked sexuality. This essay further problematizes masculinity by focusing on the plight of Indo Caribbean men and the contradictions and negotiations that exist within gender performances, national identity and class positioning.

In choosing to encompass the material of our volume within the geographical boundaries of India, it is necessary to address the question of essayist heritage. In the next essay "Gay Writing and the Idea of Doubleness," Akhil Katyal addresses the question of whether writing on Indian masculinity can be appropriated by the *pardesi* hand. Examining whether the par (other) and des (country) outsider extends not simply to the non–Indian but to the non-resident Indian. In his essay, Katyal illustrates this through a paper that draws on an extended personal interview with Hoshang Merchant conducted in Hyderabad in July 2010. Hoshang recounts the relationship he shared with Kashmiri-American poet Agha Shahid Ali and the impact on their friendship in the period after Ali turned down the offer of contributing to India's first collection of gay writing in 1999, driven by an apprehension of coming out to his father. Narrating the episode, Katyal writes, "'Perfidies,' he told me, campily, 'are never forgiven even if they can be understood.'" Katyal asks who is permitted to legitimately write a "gay story," why writing on masculinity appears to predominantly emphasize homosexuality, and questioning the fascination that exists as to the sexuality (or for that matter the gender) of the writer.

Tanmayee Banerjee's essay, "Negotiations of Masculinity in Riwik Ghatak's Partition Trilogy," reflects on *Meghe Dhaka Tara* (The Cloud-Capped Star), *KomalGandhar* (E-Flat) and *Subarnarekha* (Golden Lining), which address the dynamics of partition. The films show, through form and content, how gender equations get problematized in the post-partition immigrant society. Through an analytical discussion on these films Banerjee argues how masculinity has to negotiate with circumstances in the post-partition unsettled order of the society, in the first film through financial dependence of the male members on the earning female member of the family; in the second film through men's dependence on women for emotional and practical support; and in the third film through reduction of the male protagonist to the state of utter helplessness and his absolute failure to "protect" and "preserve." Banerjee further contends that the patriarchal paradigm suffered a restructuring in the immigrant families which migrated to West Bengal (India) from East Pakistan (now Bangladesh) after the 1947 partition of Bengal followed by the independence of India. It was due to the female members assuming the controlling center of these families either through obvious ways such as earning money or subtle ways of taking control of situations. Banerjee argues that these masculinities are in crisis and it is only through their relationships with women that they reach a point of resolution and assert their masculinity.

Sayantan Dasgupta, in "Masculinizing the (Post)colonial Subject: The *Amar Chitra Katha* Comic Book," investigates a popular comic book series that focuses on Indian history and mythology, to see how it locates itself in the context of gender politics and stereotyping. Dasgupta argues that this comic book series, which is written primarily for children, situates itself firmly within the politics of nationalism and finds itself engaging with various discursive practices related to the formation of a national identity, specifically within the template of a colonial history. In one of these discourses, the *Amar Chitra Katha* seems to engage with the Orientalist construction of colonial subject races as effeminate, emasculated and passive. Predictably enough, the

Amar Chitra Katha responds to this by attempting to (re)construct an alternative model of history where the "true" Indian is shown to be a martial fellow. This construction, as Dasgupta points out, manifests itself in varied ways with regard to the various groups (Rajput, Mughal, Sikh, etc.), imbuing the *Amar Chitra Katha* iconography with a gender angle that cannot be ignored.

The final essay of this volume, "Rethinking the Circuits of Male Desire Across Multiple *Dostanas*" by Dashini Jeyathurai, looks at two productions of the popular Bollywood film *Dostana* (Friendship) in 1980 and 2008 and traces the "invisible" male triangle. The 2008 *Dostana* has received widespread scholarly attention as a significant queer text in mainstream Indian cinema (Baker, 2012; Dudrah, 2012; Dasgupta, 2012; Ghosh, 2011), which simultaneously invokes "the phobic and the erotic" (Ghosh, 2011:65). *Dostana* uses the male body to arouse an active desire from the film's viewers. Male bonding has always been a primary feature of Bollywood cinema as described earlier in this introduction. Like most Bollywood films, friendship is celebrated in this film; however the physical intimacy is inscribed within a pleasurable spectacle which offers the viewers multiple locations of identification. It is useful to emphasize that the act of seeing and deriving pleasure needs to be seen as dialectic with an ever slipping trajectory of signification sliding the pleasure of cinema on to ambiguous realms of intertextuality. John Abraham demonstrates this successfully in the semi-nude sequences of the film. Jeyathurai offers to read the "invisible" third character in both films who is introduced as the "other" to codify male desire and highlight the supremacy of the "dostana" (friendship) shared by the two leading men. She concludes by saying that both films tease the implications of a cinema space that is increasingly masculinized and eroticized and invites us to consider how the homoeroticism of the genre may offer a viable language with which to narrate male queerness.

Concluding Remarks

All essays in this volume demonstrate how reading masculinity from a gender and queer studies approach provides particular insights about power relations, representation politics and nationalist agendas within the backdrop of cultural complexity. The explorations in this volume, as Ruth Vanita in the Foreword mentions, move in many directions. We do not and cannot claim this work to be representative of all the changes that have been happening but hope some of the issues brought up in this volume will open up new areas for further enquiry. It is clear from the essays in this volume that the time is ripe for a comprehensive approach to the challenges which masculinity studies pose for the Indian male. This volume identifies some issues which may help towards its understanding. In particular it draws attention to

(a) Thinking outside the bipolar box
(b) Identifying gender as an integrated narrative

The study of masculinities as a constructive response to feminism has come a long way since it first emerged out of the woodwork in the 1980s. There is already a strong growing scholarship in the area including some seminal work on Indian masculinities (Srivastava, 2004; Chopra, Osella and Osella, 2004; Osella and Osella, 2006, Kulkarni, 2007). Kavita Daiya proposes that while violence by men against women has gained ascendancy in recent academic discussions, there needs to be a more deliberate focus on the violence suffered by male bodies in the public sphere (2006, 2008).

The question of intersectionality and gender as an integrated narrative permeates almost all the essays in this volume in diverse ways. It is also evident that research on gender is constantly reinventing itself as it seeks to reach beyond itself and engage the global (as Ansari and Nair's essays demonstrate). The contributors have demonstrated this trend from their diverse vantage points. It also emphasizes what is distinctly and characteristically local and place bound in fascinating ways. This dialogue between the global and local approaches towards masculinity and gender is crucial to a proper understanding of the nature and significance of masculine culture in India.

Along with this, the issue of commodification also becomes a salient issue in the re-description of masculinity. This is demonstrated through the hyper-masculinized bodies that are displayed in television advertisements, films and magazines. Gokulsing and Dissanayake argue that "in contemporary capitalist societies, popular culture operates within the space of consumerism. Therefore the manifold relations that exist between consumption and popular culture need to be recognised and explored" (2009: 278). Our identities and subjectivities are after all constructed by what we consume. As Patnaik has noted (in this volume), the media and by extension popular culture plays a huge role in promoting certain body types and deriding others.

This collection also explored the ideals of masculinity that are embedded and imbibed by young Indian school-going boys who are introduced to these ideals through popular comic books like *Amar Chitra Katha* (Sayantan Dasgupta, this volume). The *Amar Chitra Katha*, which remains one of India's leading comic book series promoting "the route to your roots" and the "glorious heritage of India" highlights and appeals to the nationalist sentiments of consumers. Karline McLain has noted that despite the appeal of this series it has also been challenged by many who see its vision of Indian ness as limited and even exclusive, "marginalisation of muslims and other non Hindu's from the national past, the recasting of women in traditional roles and the privileging of middle class, upper caste Hindu culture" (2009: 159). We see again the pressing need for an intersectional focus within masculinity studies. The understanding of gender discourses, especially those relating to masculinity necessitates the comprehension of the "materialities of discourse and their relations to power" (Gokulsing and Dissanayake, 2009: 278). As one reads the essays in this volume, these facets of exploration need to be kept in mind.

Much of the literature on gender is at the level of individuals (See Butler, 2004, for example). More needs to be done at the intersectional level. Variables such as class, caste, disability, age, nationality and identity need to be explored at the intersection of policy and politics. Masculinity cannot be studied without acknowledging this intersectionality and masculine studies like women's studies needs to engage with queer identities, class differences and so on. As Rukmini Sen (2013) in response to the 2012 Delhi rape case puts it:

> Will some of the people who have vented their anger in protest against the gang rape of the medical student raise at least their voice in support of a sex worker's livelihood, a heterosexual person's right to live with a partner without marriage, a lesbian or gay person's right to choose a partner ... and not pass moral judgements on these groups of people?

Sen's call for an intersectional focus is what the contributors and the editors have tried to do when putting together this volume. In addressing masculine cultures, it is imperative to situate this within a national, class/caste framework. In putting together this collection, we were motivated by a desire to capture the complex operations of gender narratives. Prime Minister Manmohan Singh's quote at the beginning of this introduction is indicative of the work that needs to be done within the field and this volume is one of the steps taken in that direction.

Note on transliteration: We have retained the various forms of transliteration adopted by the individual authors.

References

Aldrich, Robert (2003). *Colonialism and Homosexuality*. London: Routledge.

Alterno, L., and R. Mittapalli (2009). *Postcolonial Indian Fiction in English and Masculinity*. New Delhi: Atlantic Publishers.

Arondekar, Anjali (2009) *For the Record: On Sexuality and the Colonial Archive in India*. Durham: Duke University Press.

Ballhatchet, Kenneth (1980). *Race, Sex and Class Under the British Raj*. London: Weidenfeld and Nicholson.

Baker, S. (2012). "Opening Closets/Dividing Camps: *Dostana* and Gay Framing in Indian Culture and Society." In R. K. Dasgupta and S. Baker (Eds.), *Popular Masculine Cultures in India: Critical Essays*. Kolkata: SetuPrakashani, 152–171.

Barthes, Roland (1967). *Elements of Semiology*. Trans. Annette Lavers and Colin Smith. New York: Hill and Wang.

Bhaskaran, Suparna (2002). "The Politics of Penetration: Section 377 and the Indian Penal Code," in Ruth Vanita (Ed.), *Queering India: Same Sex Love and Eroticism in Indian Culture and Society*. London: Routledge, 15–29.

Bradley, Harriet (2nd Edition) (2013). *Gender*. Cambridge: Polity Press.

Brittan, A. (1989). *Masculinity and Power*. London: Wiley and Sons.

Butler, J. (2004). *Undoing Gender*. London: Routledge.

Chopra, Radhika, F. Osella, C. Osella (Eds.) (2004). *South Asian Masculinities: Context of Change, Sites of Continuity*. New Delhi: Kali.

Clare, Anthony (2001) *On Men: Masculinity in Crisis*. London: Chatto and Windus.

Connell, R. (1995). *Masculinities*. Berkeley: University of California Press.

_____ (1996). "Teaching the Boys: New Research on Masculinity, and Gender Strategies for Schools." *Teachers College Record*. 98 (2): 206–236.

Crenshaw, K. (1989). "Demarginalising the Intersection of Race and Sex: A Black Feminist Critique of Antidiscrimination Doctrine, Feminist Theory and Antiracist Politics." *University of Chicago Legal Forum*, 139–167.

Daiya, Kavita (2006). "Postcolonial Masculinity: 1947, Partition Violence and Nationalism in the Indian Public Sphere." *Genders*. Accessed on 07 June 2012 at <http://www.genders.org/g43/g43_daiya.html>.

_____ (2008). *Violent Belongings: Partition, Gender and National Culture in Postcolonial India*. Philadelphia: Temple University Press.

Dasgupta, R.K. (2012). "The Queer Rhetoric of Bollywood: A Case of Mistaken Identity." *InterAlia: A Journal of Queer Studies*. 7: 1–24.

Desai, Meghnad (2004). *Nehru's Hero: Dilip Kumar in the Life of India*. New Delhi: Roli Books.

Dudrah, R. (2012). *Bollywood Travels: Culture, Diaspora and Border Crossings in Popular Hindi Cinema*. London: Routledge.

Elliott, Anthony (2009). *Contemporary Social Theory*. London: Routledge.

Feasey, R. (2008). *Masculinity and Popular Television*. Edinburgh: Edinburgh University Press.

Fulcher, J., and J. Scott (2d ed.) (2003). *Sociology*. Oxford University Press.

Ghosh, S. (2002). "Queer Pleasure for Queer People: Film, Television and Queer Sexuality in India." in Ruth Vanita (Ed.) *Queering India: Same Sex Love and Eroticism in Indian Culture and Society*. London: Routledge, 207–221.

_____ (2011). "Bollywood Cinema and Queer Sexualities." in R. Leckey and K. Brooks (Eds.), *Queer Theory, Law, Culture, Empire*. London: Routledge, 55–68.

Gokulsing, Moti, and Wimal Dissanayake (2009). *Popular Culture in a Globalised India*. London: Routledge.

_____, and _____ (2012). *From Aan to Lagaan and Beyond: A Guide to the Study of Indian Cinema*. Staffordshire: Trentham.

John, Mary E., and Janaki Nair. (1998). "Introduction," in M. John and J. Nair (Eds.), *A Question of Silence?: The Sexual Economies of Modern India*. New Delhi: Kali for Women, 1–51.

Kakar, Sudhir (2007). *Indian Identity: Three Studies in Psychology*. New Delhi: Penguin.

Kavi, Ashok Row (2000). "The Changing Image of Hero in Hindi Film." *Journal of Homosexuality*. 29 (3/4): 307–312.

Knudsen, S. V (2006). "Intersectionality: A Theoretical Inspiration in the Analysis of Minority Cultures and Identities in Textbooks," in E. Bruillard, B. Aamotsbakken, S.V. Knudsen and M. Horsley (Eds.) *Caught in the Web or Lost in the Textbook*. Caen: IARTEM, 31–76.

Kulkarni, Mangesh (2007). "Indian Masculinities: A Million Mutations Now?" in Ravindra R. P. et al. (Eds.), *Breaking the Moulds*. Delhi: Books for Change. 204–212.

Macaulay, T. B. (1880) *Critical, Historical and Miscellaneous Essays and Poems*. Vol. 2. Boston: Estes and Lauriat.

Mclain, Karline (2009). "Gods, Kings and Local Telegu Guys: Competing Visions of the Heroic in Indian Comic Books," in K.M. Gokulsing and W. Dissanayake (Eds.) *Popular Culture in a Globalised India*. London: Routledge, 157–173.

Mclintock, Anne (1995). *Imperial Leather: Race, Gender and Sexuality in the Colonial Contest.* London: Routledge.

Nandy, Ashis (1983). *The Intimate Enemy: Loss and Recovery of Self Under Colonialism.* New Delhi: Oxford University Press.

Osella, F., and C. Osella (Eds.) (2006). *Men and Masculinities in South India.* London: Anthem Press.

O'Sullivan, T. (2001). *Key Concepts in Communication and Cultural Studies.* London: Routledge.

Pradhan, M., and U. Ram (2010). "Perceived Gender Role That Shape Youth Sexual Behaviour: Evidence from Rural Orissa, India." *Journal of Adolescence.* 33(4): 543–551.

Ray, Sangeeta (2000). *En-Gendering India: Woman and Nation in Colonial and Postcolonial Narratives.* Durham: Duke University Press.

Segal, Lynne (1999). *Why Feminism? Gender, Psychology, Politics.* New York: Columbia University Press.

Sen, Rukmini (2013). "The Need for an Everyday Culture of Protest." *Economic and Political Weekly.* XLVIII (2). Accessed on 31 January2013 at http://www.epw.in/web-exclusives/need-everyday-culture-protest.html.

Sethi, Rumina (2011). *Politics of Postcolonialism.* London: Polity.

Simon, B. (2003). *Identity in Modern Society: A Social Psychological Perspective.* Oxford: Wiley Blackwell.

Sinha, Mrinalini (1995). *Colonial Masculinity: The Manly Englishman and the Effeminate Bengali.* Manchester: Manchester University Press.

Spivak, Gayatri (1988). "Can the Subaltern Speak?" In C. Nelson and L. Grossberg (Eds.), *Marxism and the Interpretation of Culture.* Urbana: University of Illinois Press.

Srivastava, Sanjay (2007). *Passionate Modernity: Sexuality, Class and Consumption in India.* London: Routledge.

_____ (Ed.) (2004). *Sexual Sites, Seminal Attitudes: Sexualities, Masculinities and Culture in South Asia.* London: Sage.

Vanita, R. (Ed.) (2002). *Queering India: Same Sex Love and Eroticism in Indian Culture and Society.* London: Routledge.

_____ (2005). *Gandhi's Tiger and Sita's Smile: Essays on Gender, Sexuality and Culture.* New Delhi: Yoda.

_____, and Saleem Kidwai (2000). *Same Sex Love in India.* London: Palgrave Macmillan.

Walby, Sylvia (1990). *Theorising Patriarchy.* Oxford: Blackwell.

"Sane Sex," the Five-Year Plan Hero and Men on Footpaths and in Gated Communities

On the Cultures of Twentieth-Century Masculinity[1]

SANJAY SRIVASTAVA

Theoretical Orientations

This essay provides an overview of the *modern* cultures of masculinity in India. It does not pretend to be exhaustive in scope, aiming rather at an extended introduction to the topic. And, though it is primarily concerned with exploring the building blocks of heterosexual masculinity, it should also be seen to be part of the wider debate about the relationship between hetero and non-heterosexual masculinities.

The concept of gender has come to be seen to offer a means of renewing feminist discourse by encouraging a more relational approach to masculinity and "feminity," as against the marginalization inherent in the project of women's studies. It also allows of the investigation, problematization and interrogation of masculinity, equally with femininity. Notwithstanding these enabling possibilities, however, gender is still largely deployed in contemporary social science discourse as a synonym for women, its relational aspect obscured and the invitation to interrogate masculinities largely ignored. This chapter proceeds from the position that the study of masculinity is important in that it "is simultaneously a place in gender relations, the practices through which men and women engage that place in gender, and the effects of these practices in bodily experiences, personality and culture" (Connell, 2005:71). Further, as the historian Rosalind O'Hanlon has pointed out, "A proper understanding of the field of power in which women have lived their lives demands that we look at men as gendered beings too" (O'Hanlon 1997:1).

Hence, the study of masculinity concerns the exploration of power relationships within the contemporary gender landscape, where the dominant ideals of masculinity impact both on women as well as on different ways of being men. This way of understanding masculinity is an exploration into the naturalization of the category "man" through which men have come to be regarded as both un-gendered and the "universal subject of human history" (O'Hanlon 1997:1).

Before proceeding further, it is important to say something about the terms "masculinity" and "patriarchy" and the relationship between the two. Masculinity refers to the *socially produced but embodied ways of being male*. It's manifestations include manners of speech, behavior, gestures, social interaction, a division of tasks proper to men and women, and an overall narrative that positions it as superior to its perceived antithesis, femininity. In order for masculinity to be positioned in a relationship of superiority to feminine identity, it is a key requirement that the latter be represented as possessing characteristics that are the binary opposite of the former. However, this is not all; dominant masculinity stands in a relationship not just to femininity but *also to those ways of being men* that are seen to deviate from the ideal. It is in this sense then masculinity possesses both external (relating to women) as well as an internal (relating to "other" men) characteristics. Both these contexts assist in bolstering what scholars have referred to as hegemonic masculine identity. Finally, it is erroneous to view femininity as the opposite of masculinity. Rather, the former should be regarded as supplement to the former: the definition of feminine qualities serve to also define masculinity.

Patriarchy refers to a *system* of social organization which is fundamentally organized around the idea of men's superiority to women. Within this system, even those who may not approximate to the male ideal (such as homosexual men) still stand to benefit from the privileges attached to being men. Though it is difficult to posit simple definitions of patriarchy and masculinity, we might say that patriarchy refers to the systemic relationship of power between men and women, whereas as masculinity concerns both inter and intra-gender relationships. And, while it cannot be argued that under patriarchy *all* forms of masculinity are equally valorized — in 1870, the colonial government in India sought to register all *hijras* and *zananas* (i.e., non-castrated transvestites) and to make them ineligible to adopt a son or act as guardians to minors[2] — there is nevertheless an overwhelming consensus regarding the superiority of men over women.

Patriarchy makes men superior, whereas masculinity is the process of producing superior men. The ideas of "making" and "producing" are crucial to the study of masculinity, for they imply the historical and social nature of gender identities. Further, the fact that masculinity must consistently be reinforced says something about the tenuous hold of gender identities. Following from this, we might also say that masculinity is *enacted* rather than expressed. When we say that something is expressed we utilize the idea that it already exists, and gender identities in particular do not already exist. There is an entire task of building and rebuilding, consolidation, representation, and enforcement. This does not, of course imply that existing formations of masculinity do not also contain instances of men's deviation from the dominant mode (see, for example Chopra 2003), rather that we still need to be attuned to whether such deviations disrupt existing frameworks or find ways of operating within them.

One of the most tenacious arguments against the "social" characterization of masculinity is that which relies on ideas of manifest biological difference. However, as Connell, points out, "the social relations of gender are not determined by biological difference but deal with it" (Connell 2005: 139–140). And that, gender "is about the linking of other fields of social practice to the nodal practices of engendering childbirth and parenting" (139–140). Biology always operates in tandem with social and cultural realities, and it is this combination that produces different ways of being. This way of positing the issues avoids constituting biology and culture as totally unrelated realms, or biology as prior to culture. It also serves to emphasize the fact that "we become human only in human society" (Padgug 1989). Finally, while it is important to avoid biological reductionism, we should also avoid the trap of "extreme difference." I refer here to academic and NGO perspectives (particularly those linked to public health activity) that posit an *absolute* difference between western and non-western concepts and identities. The long history of interaction between different cultures suggests that though the specificities of history and culture are important, we should also be mindful that contemporary identity politics is played out in *zones of interaction* that fill up with messages and behaviors from diverse sources, including the processes we now refer to as globalization. Hence, as one anthropologist has pointed out, "Rather than trying to rescue an image of a purely indigenous sexuality, distinct and untainted by 'outside' Western influence, it is more useful to ask what kinds of interactions, connections and conflicts emerge in the ... porous zones" (Pigg 2005:54).

To return to the idea of the social nature of gender, of those recent discussions that have foregrounded enactment as a significant aspect of gender, the one that relates to performance has been particularly influential. The theoretical discussion on gender as performance (or enactment) owes much to the work of Judith Butler (1999) who has sought to move discussion of gender and sexuality from notions of depth to surface. Butler also argues against the separation of gender and sexuality. She suggests that "The regulation of gender has always been part of the work of heterosexist normativity and to insist upon a radical separation of gender and sexuality is to miss the opportunity to analyze that particular operation of homophobic power" (Butler 1999: 186). These — performance, the yoking of gender and sexuality within the same analytical framework — are important ideas and will be discussed in different contexts in this essay.

However, it is also important to recognize the limits of performativity as a framework of analysis. For, as Blackwood and Wierenga (1999) point out, "Although performance theory is interested in unraveling the workings of gender, it cannot explain how people of different races, classes, and cultures and in different historical periods experience their bodies and their sexuality" (Blackwood and Wieringa 1999: 14). That is to say, while performance theory offers significant correctives to biologism and heteronormativity, it may be far too general a framework to offer insights into the specificities of identity and behavior. So, for example, if gender identities are fluid — as performance theory would imply — then how do we explain the fact that "butch women" in Jakarta base themselves on mythical idealized *male* figures? That is, that their sense of being depends upon on essentialized representations of manliness (Wieringa 2007). And, further, why is it that a *biologically female* transgendered person from Sri Lanka — who wishes to be recognized as male — bases his idea of manliness around notions of physical strength and aggression (Wijewardene 2007)? In other words, gender identities on the ground must account for the social and historical contexts within which performing subjects are nurtured, and this requires more nuanced understanding of what makes the everyday.

Masculinities and History

Contemporary understanding of masculinity must relate to its history. In all cultures, including European, a wide variety of conceptions of masculinity existed before the advent of the modern era. Many forms of expression — body appearance, gestures, voice, and so on — were seen to be part of maleness. In fact, some theorists now argue for a strong connection between modernity and currently dominant form of masculinity. It has been suggested that the binarism and essentialism of modern thought that characterized diverse fields of activity also had a strong influence upon ideas of gender identity. This was manifested in a "separation of reason from nature [which] works to divide men from their emotions and feelings which become threatening to [their] identities as men ... [men are exhorted to] disdain emotions and feelings a signs of weakness and so as potentially compromising [their] sense of male identity" (Seidler 1994: x–xi).

Increasingly, in terms of the Enlightenment discourse, this came to be expressed in terms of a split between being scientific and rational and being unscientific and irrational. And further, it was accompanied by the idea that the only "real" things were those that could be measured and quantified. Indeed, for influential thinkers such as Francis Bacon, science itself came to be seen as a new masculine philosophy (Seidler 1994:6). Modernist social theory has been greatly influenced by developments in the seventeenth and eighteenth centuries in terms of ideas of reason, science, emotions, quantification, and so on. This realm of knowledge has been the crucible for the making of gender identities and within which, for example, men become characterized as non-emotional and rational, and women as their opposite.

While social theory and historical analysis based upon western contexts provides useful background, it is frequently inadequate for an understanding of gendered complexities in other parts of the world. We might, here, begin with the colonial context. The colonial era was particularly important in the career of modern masculinity. It can be argued that colonialism consolidated hegemonic masculinity which combined the valorization of science, the feminization of non–European people, and the role of males in expressing their masculinity. In many ways then colonialism becomes an expression of the masculine ideal which had been developing in Europe through the seventeenth and eighteenth centuries. Critical studies of colonialism also suggest that it is impossible to understand contemporary *European* male identity without also understanding the colonial encounter. However, we should not conclude from this that, colonial powers, such as the British in India, invented certain types of masculine cultures and introduced them into the culture of the colonies; and that certain ideas that came to be associated with masculinity — such as being war-like — simply did not exist before colonialism. As Rosalind O'Hanlon has argued, for example, "martial masculinity" (O'Hanlon 1997: 17) *was* an important aspect of pre-colonial life, one which the colonizers built upon and incorporated within the discourses of colonial masculinity.

Nevertheless, it is important to understand the *intensification* of certain forms of discourses around masculinity that occurred during colonialism and their continued circulation during our own time. The term colonial masculinity expresses the importance of the relationship between two social contexts, colonialism and masculinity. Colonial masculinity does not simply refer to the ways in which colonial processes produced certain ideas about natives; rather, this term also suggests that colonialism influenced the identities of both the colonized as well as the colonizers. It is in this sense that it was suggested above that the making of British male identities during the nineteenth century cannot be understood in isolation from the events and processes of the colonial era. One scholar speaks of this relationship between European identity and the colonial sphere by asking us to "rethink European cultural genealogies across the board and to question whether the key symbols of modern western societies — liberalism, nationalism, state welfare, citizenship, culture, and 'Europeanness' itself— were not clarified among Europe's colonial exiles and by those colonized classes caught in their pedagogic net in Asia" (Stoler 1995:16). Keeping the above in mind, let us briefly explore some of the contexts of colonial masculinity.

The nineteenth century British public school presents us with a rich site for the analysis of gender configurations during the colonial era. For these institutions not only produced the (elite) personnel for the colonial enterprise — administrators and soldiers that manned the levers of empire — but they also manufactured a coherent discourse on the connection between gender, religious identity, and the colonial civilizing mission. The British public school was crucial in the development of what has been referred to as "muscular Christianity" and "moral manliness" through which colonialism came to be identified both as divine calling as well as a rite of passage for "real" men. The ideal of moral manhood (Mangan 1986: 147) took on the nature of an imperative that defined the essence of elite British male-hood, and, explained the glittering successes of the imperial enterprise. A race filled with moral and physical certitude, instilled on the playing fields of the English public school, now sallied forth to sow the effete, tropical, winds with the manly seeds of a more robust environment. The following verse from a poem by Sir Henry Newbolt — frequently reproduced in boarding school magazines in Great Britain amply demonstrates the contexts within which upper-class British masculinity was sought to be located during the nineteenth century:

> Say not 'tis brutal, our noble game
> When it fans our English valour's flame
> How many a charge through the ranks of the foe
> Have been made by a warrior who years ago
> Hurried the leather from hand to hand
> And 'gainst heavy odds made sturdy stand
> 'Neath Old England's banner in every land
> Our football players to guard it stand
> [quoted in Emsley 2007: 49].

The public school emphasis of physical prowess as a significant ingredient of leadership articulated well with the discourses of imperialism where "manly men" were to be in charge of the world's affairs. As "real" men, the colonizers possessed a justification for bringing vast areas of the world under colonial rule, for not only were they bringing civilization to these areas, they were also the harbingers of scientific thinking to people who had earlier been unscientific and hence wanting as human beings. "It is this vision of rationality as a relationship of *superiority*," Victor Seidler says,

> that gets embedded within modernity and which helps organise our relationship with the self within western culture. It creates its own tacit superiority as we learn to appropriate reason and science as our own. It worked to legitimate colonialism as it served to lower others in western eyes as being closer to nature and therefore as being in need of the "civilisation" that only the west could bring [Seidler 1994:16].

Within the colonial sphere itself, the obverse of the masculinization of Britishness, was the feminization of the natives, where the latter term refers to the attribution of "women like" traits to women in the context of the lower value placed on feminine gender identity. Hence, whether in Asia, or in other parts of the colonized world, there emerged a remarkably consistent discourse on the native's incapacity for self-government and informed decision making due to their inherent effeminacy (see, for example, Sinha 1997). This argument was bolstered by a number of others that derived from a variety of pseudo-sciences (such as colonial psychology and psychiatry) that sought to provide the proof of this position.

As one historian has pointed out, the process of the feminization of the native has a history that is intimately connected to a number of perspectives on the nature of the non-western milieu that had been developing over a period of time. So, at the close of the eighteenth century, Robert Orme, official historian of the East India Company was to speak of Indians as "people born under a sun too sultry to admit the exercise and fatigues necessary to form a robust nation" (quoted in Sen 2004:77). And that such people,

> were naturally weak in their constitution. As a result of this general lack of strength, the most popular source of livelihood was the manufacture of cloth, spinning and weaving. The weavers of India were deprived of the tools and machine skills available in England or other parts of Europe, yet their cloth was of exceptional quality. Such remarkable skills were accounted for in the fact that the Indians in the form of their labouring bodies possessed qualities unique to women and children [Sen 2004:77].

However, while some natives were feminized, others were represented as "martial races" (Omissi 1991) and hence worthy of respect, even though they could not be regarded as equals of the British since they did not possess sufficient *intellectual* prowess. The martial races idea — one that was never fixed but changed according to circumstances — was particularly deployed in India in the aftermath of the 1857 mutiny, and in light of the subsequent reorganization of the Indian army. New groups came to be identified as particularly suitable for making war, while others — usually those seen to be the trouble makers during the mutiny — were effectively excised from recruiting mechanisms. The Sikhs and Gurkhas — martial races to this day — benefited from the context produced by post–1857 political anxiety over native loyalty and an earlier history of "racial hygiene" (Omissi 1991) that decreed that pure races produced the best kind of military men. As historians have emphasized, the taint of effeminacy fell most heavily upon those sections of the native populations who were seen to have formal education of a similar kind to the rulers, and hence conversant with the ideas of freedom and liberty which Europeans characterized as the legacy of the Enlightenment. The "effeminate Bengali" (Sinha 1997) was, of course, only the best known of a number of such stereotypes that circulated during the colonial era.

Closely allied to the effeminacy perspective was the colonial discourse on non-heterosexual masculinity. Following an European history of the production of the homosexual as a distinct identity, one that an influential line of thinking (Foucault 1990) has identified as closely linked to the rise of a normalized bourgeois identity during the eighteenth and nineteenth centuries, the colonial sphere saw a similar stigmatization of non-heterosexual masculinity. It is now a common enough observation that Section 377 of the Indian Penal Code that prohibits "unnatural sex" is, in fact, a colonial artifact, brought into law in 1861. The relative lack of censure regarding homosexual relationships as a fact of pre-colonial Indian life — an aspect remarked upon by many historians — slowly gave way to the *public* and legal heteronormativity.[3]

The colonial era in India did not, however, completely overwrite those indigenous contexts where gender identities continued to be ambiguously inflected. The example of the transvestite performer in the Parsi, Gujarati, and Marathi theatres during the late nineteenth and early twentieth centuries is a case in point. During this period, Kathryn Hansen points out, there existed a public cultural space of "transgender identification and the homoerotic gaze" (Hansen 2004:100) that was sustained by a number of highly celebrated *male* performers such as Naslu Sarkari, Jayashankar Sundari, and Bal Gandharva. Hansen further notes that "The Pleasures of the homoerotic gaze and transgender performance were linked in the urban theatre with the satisfactions of social and economic privilege. Both Jayashankar Sundari and Bal Gandharva, rather than bearing any stigma, became national icons and recipients of the Padma Bhushan" (118–119). Finally in this context, it is important to note Hansen's contention that the popularity of the transvestite male performer cannot be simply attributed to the lack of availability of female performers; rather, she suggests, that may, actually, have been a preference for female impersonators who, in fact, competed with women actors.

Notwithstanding the existence of hybrid spaces such as the above, it is correct to say that the dominant tendency among the Indian intelligentsia of the period was to accept the rigid binaries of gender identity that colonialism intensified; after all, the tradition of the transvestite performer did decline, his place eventually taken by women actors doing women's roles. Perhaps the most salient context within which masculine identities became codified according to the colonial discourse was that of nationalism. National identity came to be seen as a way of reconstituting the subject position of Indians on a number of fronts, and gender was one of these. So, the nationalist response to the British characterization of "Indian effeminacy" was to both to seek to provide proof to the contrary as well as embark upon measures of improving and rejuvenating Indian masculinity. Rather than interrogate the colonial model, nationalists implicitly, agreed with its premise that Indians lacked manliness and sought to rectify this defect through various means.

Historians have pointed out that this "self-image of effeteness" (Roselli 1980) came to be widely accepted among nineteenth century Indian (Hindu) intelligentsia, and many came to believe that the emasculation was, among other things, due to the long history Muslim rule which had reduced Hindus to the status of a subject population. As suggested above, attempts at rectification were many and varied. So, one response was connected to the acceptance of the association between science and masculinity, and consisted in promoting the spread of western science. Indeed, being scientific also became an indispensable sign of Indian modernity. Social and religious thinkers such as Swami Vivekananda and Dayanand Saraswati sought evidence for Indian manliness and rationality in ancient texts; and institutions such as Doon School, established in 1935 with explicitly nationalist aims to produce an Indian boarding school for the training of a modern intelligentsia, became important sites for the development of a post-colonial scientific masculinity (Srivastava 1998).

In addition to the project of making the Indian mind masculine, there were also efforts at instituting new regimes of physical education through which the male body could be restored its lost masculinity. Institutions such as the Samarth Vyamshala Mandir ("The Temple of Complete Physical Exercise") located in Shivaji Park in central Mumbai, established in 1925 by P. L. Kale, were part of the nationalist attempts at reconstituting a lost Hindu masculinity. Of course, there already existed a long tradition of physical culture in India as embodied, for example, in the tradition of wrestling (Alter 1992), and, in some cases, the nationalist version of a suitable physical culture for a rejuvenated Indian masculinity relied on this tradition. However, it also went beyond it to forge a particularly modernist dialogue regarding the role of physical activity in the making of a new masculinity that would contribute to nation-building (Alter 2000).

An important adjunct to the consolidation of ideas of colonial masculinity was, unsurprisingly, the concurrent worsening of women's position in society. The project of Indian modernity — in whatever field — became, in effect, a "fraternal contract" (Pateman 1989) that intensified and ossified existing gender hierarchies. Let us take one instance of this process of the conjoining of masculinity, modernity, and gender power which has concrete consequences for our own era. Feminist scholars have argued that the imposition of English law upon an indigenous system, though it was commonly seen as a sign of progress may, in fact, have worsened the situation for women who enjoyed certain rights and freedoms under customary law (Agnes 2001). In particular, as Agnes points out, an aspect that was most severely affected was women's right to property that, for example under customary Muslim law, was much stronger than that which came to pass under the modern code. The politics of masculinity in the contemporary period, Agnes further suggests, is responsible for the situation where efforts to restore those rights of women alienated during the colonial period through colonial law are condemned as the imposition of Western values (Srivastava 2003).

The above points to a situation where the colonial cultural politics of masculinity gave way to postcolonial concerns that both built upon but also departed — as they had to — from preoccupations of the colonial era. The discussion that follows outlines these various trajectories of the intertwining of modernity and masculinity in India.

Sane, Upper Caste Masculine-Sexuality

The opening decades of the twentieth century in India witnessed a body of sex-literature whose inspiration derived partly from the work of European writers and activists such as Havelock Ellis and Margaret Sanger. It was a context that brought together sexuality, *Swarajya*, eugenics and masculinity. This was the field explored, for example, by N. S. Phadke, Professor of Mental and Moral Philosophy at Rajaram College in Kolhapur, Maharashtra. The Foreword to Phadke's 1927 book, *Sex Problem in India. Being a Plea for a Eugenic Movement in India and a Study of All Theoretical and Practical Questions Pertaining to Eugenics* was written by Margaret Sanger, "the pioneer birth controller" (Haste 1992: 24), a fact that succinctly illustrates the localization of Western ideas in an altogether different context. Phadke pointed out that his discussion was concerned with the issue of how to maintain the vigor of a "declining race," for "who could deny that physical strength and military power will be for us an indispensable instrument to keep *Swarajya* after it is won?" (Phadke 1927: 8).

In many ways, Phadke articulated two important and recurrent themes of twentieth century nationalist discourse, viz. that of "ancient Indian wisdom," and the importance of "scientific thinking" for the development of a post-colonial society; philosopher-president Radhakrishnan's The *Hindu View of Life* (1975), presents a good example of this, as do the views of the founders of modernizing institutions such as the Doon School (Srivastava 1998), and reformist movements such as the Brahmo Samaj and the Arya Samaj. So, Phadke was to suggest that "any attempt to work out a Eugenic programme in India" will have to take careful account of the principle of Heredity; and the Indian Eugenist will have "to subject the present Indian marriage institution to impartial and thorough-going criticism, and make constructive suggestions for its reform, induce the people to overhaul the whole mass of conventions and ideas about the act of procreation, and inspire them to leave the orthodox superstitious attitude towards sex questions for a scientific and healthy one" (Phadke 1927: 14–15). "It need never be supposed," he added,

> that the ancient Aryans were ignorant of the first principles of Eugenics and that India will have to learn them anew at the feet of the Western scholars. [For] even in the Vedic and Puranic times our ancestors had realised the value of Eugenic principles with remarkable fullness of vision and depth of anxious insight, and ... had applied them to social laws and customs with conspicuous skill and foresight. ... a goodly harvest of Eugenic literature can be collected from Manu, Yadnyavalkya and other Smritis, some Brahmanas, the Ashvalayan Griha Sutras, medical treatises like the Vagbhatas and Sushruta, and the great epic of Mahabharata [1927: 18–19].

Phadke's was not, by any means, a lonely voice, and the opening decades of the twentieth century witnessed a large body of sex literature that also engaged with the western theories and writers. Others, such as the medical doctor turned sexologist A. P. Pillay (1889–1956), sought to promote the ideas of rational sexual and gender identities as ingredients of modern social life. Pillay's *The Art of Love and Sane Sex Living* (1948), which carried glowing endorsements from, among others, the anthropologist Verrier Elwin, sought to inform the public that "the irksome religious dogmatism and anti-sexual taboos and tyranny still persisting are incompatible with biological needs and scientific findings" (from the inside front cover of the book). The issue of the ideal (middle-class) masculine identity was outlined through a combination of scientific and psycho-social discourses, with a particular regard to the sexual "satisfaction" of women as constitutive of such identity. Going by the fact that this publication achieved fifteen editions — and that Pillay was one of the guiding lights behind the Family Planning Association of India — we may assume that such works were extremely popular among the educated middle-classes in early twentieth century India.

Pillay's monograph was published in Bombay and, given the corpus of similar publications, Maharashtra was a particularly fertile site for negotiations of modernity that were elaborated through explorations of sexual and masculine cultures. There is a specific subtext to such works, of which the Phadke and Pillay texts are the most prominent examples. Within them, there is both a concern for the nature of Indian masculinity after *Swarajya*, and also the play of the politics of *upper caste masculinity* at a time when a number of social reform movements in western and South India expressed their concerns through the matrices caste oppression and self-respect. A plea for a Eugenic movement and for rational sex in this context should alert us, then, to a number of overlapping contexts and anxieties of early twentieth-century Indian life. So, for example, Phadke's suggestion that the caste system was validated by modern science in the form of eugenics says a great deal about the perceptions of threat experienced by upper caste men from anti-caste and anti–Brahminical movements of the period.

Pillay's was one of the earliest attempts to formulate the idea of modern masculinity that was also quite distinct from the traditional concerns with semen and its contribution to the formation — or dissipation — of maleness. Pillay's project was tightly bound to the notion of a "scientific-egalitarianism" where the male body was capable of bringing about social change through bodily practice. However, though the male body was positioned within the domestic space — via the relationship between men and women — it was simultaneously abstracted from the power relationships of gender in terms of work and reproduction. So, equality here was, in a sense, positioned purely through the agency of pleasure, excluding all notions of work; men and women are equal, Pillay was to implicitly suggest, in terms of their capacity for sexual pleasure, and the realm of the sexual is unconnected to the wider social sphere within which gender relationships might be unequal. In this way, we might think of masculinities whose pleasures and powers are connected to granting the gift of pleasure to women without necessarily diluting the *ability* to grant, and to take away.

From Scientific Masculinity to Homo Economicus: The Five-Year Plan Hero

Science as an aspect of the culture of Indian modernity has, of course, a well-established history in India (see, for example, Vishwanathan 1988, Srivastava 1998, Prakash 1999). In order to better grasp the complexity of post-colonial gender politics — especially in the context of masculine identity — it is particularly important to engage with the cultural discourse of science and rationality in the life of the modernizing nation-state. The project of the transformation of the native to the citizen was, of course, a gendered one, and science and reason played a particularly important role in defining the contours of modern subjectivity in India. The national heroes of postcolonial modernity were, typically, men such as P. C. Mahalanobis (1893–1972), an active Brahmo Samaji,[4] keen researcher of anthropometry, founder of the Indian Statistical Institute, and a leading influence upon the formulation of the second Five-Year Plan (Rudra 1996; see also Chatterjee (1993) chapter ten, for a discussion of planning in India).

It is the context of twentieth century development theory, as expressed through the post-independence planning regime and concurrently articulated in the Hindi films of the 1950s and 1960s, that provides the next rung of my discussion. What is of significance is the relatively *popular* currency of ideas that located Indian modernity,— and sought its meaning— in the spirit of a scientific world-view. In another work on the career of India's most famous "playback" singer, Lata Mangeshkar (2006), I have noted the emergence during the immediate post-independence period of a masculine type I have referred to as the Five-Year Plan (FYP) Hero, and have suggested that Lata's little girl voice should be counterpoised not just to any postcolonized masculinity, but to quite a specific one, that of the FYP Hero. This hero of Indian films represented a particular formulation of Indian masculinity where manliness came to attach not to bodily representations or aggressive behavior but, rather, to being scientific This was the idea of a middle-class epistemological or science-based masculinity as it emerged from sites as the Doon School (see Srivastava 1998). One of the ways in which this came to be represented on screen was through the operation of very specific spatial strategies, where roads and highways and metropolitan spaces came to be the "natural" habitat of the FYP Hero. As well, an important strand in 1950s and 1960s films was the profession of the hero: quite often he was an engineer (building roads or dams), a doctor, a scientist, or a bureaucrat. In significant instances, the filmic presence of the hero was one which could be quite easily characterized as camp. However, the camp persona of the heterosexual hero could co-exist quite comfortably with a nationalist ideology which identified post-independence manliness as linked to the "new" knowledges of science which, it was held, would transform the irrational native into the modern citizen. In the field of popular culture, the immediate post-independence period was particularly important in terms of representations of what could be called the aesthetic of planning and development.

For a fuller understanding of the symbolism of the filmic woman who embodies the voice of Lata Mangeshkar, we have to turn to the FYP Hero, whose identity, I suggest, is strongly linked to the nationalist economic development philosophy reified in the formulation and implementation of the Five-Year Plans.[5] The iconic presence of the FYP Hero gained some its legitimacy through both the Keynesian *and* the neo-classical models of economic thought, and he stood both for government intervention and for delayed gratification through the re-investment of savings for the "national" good.[6] The FYP Hero represents, in a broad sense, a particular formulation of Indian masculinity where manliness comes to attach not to bodily representations or aggressive behavior but, rather, to being scientific and rational (Srivastava 1996).

In the Indian case, economic development policies, especially in the guise of the Soviet inspired Five-Year Plans, traced a particular lineage to the world of science through, among others, the agency of mediating figures such as Mahalanobis, as mentioned above. One of the ways in which the scientific nature of the FYP Hero came to be represented on the screen was through the operation of very specific spatial strategies. An important aspect of this strategy was the iconic use of roads and highways in Hindi films of the 1950s and 1960s. My reference is to the bitumen road as a place of encounter between the hero and the heroine, as the backdrop to crucial song sequences, and as the linear space which provided the musical interlude for the display of the FYP Hero's technological aptitude as he adeptly handled that epitome of modernist desire — the motor car. Indeed, roads and highways in these films seem to carry such an aura of a planned modernity — all those aspirations of progressing in both literal and figurative senses — that the woman at the steering wheel and women on bicycles riding along the open highway become one of the most powerfully evocative representations of the modern Indian womanhood; these women come to embody a manual dexterity which marks them as visibly different.

The recurring association between the road/highway and the FYP hero serves to emphasize another point: that of his "natural" milieu: the metropolis.[7] We get some idea of the metropolis as a structuring trope through a series of post-independence Hindi films. So, "in films such as *Shri 420* (1955, Raj Kapoor), *New Delhi* (1956, Mohan Segal), *Sujata* (1959, Bimal Roy) and *Anuradha* (1960, Hrishikesh Mukherjee), the struggle over meaning and being in a post-colonial society takes place in a context where the metropolis is always a willful presence" (Srivastava 1998:165). Here, as in other films, the metropolis is, by turns, a site of decadence and extravagance luring innocent people into its web, a progressive influence upon "backward" intellects, and the promise of a contractual civil society that would undermine the atavism of kin and caste affiliations, ostensibly typified by the cinematic village. But perhaps, most importantly, the metropolis is also home to the modern, male, improver, the FYP hero.

Spatial strategies are particularly important representational tools in these films, one where, as has been noted in another discussion, "the aura of the metropolis manifests itself through a new language of cinematic space, [and] where striation and secularisation become important expressive principles" (Srivastava 1998:165). So, the opening shots of *New Delhi*, establish the sense of the post-colonial modernity the hero hopes to find in the milieu of the actual city. It is a modernity that expresses itself through the measured grid of roads, traffic lights and footpaths; and the camera, the hero, and the audience look out at these landmarks from a car being driven along major thoroughfares along which are dotted office buildings and other memorials to the nation-state. In *New Delhi*/New Delhi, economic planning and city planning come together "at a juncture where state intervention and a geometrical sensibility of modernity produce a peculiarly post-colonial nationalist aesthetics" (Srivastava 1998:166).

In some instances, the aura of the city is figured as the capacity of the male body to infiltrate those national spaces — such as the village — that may still be under the sway of "primitive" influences. Here, the metropolitan male body hurtles along national highways and train tracks, *en route* to the cinematic village; his object of social transformation is to be achieved through the transformation of personalities, and his presence as metropolitan virtues incarnate is the chief therapy. The hero is both an instrument of change as well as its personification. His metropolitan male body *is* the nation: it is an organic illustration of the transformation of local identities into the larger national self.

In the context of popular culture constructions of masculinity — and masculine sexual identity — the time of the FYP Hero had run its course by the late sixties. Of course, even during the height of his popularity, the economically and sexually frugal savior of the nation — who also saved on its behalf — had been shadowed by the vigorous and nihilist on-screen persona of Shammi Kapoor (1931–2011). However, the most decisive blow to the FYP Hero's identity as a culturally meaningful icon was delivered by the complex screen presence we now designate under the rubric "Amitabh Bachchan." The grounds for the articulation of "Bachchan-ness" were, however, prepared in a number of ways throughout the late 1960s and into the 1970s. So, for example, credit is due to the antics of the vehemently exuberant Jeetendra (b. 1942), and the slow but steady filmic journey of Dharmendra (b. 1935) from the "softness" of *Bandini* (1963; d. Bimal Roy) to the muscular jocularity of *Sholay* (1975; d. Ramesh Sippy). Of course, an important context in popular culture representations of masculinity during this period was the very real shift in creative class consciousness, with the lower classes finding an important niche both as characters and as audiences (on this see Mishra 2002).

The Demise of the Five-Year Plan Hero

It has been variously noted that Amitabh Bachchan's success lies in the anti-state, "angry-young man" presence of his on-screen persona (Prasad

1998). This is not doubt true. However, I would also like to speculate that Amitabh Bachchan brought to the screen some other very significant aspects of small-town masculinity, ones that have to do with the consuming and expressive capacities of the previously unrepresented provincial male body. In particular, this relates to skin color, language, homoeroticism, and an *incipient* relationship with commodities. Let me begin with anecdotal fieldwork. In various discussions about the appeal of Amitabh Bachchan with men in Patna and Lucknow, I have yet to come across a single instance of where their responses were articulated in terms of his anti-statism. In fact, I would like to suggest that in non-metropolitan areas (and indeed in larger cities), the state, simultaneously as it loathed, is also an object of great desire. There are the every-day complaints about its arbitrariness and high-handedness, but over-riding these is an almost sensuous craving to be recognized, touched, fondled, and assimilated by it. The loving detail with which newspapers — particularly in smaller towns — report the movements of the District Magistrate, the Superintendent of Police, the housing board chairman, the Cane Commissioner, the Revenue Commissioner, the Station House Officer, and a variety of other officials, reflect the situation of constraint and desire with respect to the state.

The two significant features that have tended to be overlooked in explanations of Bachchan's popularity have to do with his skin color and his language. We must remember that Bachchan was perhaps the first of the non-fair heroes on the Hindi cinema screen. Even in *Teesri Kasam* (1966, Basu Bhattacharya), the role of a Bihari villager is played by a very unlikely Raj Kapoor. Through the late 1970s and 1980s the Bachchan persona foregrounded the provincial-male-body-in-the-city. It was a one that was easily recognizable by the color of his skin and the distinct Allahabadi Hindi. The latter aspect became such an indispensable part of the Bachchan persona that in, say, *Namak Halal* (1982, Prakash Mehra), though Bachchan's on screen character (Arjun) starts off being a Haryanavi, as the film progresses, the "Jat" accent gives way to an Allahabadi lilt. So, both through his coloration and his language, the on-screen Bachchan marks an important move away from the Five-Year Plan Hero. There is an additional aspects that particularly relates to the death of the Five Year Plan Hero. This concerns the unambiguously heterosexual nature of the latter. An aspect of Bachchan's on-screen appeal lay in his ability to tap into the symbolic world of homoeroticism that finds play in a number of *provincial* contexts in India. Homoerotic representations can be found in contexts as diverse as marriage linked tomfoolery, everyday humor, celebrations surrounding festivals such as *Holi* (Cohen 1995), and the persistence of the Hijra imagery in a wider variety of contexts (Ghosh 2002). Bachchan was the first *hero* to openly express a homoerotic aura in several of his films. Most commonly, this was through "techniques of the body" (Mauss

1937/1973): cross-dressing, certain ways of walking, gesticulating (the hand-clap), and facial demeanor. That is to say, in films such as *Namak Halal* (1982, Prakash Mehra) and *Don* (1978, Chandra Barot), Amitabh Bachchan tapped into an ambiguous sexual canvas in a manner which, if not taboo for a leading man, was certainly extremely unusual, with such representations confined to minor characters or comedic roles.

What I wish to suggest is that a significant aspect of the Bachchan phe-nomenon concerns the representation of provincial masculinity in a metro-politan milieu. And, further, the provincial man comes to be associated with various forms of action, commerce, and individualism. Hence, the Bachchan hero moves — physically — through a world of container terminals, five-star hotels, wedding cakes, fancy shoes, international brand alcohol, dance halls, casinos, airports, and other sites and objects of industrial production *and* con-sumption. The Bachchan hero is the first generation consumer, having recently broken the shackles of the savings-regime of the FYP political economy. He is as much anti-statist in taking the law into his own hands, as announcing the beginnings of a consumerist agenda. His significance lies in the iconization of the loss of faith in the intentions and capacities of the FYP state, as well as the establishment of the provincial male as a potential participant in con-sumerism. Further, through Bachchan's body, metropolitan and provincial spaces become intertwined: provincial masculinity haunts metropolitan spaces, seeking to share in its fortune, interrogating its life-ways, and taking up res-idence in its Jhuggi-Jhopri (shanty) localities. It is to this latter context I now wish to turn in order to move to another register of analysis: that of ethnog-raphy of the city. The next section explores this context through an account of certain contexts of urban subaltern masculinities.

Footpath Desires and the Erotics of Modernity

The FYP Hero model of masculinity was located within the Keynesian model of economic thought, representing both government intervention and delayed gratification through re-investment of savings for the national good. While the FYP Hero was not asexual, his sexual self could only be read as the preoccupation with reproduction: he was the father of the nation. We might say, then, that the putative Indian concern with "semen anxiety"— regarding wastage of an essential fluid — is particularly relevant for the personality and preoccupations of the FYP Hero.[8] For, his manly vigor derived from his ability to sublimate non-reproductive desire — which may lead to semen wastage — into the service of the nation; it is the constant risk of non-sublimation (rep-resented by the vamp, for example) that was the source of anxiety. In this section, I reflect upon the *determinative* status of semen anxiety as constitutive of Indian male identity. I would like to suggest that the political and cultural economies of contemporary urban masculinities calls for analytical frameworks that include consumption as an important variable, and that the scholarly focus on semen anxiety misses out on important dimensions of the relationship between masculinity and modernity. The discussion will proceed through focusing upon material I will refer to as "footpath pornography."

The publications I refer to as footpath pornography are Hindi language booklets that are available all over North India. Typically, they are cheap to acquire (with prices ranging from Rs. 10–30), and are poorly printed and bound. They are, as my naming of the genre indicates, most frequently available at make-shift book-stalls that crowd the footpaths surrounding some of the busiest transit areas of the city — such as railways stations and inter-state bus stands — as well as commercial and small-scale industrial localities. The booklets are part of a world of ceaseless circulation: for, their purchasers most frequently acquire them in between, say, catching a bus or a train, and, as commodities, they circulate among men who are themselves vulnerable to frequent changes of employment and residence. Another aspect to their life as circulating commodities is that the publishers frequently disappear, switch trade, and commonly have their material carted away by the police.

While the audience for this material can be varied in terms of class, a very sizable section consists of young men of limited means, quite often living in slums and shanty towns under conditions of great insecurity of tenancy and landholding, and working as factory labor and in a variety of other casual (or "informal") occupations. Theirs is a world of constant and enforced mobility: changes in market conditions lead to frequent job losses and changes in government land policies lead to evictions from their "unauthorized" places of settlement. Booklet cover photographs often portray European women or versions of westernized Indian women in poses of "rapture" and "seduction." The authorship of the booklets is exclusively male. And, given their status as goods that are on public display and hence must be purchased in public, it is men who are also the purchasers.

In the majority of cases, the presentation of the footpath literature — despite its apparent intent — is not much like material that appears likely to elicit a sexual response. So, while the covers advertise for photos inside, these are mostly line-drawings printed on poor quality paper. Further, the printing itself is of haphazard quality, with frequently blurred images and bleeding colors. What, then, is the work of the low-quality image produced through the aegis of low-grade mechanical reproduction? And, what kinds of masculinities does it speak to? I suggest here that the booklets address a masculine context that is located within an — what might be called — an erotics of modernity.

The power of the footpath image derives, I suggest, from its *inability* to present a "realistic" representation of desire. As noted above, the women in these images are usually western or westernized Indian types. There is, therefore, an enormous distance of class and culture between the viewers (and readers) of such material and the female objects of desire. Indeed, the crux of the fantasy lies in the complete inaccessibility to the subaltern males whom I posit as the key readership for footpath pornography. In turn, the lack of realism of the printed material merely extends the logic of distance between the representations and the viewer: unattainable women (and desires) seem even more so through the lack of verisimilitude between the image and the possible objects of desire. What is "foreign," remains so. This distance is, in turn, the productive site of an erotic culture that is both produced through the material (or, mechanical) and cultural conditions of Indian modernity and produces modernity itself as erotic.[9]

Let us turn to the women of the booklets in order to explore this aspect. A wide variety of women jostle for male attention both in visual and narrative forms. Typically (and as noted above), visual representations consists of European women, or westernized Indian women. There is the continuity here with Indian cinema and the persona of the vamp, the most famous of whom was Helen, the Anglo-Indian actress who was famous for her western dance numbers. Helen constituted a displacement of Indian male desire: a western looking woman who was the focus of the desire that was unbecoming of the traditional Indian woman. The *Indian* woman was the object of a more permanent desire for domesticity whereas the western woman embodied a desire that was fleeting: she was more suitable as mistress and girlfriend.

The footpath booklets carry ample examples of the cultural complex we might loosely referred to "Helen-ness." This concerns the wanting and not-wanting the western or the westernized Indian woman. The story below is taken from the *Raat Ki Rani Digest* (Queen of the Night Digest) by Mast Ram (The Merry One; no publisher, no date). It carries the title "Pyaar ka Bhoot" (The Obsession of Love). The proponents of the story are Tejinder, a wealthy young Sikh who has an electronics business in Wazirpur, an outlying industrial and residential area of Delhi, and Shirley George, a Keralite Christian who lives in an apartment in affluent South Extension. In the story, "Shirley" is written as "Shir-lay," an error in transliteration that tells us something about the social and cultural distance of the booklet reader — and, in this case, the author — from the world of women named Shirley and, of course, Helen. It is this distance that is at the heart of the desire under discussion.

Shirley's modern persona is established in a number of ways: she is a Christian, lives alone (and in an up-market locality, hence combining personal autonomy with financial independence), and has been seen riding pillion on a motorcycle near the Army Officers Club in the Cantonment area of Delhi's Dhaula Kuan. The discourse of autonomy which often accompanies the idea of army women in India completes the picture of a woman of the city, astride (not side-saddle) a motorcycle with an unrelated male; she is dangerous and desirable in some indefinable manner.[10] Further, she is undertaking a course in beauty and make-up run by the (real life) herbal remedies entrepreneur, Shahnaz Hussain.

Tejinder is, through his Sikhness, an epitome of virile Indian manhood. However, in contrast to Shirley's modernist guile, his is an ingenuous masculinity, exemplified by the honest labor that has gone in to the making of his worldly success. Through a series of events, Tejinder and Shirley meet and launch upon a relationship, the course of which progresses through many car rides during which Shirley shares the front seat with her arm around her beau. There are frequent overnight stays in hotels where the lovers share passionate sex, whisky and that persistent symbol of the Indian modernist diet, omelets; Shirley's modernity is, then, of an un-remediable sort, more than skin deep, having been ingested through whisky and omelet and now lodged deep within her innards. It is not something just for show.

The affair proceeds apace and the pair visit Switzerland for a holiday. Shirley asks Tejinder for five thousand dollars which, she says, her father requires, but Tejinder thinks it is to pay a debt incurred as a result of her European shopping spree. He declines. Soon after, Shirley refuses to see him any longer. One day, Tejinder runs into her at a five-star hotel, playing cards and drinking in the company of an army man, Captain Arvind Kumar. He asks what became of their declarations of undying love for each other. Shirley replies that she will never be a slave to one man, and, shouts at him to "get lost." Crestfallen, Tejinder leaves. Some days later, Tejinder is arrested by the police, accused of kidnap and rape. Despite the false allegations made by Shirley, the author tells us, Tejinder's received an extended jail sentence. In jail, the story concludes, he lost the best years of his youth, and, he was also rid of the obsession of love.

Tejinder's tale of woe in not an unfamiliar one in footpath pornography, pitting, as it does, a traditional and pure Indian masculinity against the wiles of well-tempered westernized femininity. The warning against "deep" modernity embodied by women such as Shirley is accompanied by the simultaneous recognition of the seductions posed by the modern woman. There is a resigned acknowledgment of the powers of Helen-ness, as well as a warning against it. Beware the omelet eating woman.

In an age of hyper-consumerism, the desire for the active and consumerist woman, such as Shirley, is also a desire to take part more intensively in the cultures of consumerism. Her deep modernity is the site of an intense erotic charge as well as threat. How to consume modern sexuality and yet remain in control of one's masculinity: how to have but not have the modern woman?

The subaltern masculine cultures of the footpath booklets are embedded within an erotics of modernity that is both the grounds of aspiration as well as a context of fear. The erotics of modernity is characterized by the scattering of desire across a number of material and symbolic registers. The thread that connects these is the intense engagement with worlds that become erotic through their apparent inaccessibility. This, in turn, conjures the figure of the subaltern male who both desires and is chastised by the objects of his desire. Maleness is made in this crucible of seeking control and encountering rebuff.

Masculinity, "Publicness," Leisure and Consumption

Staying with the themes of consumerism and public spaces, this final section explores the relationship between masculinity and new cultures of middle-classness. Feminist scholarship has usefully suggested that the discourse of safety that is companion to the issue of women's access to public spaces is mired both in patriarchal and masculinist notions of protecting women (and hence men's honor), as well as classed notions of urban threats to "respectable" women (Phadke 2007). The offer of "safety" seeks to guard women's "reputation," and hence brings with it, among other restrictions, a "desexualised version of public visibility" (Phadke 2007). It is desexualized in the sense that women — unlike men — are prohibited from public expressions of sexuality. The choice is clear-cut: women should be safe in public spaces, but this also entails proper conduct on their part. It is in this regard that we need to consider some newer contexts that relate to women's access to public spaces and the politics of masculinity that surrounds it.

The rise of a new consumer culture that includes a larger section of the population than before has entailed the production of both new spaces as well as new identities. In terms of the former, they include new spaces of residence, leisure and shopping, and with regard to the latter, the relatively recent figure of the "consuming woman." The hectic construction activity that relates to gated residential communities and shopping malls are important to consider in this context. An extraordinary range of large and small cities across the country — with equally mind-boggling inventory of land area under construction, or completed — constitute sites of such activity. The Lucknow-based Sahara corporation has plans for the "world's largest chain of well-planned self sufficient high quality townships across 217 cities in the country" (Ahmedabad: 104 acres; Coimbatore, Kerala: 103 acres; Lucknow: 200 acres); it has already constructed the Amby Valley township near the city of Pune in Maharashtra on 10,000 acres which is described as "independent India's first planned, self contained, aspirational city, remarkable for its unsurpassed grandeur and plush signature features." In the Rajasthan township of Bhiwadi, some 60 kilometers from Delhi, no less than eleven real estate companies are reported to have launched *gated* residential projects in different price ranges, hoping to cash in on the proposed development of a number of "Export Processing Zones" and "Special Economic Zones" by large corporations such as Reliance and Omaxe.[11] The Omaxe group has residential projects in twenty-two cities across nine states in north and central India. These include the Omaxe Riviera (Rudrapur, Uttarakhand) and Omaxe Park Woods in Baddi (Himachal Pradesh), a township that is "home to some of the top industries like Nicolas Piramal, Bajaj Consumer Care, Ranbaxy, Dr. REDDY'S Lab, Torrent Pharmaceuticals, TVS Motors, Colgate Palmolive, Dabur India, Cipla, Cadbury's, Wipro, Wockhardt, Procter & Gamble, Marc Enterprises etc."[12] The Omaxe Heights in Lucknow offers an "in-house club with swimming pool and wave pool, tennis court, basketball court, banquet/community hall, squash court, steam room, Jacuzzi, gymnasium and television lounge."

With respect to shopping malls, while their numbers in India are not comparable to North America, it is not for want of local ambitions. So, before the economic downturn of the past few years, retail operators and mall entrepreneurs had predicted there would be around 700 malls in India by end of 2010 (Goswami 2009). At present, there are 172 malls already operating in India that "offer 52 million square feet of space" (ibid.: 12), and by the first quarter of 2011, this number was expected to rise to 350. At present, North India has 79 malls, western India 56, the eastern region 16, and south India 21. South India is expected to treble the number of malls (to 72) by this time, registering the fastest rate of growth. The National Capital Region has the most number of malls in the northern region, with Gurgaon home to eleven (compared to Jaipur's five and Lucknow's three).

The promises of spatial modernity held out by gated communities and malls have important consequences for our thinking on the relationship between space and gender. A significant aspect of the spatial narrative of consumerism is the concurrent one of the consuming woman. And, while the consuming woman is usually imagined as a middle-class figure, the aspiration to be one is not limited to the traditional middle classes. Indeed, for many younger women from lower socio-economic backgrounds, the idea of being middle class (which itself is a complex notion in the Indian context) is tightly bound up with being able to take part in the new consumerism (see, for example, SWSJU 2010). Further, the consuming woman is an object of great interest and research among marketing and advertising companies (Srivastava 2007).

The most significant social characteristic of the new spaces of consumerism is their invitation to *all* consumers to participate equally in the *public* life of such spaces. A consumerist democracy is the key to both profitability and an implicit justification for an activity that, historically, has been looked at with suspicion. However, it is also the site for male anxiety regarding the consuming woman. For, the consuming woman is one who spends upon herself, rather than necessarily furthering the interests and welfare of the family (and particularly the males among them). "Professional women," as Tanika Sarkar points out, now "have access to unprecedented self-reliance, [but] even housewives, faced with the ad culture and the shopping arcades, seek out things that are specially meant for themselves" (Sarkar 1995: 212–13). Contemporary economic and cultural changes pose an interesting challenge to masculine notions of the self: consumption is a good thing and none should be excluded, but what about the consuming woman who appears to "spend like a man"?

In some instances, masculinist discourse resolves the potential threat of the consuming public woman through the notion of the traditional-modern woman, where the woman as consumer is, nevertheless, positioned as being able to strike a balance between her public activities and her responsibilities towards the home. Within this discourse, the modern woman can, when required, "come back" to being a good housewife. In other cases, certain spaces such as gated communities are able, through strict control over space, to produce a safe realm for women. However, given the male dominated nature of the Residents Welfare Associations (RWAs) of the gated communities that are responsible for safety and security, the rules of protection referred to in the opening paragraph of this section apply. Also, while women residents are afforded protection within gated communities, the same may not apply to the female domestic workers who work within them; class and gender intersect in important ways in the making of masculine cultures.

The development of privatized public spaces such as gated communities and shopping malls are often looked upon with favor in as much as they are positioned alongside the dangers of the street and the bazaar. RWAs in gated residential enclaves work towards producing a sense of the public through organizing a variety of activities — religious and non-religious — that mimic the activities of the street. What makes possible the ersatz pell-mell of the street within the enclave is the circulation of the discourse of consumerist choice and intent that is *uninterrupted* by the "distractions" of the street, including the need for constant vigilance against putative others. It is within this crucible — where the street is not the street — that the public women of the gated community can be both the guardians of tradition *and* take part in the sexualized presentations of the self; the morning after elaborately dressed women have performed the rituals of *Karva-Chauth* (to ensure their husbands' well-being), they pace the condominium grounds on their exercise rounds dressed in skin-hugging clothing. And, unlike the constraint placed on women at street celebrations of the spring festival of *Holi* (that can also involve a sexual economy of fun [Cohen 1995]), at corporate-sponsored *Holi melas* (fairs) in many gated communities, men *and* women dance together to Bollywood songs on an open-air stage. The broader context of this is a particular kind of gender politics — built out of masculine and patriarchal strictures — that relates to the perceived ability to move between the worlds of "tradition" and modernity (see Srivastava 2007) by exercising choice. Through the notion of choice, consumerist modernity and its spaces offer women the possibility of both maintaining their reputation and taking part in "disreputable" activities denied by the open street. It is in this sense that contemporary middle-class notions of urban citizenship reformulates the "fraternal social contract" (Pateman 1989) within its masculinist terms to include the consuming woman within its remit; the manageable female consumer-citizen finds considerable play in RWA discourses of the making of the global city and its inhabitants.

Masculinities and Modernities

This selective history and ethnography of Indian masculinity has sought to suggest that the topic cannot be understood through focusing on men's identity as men. Rather, an exploration of male subjectivity requires close attention to a number of different contexts of cultural and political economy. Our objective is best served through approaching the issue through an interdisciplinary method that treats "masculinity" as the complex site for the unfolding of a number of different processes. These include different strategies of engaging with colonialism and the search of a national identity, the politics of caste and the valorization of science in the making of Indian modernity, post-colonial cultures of "nation-building," and the more recent efflorescence of commodity cultures. This is not the most "concise" way of navigating to the issue of masculine identity, but to proceed otherwise is to do injustice to the lessons of feminism and other critical positions within social theory.

Notes

1. This essay is an amalgam of a number of different essays written earlier and has not appeared in print in this form. As well, there are parts of the discussion which are completely new and have not appeared in print in any form.

2. "Extract from the Abstract of the Proceedings of the Council of the Governor General of India, assembled for the purpose of making Laws and Regulations under the provisions of the Act of Parliament 24 & 25 Vic., cap. 67, dated 3rd October 1870." Home Department

Files, National Archives of India, New Delhi (hereafter NAI). No. 1744, 27 September 1870. (Emphasis added). See also Nigam 1995.

3. It should be pointed out that it is *male* homosexuality that is being explicitly referred to here. The possibility of female homosexuality, though amply documented by writers and scholars, did not, for various reason engage much public attention; one of these, no doubt, was the naturalization of maleness as the crucial gender identity to be nurtured and protected.

4. See Srivastava (1998) for a discussion of the connections between the Brahmo Samaj and "modern" Indian identity as promulgated through educational institutions such as the Doon School.

5. Masculinity has had a varied career in Hindi films; for some other examples see Chakravarty (1993), especially Chapter Six, and Kakar (1990). It should also be added that the singing voices that most typified the FYP hero were those provided by Mohammad Rafi and the "earlier" Kishor Kumar. And, that the dominance of Lata's voice was part of the same process that established the styles popularized by Rafi and Kishor Kumar as the norms for male singers.

6. I am following standard and somewhat simplified notions of "Keyensian" and "neo-classical" models of economic thought. See for example, Samuelson 1992.

7. The following discussion has been adapted from Srivastava 1998, 165–167.

8. On the different ways in which this idea has been formulated see, for example, Alter 1992 and 2000, Carstairs 1958, Kakar 1990, and Parekh 1989.

9. My reference here is to "modernity" as a subjective — and shifting — experience of time and place. Of course, we might say that its apparent antithesis, "tradition," is also a product of modernist discourse. In my discussion, however, I treat the two terms as ones that have popular currency in India and are perceived as embodying different characteristics with relation to, say, male and female attributes, technology, governance, domestic arrangements, sexuality etc. See, for example, Chandra 1992 for India, and Berman 1983 for the western context.

10. We could speculate that Shirley is also heir to the popular image of the "loose" Malayalee woman of the soft-porn Malayalam cinema of the 1970s and 1980s which was quite widely screened in North India. I am thankful to S. Sanjeev for reminding me of this aspect.

11. www.indiarealitynews.com. Last accessed 15 August 2009.

12. www.omaxe.com. Last accessed 11 July 2009.

References

Agnes, Flavia (2001). "Women, Marriage, and the Subordination of Rights." In Partha Chatterjee and Pradeep Jeganathan (Eds.), *Community, Gender and Violence: Subaltern Studies XI.* London: Hurst and Company.

Alter, Joseph (1992). *The Wrestler's Body.* Chicago: University of Chicago Press.

_____. (2000). *Gandhi's Body. Sex, Diet, and the Politics of Nationalism.* Philadelphia: University of Pennsylvania Press.

Berman, Marshall (1983). *All That Is Solid Melts into Air: The Experience of Modernity.* New York: Verso.

Blackwood, Evelyn, and Saskia Wieringa (1999). *Same Sex Relations and Female Desires: Transgender Practices Across Cultures.* New York: Columbia University Press.

Butler, Judith (1999). *Gender Trouble. Feminism and the Subversion of Identity.* London and New York: Routledge.

Carstairs, M. G. (1958). *The Twice Born.* London: Hogarth Press.

Chakravarty, Sumita S. (1993). *National Identity in Indian Popular Cinema 1947–1987.* Austin: University of Texas Press.

Chandra, Sudhir (1992). *The Oppressive Present. Literature and Social Consciousness in Colonial India.* Delhi: Oxford University Press.

Chatterjee, Partha (1993). *The Nation and Its Fragments: Colonial and Postcolonial Histories.* Princeton, NJ: Princeton University Press.

Chopra, Radhika (2003). *From Violence to Supportive Practices. Families, Gender and Masculinities in India*. New Delhi: UNIFEM.

Cohen, Lawrence (1995.) "Holi in Banaras and the *Mahaland* of Modernity," *GLQ,* 2: 399–424.

Connell, Robert W. (2005). *Masculinities*. Cambridge: Polity Press.

Dutta, D. (2004). "Effects of Globalisation on Employment and Poverty in Dualistic Economies: The Case of India." In C. Tisdell and R. Sen (Eds.), *Economic Globalisation: Social Conflicts, Labour and Environmental Issues*. Cambridge, UK: Edward Elgar.

Emsley, Clive (2007). *Hard Men. The English and Violence Since 1750*. Continuum International Publishing: London.

Ghosh, Shohini (2002). "Queer Pleasure for Queer People: Film, Television and Queer Sexuality in India." In Ruth Vanita (Ed.), *Queering India; Same Sex Love and Eroticism in Indian Culture and Society*. New York: Routledge.

Goswami, Joydeep (2009). "India's Rich Diversity." In Amitbh Taneja (Ed.), *Operational Shopping Centres and Malls Next*. New Delhi: IMAGES Group.

Hansen, Kathryn (2004). "Theatrical Transvestism in the Parsi, Gujarati and Marathi Theatres (1850–1940)." In Sanjay Srivastava (Ed.), Sexual Sites, Seminal Attitudes. Sexualities, Masculinities and Culture in South Asia. New Delhi: Sage.

Haste, Cate (1992). *Rules of Desire, Sex in Britain. World War I to the Present*. London: Pimlico.

Kakar, Sudhir (1990). *Intimate Relations. Exploring Indian Sexuality*. Chicago: University of Chicago Press.

Mangan, J. A. (1986). *The Games Ethic and Imperialism: Aspects of Diffusion of an Ideal*. Harmondsworth: Viking Press.

Mishra, Vijay (2002). *Bollywood Cinema: Temples of Desire*. New York and London: Routledge.

Mauss, Marcel (1937/1973). "Techniques of the Body," *Economy and Society* 2: 71–88.

Nigam, Sanjay (1990). "Disciplining and Policing the 'Criminals by Birth,' Part 1: The Making of a Colonial Stereotype — the Criminal Tribes and Castes of North India." *Indian Economic and Social History Review*, Vol. 27, No. 2: 131–64.

O'Hanlon, Rosalind (1997). "Issues of Masculinity in North India History." *Indian Journal of Gender Studies* 4: 1–19.

Omissi, David (1991). "'Martial Races': Ethnicity and Security in Colonial India 1858–1939," War and Society 9 (1): 1–27.

Pateman, Carol (1989). *The Disorder of Women: Democracy, Feminism, and Political Theory*. Stanford: Stanford University Press.

Parekh, Bhikhu (1989). *Colonialism, Tradition and Reform. An Analysis of Gandhi's Political Discourse*. New Delhi: Sage Publications.

Phadke, N. S. (1927). *Sex Problem in India. Being a Plea for a Eugenic Movement in India and a Study of All Theoretical and Practical Questions Pertaining to Eugenics*. Bombay: D. B. Taraporevala Sons.

Phadke, Shilpa (2007). "Dangerous Liaisons: Women and Men, Risk and Reputation in Mumbai," *Economic and Political Weekly*, vol. xlii, no. 17, pp. 1510–18.

Pigg, Stacey (2005). "Globalizing the Facts of Life." In Vincanne Adams and Stacey Pigg (Eds.), *Sex in Development: Science, Sexuality and Morality in Global Perspective*. Durham, NC: Duke University Press.

Pillay, A. P. (1948). *The Art of Love and Sane Sex Living. Based on Ancient Precepts and Modern Teachings*. Bombay: D. B Taraporevala Sons.

Prakash, Gyan (1999). *Another Reason: Science and the Imagination of Modern India*. Princeton, NJ: Princeton University Press.

Prasad, Madhava (1998). *Ideology of the Hindi Film: A Historical Construction*. Delhi: Oxford University Press.

Radhakrishnan, S. (1975). *The Hindu View of Life*. New York: Macmillan.

Roselli, J. (1980). "The Self-Image of Effeteness: Physical Education and Nationalism in Nineteenth-Century Bengal," *Past and Present* 86: 121–148.

Rudra, Ashok (1996). *Prasanta Chandra Mahalanobis: A Biography*. Delhi: Oxford University Press.

Samuelson, P. A. (1992). *Economics*. 3rd Australian edition. Sydney: McGraw Hill.

Sarkar, Tanika (1995). "Heroic Women, Mother Goddesses: Family and Organisation in HIndutva Politics." In Tanika Sarkar and Urvashi Butalia (Eds.), *Women and the Hindu Right: A Collection of Essays*. New Delhi: Kali for Women.

Seidler, Victor J. (1994). *Unreasonable Men. Masculinity and Social Theory*. London: Routledge.

Sen, Sudipta (2004). "Colonial Aversions and Domestic Desires: Blood, Race, Sex and the Decline of Intimacy in Early British India." In Sanjay Srivastava (Ed.), *Sexual Sites, Seminal Attitudes. Sexualities, Masculinities and Culture in South Asia*. New Delhi: Sage.

Sengupta, Mitu (2008). "How the State Changed Its Mind: Power, Politics and the Origins of India's Market Reforms," *Economic and Political Weekly* 43 (21): 35–42.

Sinha, Mrinalini (1997). The "Manly Englishman" and the "Effeminate Bengali" in Late Nineteenth Century. New Delhi: Kali for Women.

Srivastava, Sanjay (1996). "The Garden of Rational Delights: The Nation as Experiment, Science as Masculinity," *Social Analysis* 39: 119–48.

_____ (1998). *Constructing Post-Colonial India. National Character and the Doon School* London: Routledge.

_____ (2003). "Schooling, Culture and Modernity." In Veena Das. A. Béteille and TN Madan (Eds.), *The Oxford India Companion to Sociology and Social Anthropology*. Oxford University Press: New Delhi.

_____ (2006). "The Voice of the Nation and the Five-Year Plan Hero: Speculations on Gender, Space, and Popular Culture." In Vinay Lal and Ashis Nandy (Eds.), *Fingerprinting Popular Culture. The Mythic and the Iconic in Indian Cinema*. Delhi: Oxford University Press.

_____ (2007). *Passionate Modernity. Sexuality, Class and Consumption in India*. Delhi: Routledge.

Vishwanathan, Shiv (1988). "On the Annals of the Laboratory State." In Ashish Nandy (Ed.), *Science, Hegemony and Violence: A Requiem for Modernity*. Delhi: Oxford University Press.

Wieringa, Saskia E. (2007). "'If there is no feeling...' The Dilemma Between Silence and Coming Out in a Working Class Butch/Femme Community in Jakarta." In M. B. Padilla et al. (Eds.), *Love and Globalisation: Transformations of Intimacy in the Contemporary World*. Nashville: Vanderbilt University Press.

Wijewardene, Shermal (2007). "But no one has explained to me who I am now...: 'Trans' Self-perceptions in Sri Lanka." In Saskia E. Wieringa, Evelyn Blackwood, and Abha Bhaiya (Eds.), *Women's Sexualities and Masculinities in a Globalizing Asia*. New York: Palgrave Macmillan.

Critical Masculinity Studies in India

Mangesh Kulkarni

The last three decades have witnessed the emergence of Critical Masculinity Studies (CMS) as an interdisciplinary field of academic inquiry (Kulkarni 2011; Kimmel, Hearn, and Connell, 2005). CMS originated in and remains largely sympathetic to feminist concerns. It is a constructive response to the diverse changes in men's lives induced by the ongoing project of women's liberation, as also by significant shifts in the economy (e.g., the transition from fordism to post-fordism) and society (e.g., changes in the structure of the family). The consequent disruption of traditional male roles (e.g., "breadwinner" and "protector") caused a crisis of hegemonic, patriarchal masculinity. The bewilderment of men buffeted by these changes found expression in various modes: as a demand for rights, a search for spiritual solace, or an unwavering commitment to the feminist cause. CMS seeks to probe the resulting predicament (and to provide some of the means needed for its resolution) by viewing it as part of the continual construction and reconstruction of masculinities across time and space.

The growing interest in CMS has given rise to an expanding corpus of scholarly output on the subject. Even a quick perusal of *Men's Lives*—a widely used anthology—or of recent issues of the Sage journal *Men and Masculinities* would indicate the variety and depth of this work in progress (Kimmel and Messner 2001). Though CMS is yet to find a secure academic foothold in India, the country requires it for at least two reasons. For one, masculinities are deeply implicated in a whole host of problems looming over the country, ranging from an abysmally low sex-ratio to communal violence. Besides, during the last two decades, the country has witnessed the emergence of men's groups, as also the publication of a significant body of writings examining various dimensions of men's lives (Kulkarni 2007; Chopra, Osella and Osella 2004).

This article offers a critical survey of the scholarly work on Indian masculinities against the background outlined above so as to formulate an agenda for future research, teaching and positive interventions in the area. The attempt is to highlight the ways in which the study of masculinities sheds new light on a wide spectrum of social phenomena ranging from colonialism and communalism to sexuality. The subsequent discussion encompasses the relevant literature generated by the social sciences and allied academic fields, as also the concerns articulated by various activist groups focusing on the gender dynamics of men and masculinities. The article takes as its point of departure the definition of masculinity provided by R. W. Connell (2005: 71): "'Masculinity' ... is simultaneously a place in gender relations, the practices through which men and women engage that place in gender, and the effects of these practices in bodily experience, personality and culture."

A Thematic Overview

Though systematic research examining different manifestations of masculinity in India is of recent origin, it has already enriched our understanding of the country's past and present in several ways. The following is an illustrative, account of certain major themes and perspectives that have emerged from the seminal work of scholars belonging to several disciplines including Psychology, History, Political Science, Sociology, Anthropology and Cultural Studies.[1] The bibliography includes publications discussed in the review and also other relevant titles pertaining to themes such as the imbrication of masculinities with education, work and health.

A. Psychological and Cultural Dynamics of Masculinities: The work of Sudhir Kakar represents the earliest and most sustained attempt to understand the psychological and cultural dynamics of masculinities in India. While he is a polymath scholar, his initial training was in psychoanalysis. In a landmark study, Kakar (1992/1978) probes the specificity of the normative matrices, family structures and socialization processes which shape the psyche of upper caste Hindu men.

According to Kakar, the closeness of the mother-son bond is an important formative influence on the mental make-up of Indian men. It stems from a variety of cultural conditions. A strongly entrenched son-preference means that the status of a married woman depends upon her ability to bear male children. Consequently, women make a considerable emotional investment in their sons. To this must be added the unusual length and intensity of maternal care received by the infant, as also the negligible role of the father in looking after young children.

An important consequence of these early childhood experiences is the

Indian man's ambivalent attitude towards the mother who is seen both as a nurturing benefactress and a threatening seductress. The modal resolution of the conflict involves a lasting identification with the mother. However, the subliminal fear of the "bad mother" is not completely erased and typically surfaces as an anxiety focused on the threatening sexuality of older or mature women. Another consequence is a permeable ego formation which generates trusting friendliness and eagerness to develop attachments. This explains the intimacy and vitality evident in Indian social relations despite widespread material deprivation.

Given the intensity and ambivalence of the relationship between mother and son, Indian boys rely on their fathers to a much greater extent than their Western counterparts in the endeavor to overcome maternal dominance and acquire a masculine identity. Hence they feel the necessity of oedipal alliance more acutely than the hostility of the Oedipus complex. Yet, the demands of the extended family require the father to maintain a certain aloofness from his son(s), creating a piquant dilemma for the latter.

Kakar's investigation into certain distinctive psychological traits of Indian men provides a useful point of departure. But his findings are largely based on limited clinical data, folklore and classical mythology. His work therefore tends to be somewhat static and ahistorical. This partly accounts for the ease with which he can reiterate the gist of his above-mentioned conjectures regarding the male psyche in a recent book on contemporary India (Kakar and Kakar 2007: 96–100) despite the significant socio-cultural transformation the country has witnessed since they were first formulated three decades ago.

The work of Ashis Nandy (1983) — who too is a psychologist and versatile scholar — tracks complex shifts in the political culture of Indian masculinities by focusing on the colonial period. He argues that one strand in the indigenous concept of manliness valorized the Brahmana in his cerebral asceticism vis-à-vis the violent and active Kshatriya who represented the feminine principle in the cosmos. Hence traditional Indian society placed limits on Kshatriya-hood as a way of life. This normative order began to change due to the impact of British colonialism which propagated hyper-masculine ideals and denigrated the colonized as infantile, devious, and effeminate people. According to the British, the positive qualities of childlikeness could be found in the loyal "martial races" of India, while childishness or feminine passive-aggression was a trait of the effete nationalists and *babus* (English educated petty officials) drawn from the non-martial races.

Indians initially responded to this quandary by giving a new salience to Kshatriyahood as true Indianness. Many of them tried to regain self-esteem by seeking hyper-masculinity or hyper–Kshatriyahood that would make sense to their compatriots and rulers. But in an unorganized, plural society, with a tradition of only contingent legitimacy for warriorhood, such a strategy was not efficacious. This is what the advocates of armed resistance discovered to their chagrin. They had isolated themselves from the society by the time Gandhi entered Indian politics.

The colonial culture's ordering of sexual identities was as follows: *Puru-shatva* (manliness) > *Naritva* (womanliness) > *Klibatva* (femininity in man). Gandhi responded through two orderings, each of which could be invoked depending on the needs of the situation. The first, borrowed from the traditions of saintliness in India, put androgyny above both *purushatva* and *naritva*. The second ordering was offered specifically as a justification of the anti-imperialist movement: *Naritva* > *Purushatva* > *Kapurushatva* (cowardice or failure of masculinity). It could make the magical power of the feminine cosmic principle available to the man who defied his cowardice by owning to his feminine self.

In sum, Nandy seems to argue that pre-colonial Indian society sustained a distinctive and composite gender order which was subsequently warped through the impact of the hyper-masculinist imperial ideology introduced by the British rulers. The nationalist response led to the inflation of the martial or Kshatriya model of masculinity that had earlier occupied a limited social space. Gandhi found a way out of this impasse by drawing on the rich resources available in the Indian tradition to create an emancipatory configuration of gender, culture and power. While Nandy's thesis remains influential, some of its presuppositions have been problematized by Rosalind O'Hanlon and Mrinalini Sinha in relation to the pre-colonial and colonial periods respectively.

B. Masculinities in the Mughal Era: In an essay marked by a deft interweaving of rich empirical material and analytical finesse, the British historian O'Hanlon has convincingly demonstrated the centrality of martial masculinity to society and politics in the late Mughal period (O'Hanlon 1997). She argues that in this period the battlefield, hunting expeditions and sports served as sites for the demonstration of the traits associated with martial valor. On the other hand, the court, the household and the harem were seen as abodes of effeteness and luxury. Contra Nandy, the code of martial masculinity was not exclusively modeled on the Kshatriya ideal, and it entered significantly into a wide variety of practices ranging from military recruitment and diplomacy to fellowship among men from different communities.

In a subsequent essay, O'Hanlon (1999) explores the ways in which norms of manhood informed the political and religious discourses of early seventeenth century Mughal north India, establishing significant links between kingship, statecraft and imperial service. To this end, she presents a case study of one high imperial servant in this period. O'Hanlon argues that the definitions of elite manliness started changing in the later seventeenth century and their nexus with imperial service frayed due to the emergence of a new urban ethos conducive to gentlemanly connoisseurship and consumption. This led to the intensification of strains in Mughal service morale.

O'Hanlon (2007a) has also explored an earlier stage of the Mughal era by investigating the linkages between kingdom, household and the body during the reign of Akbar. Her intention is to examine the composite character of Mughal political culture from the perspectives of gender and the body. She argues that Akbar drew on contemporary *akhlaqui* literature (ethical digests which offered advice on the acquisition of virtue) to create a socially inclusive model of masculine virtue which cut across law, religion, caste and region. The model emphasized the natural inner purity of the male body, and the ways of achieving moral and human perfection in the three homologous worlds that men inhabited as governors: the individual body, the household and the kingdom.

In her most recent work on the subject, O'Hanlon (2007b) draws on a wide range of sources — Sanskrit, Indo-Persian, Marathi and Indian English— to map the socio-economic and political ramifications of military sports and the history of the martial body in pre-colonial and colonial India. She underscores the importance traditionally attached to the cultivation of the bodily skills required in cavalry warfare and the concomitant development of a country-wide network that provided patronage and employment to the fighting specialists equipped with such skills. O'Hanlon argues that wrestling and allied exercises which were widely diffused and had become a vital complement to military preparation in the early modern period, dwindled in the aftermath of colonial demilitarization. This in turn led to the displacement of distinctive cultures of the body, as well as the depletion of mobility and honorable employment. The subsequent nationalist attempts to "recover" the older martial physical culture were driven by anxieties about Indian racial decline and the need for programs aimed at racial self-strengthening. This is precisely Mrinalini Sinha's point of departure.

C. Politics of Colonial Masculinities: Building on the pioneering work of Rosselli (1980), Sinha — a historian of Indian origin, currently based in the U.S.— has pointed out that "British manliness" and "Indian effeminacy" were conjointly constructed through political contestation within the imperial social formation (Sinha 1997). It is well known that the British categorized Indian people in terms of "martial" and "non-martial" races. In this invidious taxonomy, the Bengali *babus* were labeled as "effeminate." Consequently, they sought to recoup their masculinity. These were not purely local developments as the struggle was imbricated with the larger colonial contest, and also with the changing dynamics of gender relations in Britain. Sinha argues that an examination of the contending conceptions of masculinity, which were formed and re-formed during the colonial period, both in Britain and in India, would give us a much better understanding of the imperial social formation.

Certain significant ramifications of colonial masculinity can be gauged by revisiting the controversy surrounding the Age of Consent Bill (1891) that was apparently aimed at curbing the evil effects of child marriage, especially in Bengal, where the British thought the institution was most widely abused. The Bill sought to protect the child wife below the age of twelve years from the perils of sexual intercourse by declaring such intercourse to be an offence on the part of the husband. The Indian response to this measure was twofold. The pro-reform section responded positively, while the traditionalists protested vehemently. The latter saw the Bill as an affront to Indian manhood and as an egregious imperialist intervention in the private domain. But even the former did not accord centrality to the agency and autonomy of Indian women; instead it treated them as objects of reform. The marginalization of women thus cut across the reformist vs. traditionalist divide and left a deep imprint on the nationalist movement.

What the British rulers sought through measures like the Age of Consent Bill was, of course, the entrenchment of their hegemony in India. But their efforts at reform were half-hearted, as they felt threatened by the emergence of feminism in Britain itself, where sensationalized cases of child prostitution had led to the mobilization of the consent debate of 1885. They thus found it expedient to make peace with Indian patriarchy through the device of an executive order which rendered the Consent Act toothless. As Sinha points out, the final upshot was that both imperialist and nationalist interventions were subsumed within the larger matrix of colonial masculinity, marking a convergence of the efforts to recuperate the feminist challenge to British masculinity with the revivalist-nationalist efforts to reassert Indian masculinity.

While Sinha sheds new light on the reconstruction of patriarchy in the imperial social formation, her critique often elides certain important dimensions of indigenous masculinity. This is evident in her insufficient engagement with the cultural and political devices through which Indians sought to defend or reconstruct masculine identities (Singha 1998).[2] Besides, her study is quite closely aligned with Partha Chatterjee's important but controversial formulation which holds that the nationalist discourse in India was predicated on a dichotomy between the spiritual/inner and material/outer spheres, and that the nationalists recognized the dominance of the British in the latter sphere, but saw the former as an inviolable repository of superior indigenous traditions and values (Chatterjee 1986).

D. Masculinities in the Matrix of Nationalism and Communalism: For a perceptive interrogation of Chatterjee's theory of nationalism, and for a nuanced account of the imbrication of masculinities with nationalist and communal moral economies, we may turn to the work of Joseph Alter — an anthropologist of Indian origin, currently based in the U.S.A. While granting the usefulness of Chatterjee's interpretation of the nationalist discourse, Alter finds his use of the term "spiritual" somewhat misleading on account of its association with the mystical and the esoteric. Though Hindu notions of somaticity, encompassing ritual, health, and social hierarchy fell within the "inner" domain of the *soi-disant* spiritual discourse of nationalism, the forces of imperial power impinged directly on bodies as material objects. Alter extends his argument by examining contemporary popular Hindi literature on *brahmacharya* and shows how the "spiritual" male body has become a focal site for a discourse of nationalism (Alter 1994a).

This literature, chiefly intended for young men, reveals an articulation of traditional life-cycle prescriptions pertaining to *dharma* and the post-colonial anxiety to shun the contaminating effects of hedonistic modernity. The discourse of celibacy here becomes part of a "somatic nationalism," geared to the resistance of dissolute Western ideologies and to the regeneration of the motherland. Central to the pursuit of celibacy is the retention of the semen, which is imbued with not just physiological, but also spiritual/moral potency. An elaborate regimen involving the right kind of diet, exercise and various other norms of conduct, such as the avoidance of pornography, is proffered to this end. It does not spring from a puritanical preoccupation with vice and virtue, but rather reflects a hydraulic and biochemical concern with the refashioning of the male body. Alter finds an exacting embodiment of such a regimen in the wrestlers of North India, with the wrestling *akhara* (gymnasium) serving as a social microcosm through which the aforementioned ideas regarding celibacy are both put into practice and propagated.

The modern purveyors of the ideology of celibacy trace the "sexual addiction" of the country's youth to the "invention" of sexuality (*à la* Foucault) in the colonial period. Whereas there was an elaborate discourse on the *art of sex* in precolonial India, what colonialism generated was an *apparatus of sexuality*, which turned sex into a socio-moral force insidiously pervading the entire cultural arena. The legacy of colonial sexuality is incarnated in the postcolonial "libertine," whose masculinity is based on pathological individualism, domination and self-gratification, leading to a sheer waste of vital fluids. The *brahmachari* (celibate male), with his commitment to self-control, balance and natural truth, represents a nationalist negation of such libertine masculinity. It is worth noting that the *brahmacharya* discourse underscores the dangers of sex in the marital framework. It severely condemns excessive indulgence (what is not required for the purpose of procreation) in this supposedly legitimate and institutionalized form of sex. By thus making the "inner domain" of the family a site of national reform, it clearly departs from what Chatterjee sees as the early nationalist emphasis on the sanctity of this domain.

The relationship between sex and social reform implicit in the *brahmacharya* discourse has a precedent in the traditional Indian ideal of the *sannyasi* (renouncer) — a *brahmachari* deriving his socio-moral authority from an ascetic control of the senses. M. K. Gandhi, who occupied a liminal position vis-à-vis the premodern and contemporary Indian discourses on sex, invoked this ideal; however, he democratically proffered it to everybody. He also endorsed the conventional importance of semen retention, although without treating semen as the repository of truth. Above all, his views on sex, drawn as much from the Hindu tradition as from certain strands of Christianity, ultimately entailed a transcendence of the body towards a spiritual horizon. They formed a unique amalgam that granted gender equality in the quest for virtue through the regulation of bio-moral substance, but arguably underwrote the new nationalist patriarchy.[3] The contemporary discourse on *brahmacharya* on the other hand, is one-dimensional in its profane pursuit of celibacy as a way to engender nationalism, and in its straightforwardly patriarchal thrust.

Alter has also provided a trenchant critique of the communal ideology underlying the physical education regimen prevalent in the Hindu nationalist Rashtriya Swayamsevak Sangh (Alter 1994b). To this end he contrasts the RSS ideology with the non-sectarian somatic nationalism of north Indian wrestlers, both of whom seem to be drawing on certain common elements of the Hindu tradition such as *brahmacharya*. The comparison clearly reveals that the former represents a curious mélange of modern Western practices (e.g., European Physical Education techniques bulk large in the RSS drill) and a warped understanding of Hindu culture that aggressively excludes other religious communities from the definition of the nation, while covertly justifying the unjust status-quo within the Hindu social fold.

In contrast, the somatic nationalism of the wrestlers is seen to be an authentically indigenous vision of a harmonious development of the self and society, syncretic in the way it cuts across communal/caste lines, and projects an inclusive, "geomoral" conception of the nation. It seeks to overcome the baleful effects of immoral modernism by developing the psychosomatic self through a micro-physics of rigorous discipline anchored in the *akahara* (gymnasium). The nation is seen as the *akahara* writ large, embodying an elemental balance in the national ecology. While this image of the nation is fashioned in terms of Hindu notions of substance and balance, it is fundamentally unlike the socio-cultural landscape visualized by the RSS or other such champions of Hindutva. It substitutes generic geomorality for the particular, communal ideology of sacred rivers, holy mountains and blessed soil, thereby offering a Hindu critique of Hindutva demagoguery through a somatic discourse.

Alter thus offers a richly textured understanding of certain important strands of Indian masculinity within an essentially ethnographic framework. However, he does not pay adequate attention to the ways in which the seemingly benign somatic nationalism of the wrestlers often translates into an active and gruesome complicity in the murder and mayhem of communal riots, which is a commonly observed occurrence in contemporary India.[4]

The foregoing overview has tried to show how the small but significant corpus of social science literature pertaining to Indian men and masculinities has contributed to the ongoing debates on a wide spectrum of issues ranging from the cultural matrix of the body, sexuality and personality formation to the politics of colonialism, nationalism and communalism. It is quite evident that further investigations along these lines would be of great cognitive value.

Organizational Initiatives

During the last two decades, Indian civil society has witnessed a slow and sporadic but significant crystallization of organizational initiatives and interventions targeting men and masculinities. They can be broadly divided into three categories: pro-feminist, gay affirmative, and those championing men's rights. This is of course a rather crude classification which conceals commonalities as well as heterogeneity in the service of analytical convenience. However, all these forms of mobilization raise important questions which the social scientists are yet to address in an adequate manner.

A. Pro-feminist Initiatives: The women's movements of the 1970s and 1980s were inspired by second-wave feminism and had wide repercussions including the sensitization of numerous young men to the ravages of patriarchy. Some of these men (and like-minded women) have launched pro-feminist initiatives with the objective of recasting patriarchal masculinities to promote women's empowerment and gender justice. Accordingly, they have been interrogating the dominant constructs of masculinity through a critique of male socialization and gender roles. They particularly seek to reduce male violence against women, children and other men, and to eliminate various expressions of sexism.

Prominent representatives of the pro-feminist tendency include Purush Uvaach (Pune), the Mumbai-based Men Against Violence and Abuse (MAVA), Men's Action to Stop Violence Against Women (MASVAW, Lucknow), and the Forum to Engage Men (FEM) — a recently formed country-wide network. The first (and the oldest) of these still largely retains its character as an informal group — started in the late 1980s, it is run by a middle-class couple who hold periodic meetings at their residence. However, the others have assumed a familiar NGO format typified by MAVA.

MAVA claims that it came into existence in response to a small advertisement in the *Indian Express* and its sister publications, which called for men who are "strongly opposed to violence towards wives from their husbands, and would like to help stop it" (MAVA 2003). Registered in March 1993 as a "Society" under the Societies Registration Act, MAVA is run by a Managing Committee of five men from various kinds of professional background. The organization has women members as well. Its primary objective has been to bring about a change in the "traditional, male dominated" attitudes of men and help stop or prevent violence or abuse of women, which is particularly rampant in the domestic sphere (Bhattacharya 2005).

MAVA's programs have included the following: free counseling and guidance to families facing marital conflict, gender sensitization programs for different target groups including school and college youth, publication of the Marathi periodical *Purush Spandana* (Men's Heartbeats), Medical Aid Drive for Dipti Khanna — a 19-year-old girl badly injured by an acid attack in 1995 — and networking with women's groups and like-minded bodies through referral of cases of domestic violence and by jointly organizing activities aimed at tackling specific gender issues (Wagle 2007). "Yuva Maitri" (Friendship among Youth) is particularly noteworthy among MAVA's recent projects. Supported by the Population Council (New York), it involved the gender sensitization and training of a group of young male students from six colleges in the Pune district.

The regular publication of *Purush Spandan* is perhaps the most significant contribution of MAVA. Published (jointly with "Purush Uvaach" from 1996 to 2006 and independently since then) annually during Diwali, *Purush Spandana* is probably the first publication of its kind in the country. It focuses on gender issues and carries reports, essays, autobiographical/biographical accounts, stories and poems voicing the ideas, views and sentiments of men from different walks of life. The periodical has received prizes from various literary bodies in the state. English translations of selected articles from the back issues are now available in the form of a book (Ravindra, Sadani, Geetali & Mukund 2007).

B. Gay-affirmative Initiatives: A number of groups have been engaged in the struggle to end discrimination against homosexual men. They seek to root out homophobia which gives rise to such discrimination. Until recently, its chief target was Section 377 of the Indian Penal Code — a colonial piece of legislation that criminalizes homosexuality. The Section, appearing under the title "Of Unnatural Offences," reads as follows: "Whoever voluntarily has carnal intercourse against the order of nature with any man, woman or animal shall be punished with imprisonment for life, or with imprisonment of either description for a term which may extend to ten years, and shall also be liable to fine. *Explanation*: Penetration is sufficient to constitute the carnal intercourse necessary to the offence described in this section" (Ratanlal and Dhirajlal 1992: 431).

The concerns of homosexual men are gaining a wider audience in the aftermath of the AIDS pandemic. Besides, the gay cause has vocal and media-savvy spokesmen like the Mumbai-based activist Ashok Row Kavi. He launched a newsletter—*Bombay Dost*—in 1991 and the Humsafar Trust in 1994 as platforms for gay men and men who have sex with men. The Trust seeks to free these men from the bane of invisibility and infamy. It is active in educating them about sexually transmitted diseases in general and HIV/ AIDS in particular. It provides them with support structures and access to health facilities.

The Humsafar Trust has gained wide recognition for its activities which include community work, outreach into the target groups, as also advocacy and research on gender and sexuality issues concerning sexual minorities. It organized the first gay men's conference in the sub-continent. It is also an active member of global networks like the International Gay and Lesbian Human Rights Commission, and the International Lesbian and Gay Association. The Trust has always sought to work with the government, the medical establishment and various social groups involved in sexual health and social empowerment.

While homosexual subcultures have been covertly present in Indian society for long, recent years have witnessed a more open acknowledgment of the gay identity. One clear indication of this change is the unconventional representation of homosexuality in the cinema and the mass media more generally. It is particularly noteworthy that a mainstream publishing house has brought out an anthology of Indian gay literature (Merchant 1999). Events like Queer Pride marches have been organized in many Indian cities to affirm the rights of lesbian, gay, bisexual and transgender people. Most significantly, the multi-pronged campaign against the anti-gay implications of Section 377 of the Indian Penal Code has drawn a positive response from the Delhi High Court. In a historic judgment delivered in 2009, the Court decriminalized private consensual sex between adults of the same sex.

C. Men's Rights Initiatives: The groups fighting for men's rights are wary of feminism. They focus on the modern constructions of gender, which they see as imposing unfair restrictions on men. Accordingly, they target the legal and social realities that seemingly place the male at a disadvantage. A widely publicized example of the men's rights tendency is the Mumbai-based Purush Hakka Samrakshan Samiti (Committee for the Protection of Men's Rights) which claims to be the first such registered body in the country.

The Samiti was formed in 1996 to fight against the allegedly gross misuse of Section 498 (A) of the Indian Penal Code and to safeguard the interests of "harassed husbands" and their relatives who were said to be victims of such misuse. It claimed that within a few years 6000 men had joined the fraternity, mostly comprising well educated, middle-class men in the 25 to 45 age group. Similar groups have emerged in many other parts of the country, and there is now a national network of those advocating men's rights — Save Indian Family Foundation (Bangalore) — which opposes a wide range of laws and policies that (it claims) are being used against men.

The controversial Section 498 (A) of the Indian Penal Code reads as follows: **Husband or relative of husband of a woman subjecting her to cruelty**— Whoever, being the husband or the relative of the husband of a woman, subject such woman to cruelty shall be punished with imprisonment for a term which may extend to three years and shall be liable to fine.

Explanation— For the purposes of this section "cruelty" means —

(a) any willful conduct which is of such a nature as is likely to drive the woman to commit suicide or to cause grave injury or danger to life, limb or health (whether mental or physical) of the woman; or

(b) harassment of the woman where such harassment is with a view to coercing her or any person related to her to meet any unlawful demand for any property or valuable security or is on account of failure by her or any person related to her to meet such demand [Ratanlal and Dhirajlal 1992: 569].

This Section — inserted in 1983 to combat the menace of dowry deaths — makes the harassment of a woman by her husband or his relatives a non-bailable, non-compoundable, cognizable offence. Police complaints filed under it may result in the immediate imprisonment of the accused.

The men's rights groups allege that the Section has been widely abused to harass and torture husbands and their family members. They see it as an unjust measure instigated by the feminists' indiscriminate emphasis on women's victimhood and men's culpability. Therefore they target women's organizations — dubbed as "home-breakers rather than protectors of women's rights"— that are alleged to be aiding and abetting the abuse of the Section through misplaced ideological fervor. What motivates their protest is an unprecedented sense of vulnerability felt by men *qua* men. They also see the said Section as the thin end of the wedge that would irreparably cleave hoary institutions like the family, ultimately leading to a breakdown of Indian culture.

The long-term remedial measures sought by the men's rights groups include the following demands: Section 498(A) should be made non-cognizable, bailable and compoundable; if a complaint filed under the Section is proved false, the complainant should pay full compensation and such a person should be punished under special legal provisions; Section 498 (B) should be added to facilitate the lodging of a complaint against harassment by the wife or her relatives; and no compensation should be granted to working women in case of separation.

The men's rights groups have organized conventions and sought publicity in other ways to further their cause in the teeth of strong opposition by feminists who see them as part of a backlash against the attempted empowerment of women (Tata Institute of Social Sciences 1999). They have sought judicial remedies and also lobbied with the Union Law and Home Ministries as well as Parliament in pursuit of their demands. While they received a setback with the passage of the Protection of Women from Domestic Violence Act (2005), it must be noted that Supreme Court judges have often passed strictures against the misuse of Section 498 A; besides, Justice Malimath Committee's Report (Committee on Reforms of Criminal Justice System, Government of India, Ministry of Home Affairs 2003) has recommended that the section be amended to make the offence it addresses bailable and compoundable. The Government's recent bid to make laws "gender-neutral" over the next few years has given the men's rights groups a major opportunity to promote their agenda.

A sociological commonality among these different men's groups is that they are predominantly of urban, middle-class provenance. But this does not necessarily prevent them from working among other social strata. Thus, many gay activists have been attentive to their lower class brethren including the *hijras*; while pro-feminist groups have been trying to address the concerns of rural and subaltern men. A section of *dalit* (ex-untouchable) men could be galvanized into action through awareness of the predicament stemming from their contradictory caste and gender locations (Rao 2006; Anandhi, Jeyaranjan and Krishnan 2002). In any case, it seems likely that the landscape of mobilized masculinities will show greater heterogeneity in the near future.

A Possible Agenda

The foregoing overview has sought to give a fair indication of the rich potential of CMS in India. This concluding section presents an agenda for further research and intervention vis-à-vis some of the issues discussed above.

The investigation of the pre-colonial, traditional matrix of Indian masculinities and its transformation under the impact of colonialism and modernity calls for a multi-pronged research strategy.[5] Kakar's writings focusing on the psycho-sexual dynamics of personality formation and social behavior indicate one element of such a strategy. It is necessary to build upon his work through theoretically informed empirical explorations attuned to the cultural flux induced by rapid urbanization, industrialization and globalization. Nandy's imaginative account of the political and cultural transactions that produced a new gestalt of masculinities during the colonial era is a hard act to follow; but it has a considerable heuristic value. O'Hanlon's exemplary excavation of the codes and practices shaping masculine conduct and linking it to wider configurations of power during the Mughal era needs to be extended to other ruling class cultures in the country.

Sinha's concern with the dialectics of gender in the imperial social formation can be fruitfully carried beyond the chronological and thematic limits she sets herself. This would entail attention to the role of the colonial state's legal and cultural apparatuses, the transcontinental circulation of ideologies like Nazism, and various currents within the nationalist movement that contributed to the restructuring of Indian masculinities. Only thus can we gain an adequate purchase on the historical constitution and political character of the new patriarchies that emerged from our encounter with colonialism.[6]

Even as Sinha draws to our attention the colonial crucible of masculinity, Alter alerts us to the plurality of discourses and specificity of sites that constitute male bodies and insert them into larger configurations like nationalism.[7] The changing plebeian discourses of virility/patriotism and practices of physical culture/masculine camaraderie would be worthy of investigation from this standpoint. Particular attention needs to be paid to their key role in the mass mobilization program of militant Hindu nationalist formations such as the Bajrang Dal and Shiv Sena.[8]

Alter's emphasis on the body needs to be complemented by an accent on the body politic. Together they require attentiveness to the fashioning of subjectivities via processes of representation, political economy and technologies of the self. The construction and reconstruction of masculine subjectivities through the mass media, diverse channels of consumerism and ersatz economies of violence should be explored in this context.[9] It would be instructive to decipher these phenomena, especially as they resonate with the dynamics of post-fordist capitalism and shape the novel forms of nationalism and communalism materializing in its interstices.[10]

As for the concerns raised by men's groups, they require urgent investigation. The initiatives of pro-feminist groups in addressing the roots of violence against women (and men) as also in the larger area of gender sensitization should be studied, refined and replicated. It is necessary to build bridges between them and the women's movement.[11] The formation of a nationwide pro-feminist men's network — Forum to Engage Men — in 2007, and the launching of the Purush Samvaad Kendra or Forum for Dialogue with Men by the Nari Samata Manch — a Pune-based women's organization — in 2008 are welcome moves in this direction.

Gay mobilization has opened up the area of alternative sexual subcultures and of sexuality in general. It has highlighted the plight of men who have sex with men and of male sex-workers in particular. Apart from providing an alternative perspective on pressing problems like the AIDS pandemic, it has stimulated thinking and action aimed at the creation of a healthy, plural order of gender/sexual relations.[12]

The emergence of men's rights groups is among other things a symptom of the social disruption caused by attempts to alter traditional gender relations through an excessive reliance on the blunt weapon of the law (cf. Radhakrishnan 2006; Menon 2007b). A dialogue with the members and sympathizers of such groups to identify and attend to their genuine grievances and constructive suggestions could be one way of engaging them in a process of conscientization. Apart from facilitating short-term amelioration, such efforts may also offer valuable lessons for the larger project of creating a gender-just social order.

An adequate interrogation of Indian masculinities would involve critical attentiveness to academic as well as activist desiderata of the sort delineated above. This is surely a tall order. But there is no avoiding it if one is to pursue CMS with the intellectual rigour and contemporary relevance it demands and deserves.

Acknowledgments

This article is an outcome of research projects sponsored by the University of Pune, India. I have made extensive use of materials available at various institutions. Apart from my own university, the latter include Tathapi (Pune), Men against Violence and Abuse (Mumbai), Centre for the Study of Culture and Society (Bangalore), Centre for the Study of Developing Societies (Delhi), Madras Institute of Development Studies (Chennai), and the National Library (Kolkata). I have greatly benefited from interaction with scholars like Professor Ashis Nandy, Professor Rosalind O'Hanlon, Professor Sanjay Srivastava, Dr. S. Anandhi, and activists such as Mr. Mohan Hirabai Hiralal, Mr. Ashok Row Kavi, Mr. Rahul Roy, and Mr. Bindumadhav Khire.

Notes

1. Other disciplines which have witnessed some work in the area include Economics (Kodoth 2004), Human Geography (Raju, Atkins, Kumar and Townsend 1999), Social Work (Joseph 2005), and Legal Studies (Narrain 2004). It is interesting to note that two pioneering books on Indian men were written in a popular vein and were authored by freelance women writers (De 1998; Mulchandani 1999).

2. This lacuna has been partly redressed by Indira Chowdhury (2001) in her insightful study of gender and the politics of culture in colonial Bengal.

3. For the author's book-length treatment of Gandhi, see Alter (2000).

4. Kakar (1996: 66–110) offers a graphic and unsettling account of this phenomenon in the context of communal riots in Hyderabad. It is based on interviews with Hindu and Muslim *pehlwans* (wrestlers) in the city. Kakar cites Alter (1992a; 1992b) in a largely adulatory fashion, and ends his essay on a note of bewilderment: "Killers in the service of their religious communities, they [the *pehlwans*] do not fit easy psychological or philosophical categories."

5. Sanjay Srivastava's work on the Doon School — a famous boarding school for boys in India — provides a critical account of the interface between masculinity and modernity in postcolonial India (Srivastava 1998).

6. G. Arunima's study of the historical reasons for the legal abolition of matriliny in twentieth-century Kerala is a path-breaking work of this kind (Arunima 2003). Also see Chakraborty (2011) and Chowdhry (2010).

7. For an adumbration of the ways in which violence was inscribed on male bodies during the communal riots in Dharavi (Mumbai) after the demolition of the Babri Masjid, see Chatterji and Mehta (2007: 105–128). Amrita Basu (2000) has used a larger canvas to examine the conundrum involving men as victims and women as agents of communal violence.

8. Hansen (1996; 2001) and Banerjee (2000; 2005) are good examples of scholarly work in this area.

9. Some of these themes are ably explored in Srivastava (2007) and Mazumdar (2007).

10. Amrit Wilson (2007) provides a useful perspective on such issues in a diasporic context.

11. Two heartening bibliographic examples of such bridge-building are a pro-feminist graphic book on men produced by Rahul Roy, Anupama Chatterjee and Sherna Dastur (2007), and a primer on masculinity in the Gender Basics series of Women Unlimited (Bhasin 2005). Also see Kulkarni (1997) and Chopra (2007).

12. Recent years have witnessed the publication of several books and articles on alternative sexualities in India. Brinda Bose and Subhabrata Bhattacharya (2007) have compiled a substantial volume on the subject. Also see Reddy (2005), Narrain and Bhan (2005), and Menon (2007a).

References

Akhtar, Salman (Ed.) (2008). *Freud Along the Ganges: Psychoanalytic Reflections on the People and Culture of India*. New Delhi: Stanza.

Alter, Joseph (1992a). *The Wrestler's Body: Identity and Ideology in North India*. Berkeley: University of California Press.

_____ (1992b). "The Sanyasi and the Indian Wrestler: The Anatomy of a Relationship," *American Ethnologist*, 16 (2), 317–336.

_____ (1994a). "Celibacy, Sexuality and the Transformation of Gender into Nationalism in North India," *The Journal of Asian Studies*, 53 (1), 45–66.

_____ (1994b). "Somatic Nationalism: Indian Wrestling and Militant Hinduism," *Modern Asian Studies*, 28 (3), 557–588.

_____. (2000). *Gandhi's Body: Sex, Diet and the Politics of Nationalism*. Philadelphia: University of Pennsylvania Press.

_____. (2011). *Moral Materialism: Sex and Masculinity in Modern India*. New Delhi: Penguin Books.

Anandhi, S., J. Jeyaranjan, and Rajan Krishnan (2002). "Work, Caste and Competing Masculinities: Notes from a Tamil Village." *Economic and Political Weekly*, Vol. 37, No. 43, Oct. 26–Nov. 1, 4397–4406.

Arunima, G. (2003). *There Comes Papa: Colonialism and the Transformation of Matriliny in Kerala, Malabar c. 1850–1940*. Hyderabad: Orient Longman.

Banerjee, Sikata (2000). *Warriors in Politics: Hindu Nationalism, Violence and the Shiv Sena in India*. Boulder, CO: Westview Press.

_____ (2005). *Make Me a Man!: Masculinity, Hinduism and Nationalism in India*. Albany: State University of New York Press.

Basu, Amrita (2000). "Engendering Communal Violence: Men as Victims, Women as Agents." In Julia Leslie and Mary McGee (Eds.).

Bharucha, Rustom (1995). "Dismantling Men: Crisis of Male Identity in 'Father, Son and Holy War.'" *Economic and Political Weekly*, July 1, 1610–1616.

Bhasin, Kamla (2005). *Exploring Masculinity*. New Delhi: Women Unlimited.

Bhattacharya, Rinki (Ed.) (2005). *Behind Closed Doors: Domestic Violence in India*. New Delhi: Sage.

Bose, Brinda, and Subhabrata Bhattacharya (Eds.) (2007). *The Phobic and the Erotic: The Politics of Sexualities in Contemporary India*. London/New York/Calcutta: Seagull Books.

Chakraborty, Chandrima (2011). *Masculinity, Asceticism, Hinduism: Past and Present Imaginings of India*. Ranikhet: Permanent Black.

Chatterjee, Partha (1986). *Nationalist Thought and the Colonial World: A Derivative Discourse*. New Delhi: Oxford University Press.

Chatterji, Roma, and Deepak Mehta (2007). *Living with Violence: An Anthropology of Events and Everyday Life*. London: Routledge.

Chopra, Radhika (Ed.) (2007). *Reframing Masculinities: Narrating the Supportive Practices of Men*. New Delhi: Orient Longman.

Chopra, Radhika, Caroline Osella, and Filippo Osella (Eds.) (2004). *South Asian Masculinities: Context of Change, Sites of Continuity*. New Delhi: Women Unlimited.

Chowdhry, Prem (2010). *Contentious Marriages and Eloping Couples: Gender, Caste and Patriarchy in Northern India*. New Delhi: Oxford University Press.

_____ (2005). "Crisis of Masculinity in Haryana: The Unmarried, the Unemployed and the Aged." *Economic and Political Weekly*, December 3, 5189–5198.

Chowdhury, Indira (2001). *The Frail Hero and Virile History: Gender and the Politics of Culture in Colonial Bengal*. New Delhi: Oxford University Press.

Committee on Reforms of Criminal Justice System, Government of India, Ministry of Home Affairs. (2003). *Report: Volume I*.

Connell, R. W. (2005). *Masculinities*. Crows Nest: Allen & Unwin.

De, Shobha (1998). *Surviving Men: The Smart Woman's Guide to Staying on Top*. New Delhi: Penguin Books.

Gupta, Charu (1998). "Articulating Hindu Masculinity and Femininity: 'Shuddhi' and 'Sangathan': Movements in United Provinces in the 1920s." *Economic and Political Weekly*, March 28, 727–735.

Hansen, Thomas Blom (1996). "Recuperating Masculinity: Hindu Nationalism, Violence and the Exorcism of the Muslim 'Other'." *Critique of Anthropology*, 16 (2), 137–172.

_____ (2001). *Violence in Urban India: Identity Politics, "Mumbai," and the Postcolonial City*. Delhi: Permanent Black.

Jaisingh, Indira, and Monica Sakhrani (Eds.) (2007). *Law of Domestic Violence*. Delhi: Universal Law Publishing Co. Pvt.

Jeffrey, Craig, Patricia Jeffery, and Roger Jeffery (2008). *Degrees Without Freedom?: Education, Masculinities and Unemployment in North India*. Stanford, CA: Stanford University Press.

Joseph, Sherry (2005). *Social Work Practice and Men Who Have Sex with Men*. New Delhi: Sage.

Kakar, Sudhir (1991). *Intimate Relations: Exploring Indian Sexuality*. New Delhi: Penguin Books.

_____ (1992/1978). *The Inner World: A Psycho-analytic Study of Childhood and Society in India*. Delhi: Oxford University Press.

_____ (1996). *The Colours of Violence*. New Delhi: Penguin Books.

Kakar, Sudhir, and Katharina Kakar (2007). *The Indians: Portrait of a People*. New Delhi: Penguin/Viking.

Kimmel, Michael S., Jeff Hearn, and Robert W. Connell (Eds.) (2005). *Handbook of Studies on Men & Masculinities*. Thousand Oaks: Sage.

Kimmel, Michael S., and Michael A. Messner (Eds.) (2001). *Men's Lives*. Boston: Allyn and Bacon.

Kodoth, Praveena (2004). *Shifting the Ground of Fatherhood: Matriliny, Men and Marriage in*

Early Twentieth Century Malabar (Working Paper 359). Trivandrum: Centre for Development Studies.

Kulkarni, Mangesh (1997). "Rethinking Masculinity After Feminism." *The Radical Humanist*, December, 61 (9), 40–43.

_____ (2001). *Male Sexuality and the Construction of Male Identity.* Pune: Tathapi.

_____ (2006). "Is There Such a Thing as the Metrosexual Male?," *Infochange Agenda*, http://infochangeindia.org/agenda/claiming-sexual-rights-in-india/is-there-such-a-thing-as-the-metrosexual-male.html, accessed on 15 May 2012.

_____ (2007). "Indian Masculinities: A Million Mutations Now?" In *Breaking the Moulds*. R. P. Ravindra, H. Sadani, V. M. Geetali and S. N. Mukund (Eds.). Delhi: Books for Change, 204–212.

_____ (2011). "Review of *Debating Masculinity*" In *Men and Masculinities*. Josep M. Armengol and Angels Carabi (Eds.). Harriman, TN: Men's Studies Press, 2009. December, 14, 634–637.

Lakshmanan, C. (2004). "Dalit Masculinities in Social Science Research: Revisiting a Tamil Village." *Economic and Political Weekly*, March 6, 1088–1092.

Leslie, Julia, and Mary McGee (Eds.) (2000). *Invented Identities: The Interplay of Gender, Religion and Politics in India.* New Delhi: Oxford University Press.

Mazumdar, Ranjani (2007). *Bombay Cinema: An Archive of the City.* Minneapolis: University of Minnesota Press.

MAVA (2003). *Souvenir on the Occasion of the 10th Anniversary of Men Against Violence and Abuse.* Mumbai.

Menon, Nivedita (Ed.) (2007a). *Sexualities.* New Delhi: Women Unlimited.

_____ (2007b). *Recovering Subversion: Feminist Politics Beyond the Law.* Ranikhet: Permanent Black.

Merchant, Hoshang (Ed.) (1999). *Yaraana: Gay Writing from India.* New Delhi: Penguin Books.

Mulchandani, Sandhya (1999). *The Indian Man: His True Colours.* New Delhi: Picus Books.

Nandy, Ashis (1983). *The Intimate Enemy: Loss and Recovery of Self Under Colonialism.* Delhi: Oxford University Press.

Narrain, Arvind (2004). *Queer: Despised Sexuality, Law and Social Change.* Bangalore: Books for Change.

_____, and Gautam Bhan (Eds.) (2005). *Because I Have a Voice: Queer Politics in India.* New Delhi: Yoda Press.

Niranjana, Tejaswini (2000). "Reworking Masculinities: Rajkumar and the Kannada Public Sphere." *Economic and Political Weekly*, November 18, 4147–4150.

O'Hanlon, Rosalind (1997). "Issues of Masculinity in North Indian History: The Bangash Nawabs of Farrukhabad," *Indian Journal of Gender Studies*, 4 (1), 1–19.

_____ (1999). "Manliness and Imperial Service in Mughal North India," *Journal of the Economic and Social History of the Orient*, 42 (1), 47–93.

_____ (2007a). "Kingdom, Household and Body: History, Gender and Imperial Service under Akbar," *Modern Asian Studies*, 41(5), 889–923.

_____ (2007b). "Military Sports and the History of the Martial Body in India," *Journal of the Economic and Social History of the Orient*, 50 (4), 490–523.

Osella, Caroline, and Filippo Osella (2006). *Men and Masculinities in South India.* New York; London: Anthem Press.

Radhakrishnan, Ratheesh (2006). "Masculinity and the Structure of the Public Domain in Kerala: A History of the Contemporary," Ph.D. Thesis submitted to the Manipal Academy of Higher Education/Centre for the Study of Culture and Society, Bangalore.

Raju, Saraswati (2001). "Negotiating with Patriarchy: Addressing Men in Reproductive and Child Health." *Economic and Political Weekly*, December 8, 4589–4592.

Raju, Saraswati, Peter J. Atkins, Naresh Kumar, and Janet G. Townsend (1999). *Atlas of Women and Men in India.* New Delhi: Kali for Women.

Rao, Anupama (Ed.) (2006). *Gender and Caste.* New Delhi: Kali for Women and Women Unlimited.

Ratanlal and Dhirajlal (1992). *The Indian Penal Code*. Nagpur: Wadhwa & Co.

Ravindra R. P., H. Sadani, V. M. Geetali, and S. N. Mukund (Eds.) (2007). *Breaking the Moulds: Indian Men Look at Patriarchy Looking at Men*. Delhi: Books for Change.

Reddy, Gayatri (2005). *With Respect to Sex: Negotiating Hijra Identity in South India*. Chicago: University of Chicago Press.

Rosselli, John (1980). "The Self-image of Effeteness: Physical Education and Nationalism in Nineteenth Century Bengal," *Past and Present*, 86, 121–48.

Roy, Rahul, Anupama Chatterjee, and Sherna Dastur (2007). *A Little Book on Men*. New Delhi: Yoda Press.

Shahani, Parmesh (2008). *Gay Bombay: Globalization, Love and (Be)longing in Contemporary India*. New Delhi: Sage.

Singh, Richa (2001). "Masculine Identity, Workers and HIV/AIDS," *Economic and Political Weekly*, June 2, 1944–1947.

Singha, Radhika (1998). "Nationalism, Colonialism and the Politics of Masculinity," *Studies in History*, 14, 127–146.

Sinha, Mrinalini (1997). *Colonial Masculinity: The "Manly Englishman" and the "Effeminate Bengali" in the Late Nineteenth Century*. New Delhi: Kali for Women.

Srivastava, Sanjay (1998). *Constructing Post-Colonial India: National Character and the Doon School*. London: Routledge.

_____ (2007). *Passionate Modernity: Sexuality, Class and Consumption in India*. New Delhi: Routledge.

Tata Institute of Social Sciences (1999). *Shades of Courage: Women and IPC Section 498 A*. Mumbai: Akshara Publications.

Van der Veer, Peter (2001). *Imperial Encounters: Religion, Nation and Empire*. Princeton, NJ: Princeton University Press.

Verma, Himanshu (2004). *The Metrosexuals: Exploring the Unexplored*. New Delhi: Red Earth.

Verma, Ravi K., Pertti J. Pelto, Stephen L. Schensul, et. al. (Eds.) (2004). *Sexuality in the Time of AIDS: Contemporary Perspectives from Communities in India*. New Delhi: Sage.

Wagle, Jatin (2007). "MAVA: Men's Movement for Gender Justice." In *Breaking the Moulds*. R. P. Ravindra, H. Sadani, V. M. Geetali, and S. N. Mukund (Eds). Delhi: Books for Change.

Wilson, Amrit (2007). *Dreams, Questions, Struggles: South Asian Women in Britain*. Hyderabad: Orient Longman.

Zwarteveen, Margreet (2011). "Questioning Masculinities in Water." *Economic and Political Weekly*, April 30, XLVI (18), 40–48.

If Singularity Is the Problem, Could Intersectionality Be the Solution?

Exploring the Mediation of Sexuality on Masculinity

Roshan das Nair

The idea that there exists *a* masculinity which is distinct from *a* femininity is one that has a certain cultural currency, which perhaps stems from the idea that men and women, as two discrete groups, are different on a number of levels and parameters. A BBC article with the headline: "What are the 78 differences between women and men?" reported that scientists had discovered "just 78 genes separate men from women," based on their decoding of the human genome. Readers were invited to suggest how these genetic differences would manifest themselves on a behavioral level. Suggestions ranged from "Men have no opinions about curtains" to "Men need a round of applause for emptying the dishwasher," "Women think E on the petrol gauge means enough" and "Men cannot watch sports and talk to their wives at the same time." Ideas such as these, however humorous, have the ability to reinforce stereotypical notions of a "difference between the sexes" discourse, without paying much attention to difference *within* each sex. However, when such intra-sex (male) differences are explored, one system of categorization that is employed is based on a sexuality binary: distinguishing the gay men from the straight men. Therefore, from breaking down one essentialist category (men) we arrive at two sub-categories (gay/straight), which are equally essentialized. If we were to further look for divisions in the gay sub-category, we may find two other commonly deployed sub–sub-categories: "straight acting" (i.e., masculine) vs. "camp" (i.e., feminine). This brings us back to the categorization of people on the basis of gender, this time gay men, as either being masculine or feminine.

In this essay, I begin by introducing the notion of "intersectionality," and how by using intersectionality as a framework to understand Indian masculinities, plurality of both the terms Indian and masculinities is exposed. The framing of masculinities is often through various lenses, one of which is sexuality. However, the coupling of sexuality and gender can be problematic when certain sexual identity labels gain dominance over others, and when sexual practices are not tied to specific identities. Using data from a web blog, I illustrate how the notion and embodiment of masculinity is troubled by same-sex sexuality and Indian ethnicity, and how deciphering male-male physical contact in homosocial spaces can pose certain challenges. Further complications arise when the dichotomy between homosexual and heterosexual is interrupted by bisexuality. In discursive practices this interruption is sometimes silenced and sometimes discredited as being inauthentic, to maintain sexuality as a dichotomous construct. Examining blog and gay networking site data, I explore how sexuality is assessed by interpreting ethnic masculinities, particularly through reading the Indian male body and its embodiment. I end with an attempt to connect psychoanalysis, race, and masculinity, to help theorize the experience of non-heterosexual masculinities amongst racial minorities in the West.

Intersectionality

The notion of intersectionality has been appropriated from African America feminist and women's studies scholars such as Kimberle Crenshaw (1991), and represents a mode of thinking and seeing multiple interconnected and mutually constitutive identities which can and do co-exist in an individual, sometimes in a state of flux. The clunkiness of the word "intersectionality" and the multiplicity of its definitions have made it a slippery concept. As Surya Monro points out, intersectionality has been conceived of "as a crossroads," "an axis of difference," or a "dynamic process" (2010: 997). Despite these differences, some commonalities can be discerned based on the central tenets of intersectionality. Young and Meyer suggest that these include notions such as: "(i) no social group is homogenous (ii) people must be located in terms of social structures that capture the power relations implied by those structures, and (iii) there are unique, non-additive effects of identifying with more than one social group" (2005: 1145). I would like to add that these effects need not only be threats or problems to an integrated identity, but can also offer transformative possibilities for agency formation and deployment, through what Diana Fisher deftly calls the "tactical-micro-practices-in-the-hyphen" (2003: 171).

The experience of living with hyphenated identities (e.g., being a *Black-gay* man), particularly when these multiple identities belong to groups considered marginalized by their status as a "minority group," can pose several challenges. Being a minority within a minority (or a "metaminority" as I call it) creates kaleidoscopic possibilities, some beautiful and others disturbing, of being-in-the-world. I have described and discussed these problems and possibilities elsewhere (das Nair & Butler, 2012a), so throughout this essay I have only examined the scope of intersectionality in addressing Indian masculinities.

When considering *Indian masculinities*, I cannot but see the fuzzy edges, or the lack of exactness, that surround both these words. While there are myriad possibilities of defining each of these words, I will mainly focus on the latter word. However, when reflecting on localizing masculinity, or indeed masculinities, within the Indian framework, my reference is not limited to India as a nation state, but as a geopolitical area which goes beyond the borders and contested national boundaries on maps. Also, in certain instances there may be greater intra-group differences within India itself (north to south from Kashmir to Kanyakumari, or west to east from Kutch to Changlang, in mainland India) than between places just across the borders of India, in "foreign" lands. Furthermore, historical and contemporaneous migration of people and ideas across borders, and its virtual counterparts in the era of globalization, global mass media and the Internet, has meant that notions of "indigenousness" is always already contested. As Connell suggests: "What happens in localities is affected by the history of whole countries, but what happens in countries is affected by the history of the world" (2000: 39).

In this essay, I use the term "singularity" in terms of grammatical number related to the noun form of a word, whereby the singular symbolizes a unitary, homogenous or monolithic construct. Therefore, I am contrasting the singular with the plural of the word; in this case, "masculinity" with "masculinities." As previously mentioned, the issue with framing "masculinity" in the singular is the problem of essentialism. Masculinity, in the singular, facilitates and maintains discourses that enshrine the triumph of biological determinism, obfuscating the role of the social contexts in which such identities are developed and performed. It also helps to stagnate the axes of power which determine what is dominant or hegemonic masculinity, and fails to recognize that not all individuals have equal potential or agency (be they genetic, biological, financial, etc.) to play out such a narrow idea of masculinity. Furthermore, it does not allow the individual to be examined from an intersectional perspective (for example the differences between Black men and White men, or Gay men and straight men, or men with and without disabilities, etc.). Although, as I have indicated, the construction, deployment, and reading of masculinity is a product of multiple permutations and combinations, in this essay I limit my analysis to only a few of these strands: sexuality, ethnicity, and diasporic representations.

Masculinit*ies*, in the plural, creates the "conditions of possibility" to carve out individual and transitory masculine discourses, tropes, etc., of gendered identity. If we have more than one masculinity, then *a* masculinity can be contrasted to another — and feminine and the female does not become the marked gender. This in itself is not unproblematic, because with more choice of being masculine, it is inevitable that hierarchies will be formed, based on power differentials, creating a hegemonic masculinity. By "hegemonic masculinity" I am not simply referring to Connell's description of it in terms of "heroic masculinity," but rather, taking it back to Gramsci (1971), and his formulation of ideological dominance and power which is socially constructed. Again, by framing *a* masculinity as being hegemonic, we return to the conundrum of singularity. Connell's hegemonic masculinity assumes one ideal that is aspirational. But as Margaret Wetherell and Nigel Edley have questioned, can Tony Blair and Gordon Brown (their examples, not mine) be considered to embody the notion of hegemonic masculinity (I'm assuming they're thinking not!), when they wielded so much power (1999: 337)?

Distancing from notions of hegemonic masculinity itself can be seen as power-play in which the man says: "I know what some people consider the ideal, I can be that if I wanted to, but I *choose* not to go there, because I'm *secure* in who I am." This is what Wetherell and Edley found in their research, whereby there was an attempt by some of their research participants to create (or recreate) the ideal of Mr. Average instead of explicitly wishing to be the heroic masculine male, which Connell considered the hegemonic category. In this sense, as Wetherell and Edley suggest, "perhaps what is most hegemonic is to be non-hegemonic!" (1999: 351). Interestingly enough, a similar finding was reported by Adam Jowett (2010) in his discursive study, which examined the dilemma of producing gay masculine identities in a world where homosexuality and masculinity are seen as being antithetical. Jowett's gay male participants acknowledged their occasional campness but attempted to explain it away (e.g., I'm camp only when I'm drunk, or with other gay men, etc.) and preferred to embody the idea of being "just a regular guy" (2010: 22–3) or Mr. Average.

So, when we think of masculinities, I think it is imperative that we also think of sexualities, because the very framing of masculinity may be related to the way in which people see their sexuality. For instance, some of Wetherell and Edley's (1999) transcripts delineate how men define their masculinity vis-à-vis their relationship with women: e.g., being masculine is about looking after the wife. Therefore, making links between male-male sexuality and masculinity and exploring the co-construction of both these constructs is essential to understand the production of gendering. As Osella and Osella argue "it makes no sense in south Asian contexts to de-link the study of sexuality from that of gendering" (2006: 2).

By regarding masculinities through the lens of sexuality, we can begin to appreciate the notion of a "hegemonic homosexuality"—a way of being "gay" which privileges some men, and disenfranchizes others, based on socially mediated power differentials. The project of intersectionality disrupts the notion of there existing a homogenous gay or unified "gay community" in India and/or the West. Lesbian, gay, bisexual, trans (LGBT) are the dominant modes of representation of "sexual minorities" in the West and increasingly in the Global South also. It is interesting to note that in India while these terms were once the prerogative of the English speaking urban middleclass, these sexual identity labels have become commonplace in most parts of India today. Notably, the terms even featured in the 2009 Delhi High Court's landmark reading down of Section 377 of the Indian Penal Code that decriminalized consensual homosexual activity. There have clearly been benefits of people coming together under the umbrella term of LGBT to create a critical mass to effect positive social change. However, by becoming the hegemonic sexual minority identity labels, they do have the power to vilify those who do not want to or cannot subscribe to these terms. Their dominance can also create a new class differential between those who can ("authentically") claim these terms and those who use indigenous forms of sexual identities or practices. But by saying this, I am not suggesting that we adopt the MSM (men who have sex with men) label as the alternative to using LGBT labels, because I think it is only a matter of time before MSM itself becomes an identity label, which then some people are going to distance themselves from. However, MSM becoming a sexual identity label in its own right can also have its advantages, for instance politicizing a minority identity and for making rights claims without needing to label themselves as being LGBT or even "queer." As Epstein has suggested, "what we call ourselves has implications for political practice" (1987: 134).

But there are many who do not like the term MSM. Young and Meyer, for instance, suggest that the problem with MSM is that it implies an "absence of community, social networks, and relationships in which same-gender pairing is shared and supported" (2005: 1145). I think the authors make two assumptions here: (i) that people pay so much credence to their same-sex sexual activities to elevate them to the level of an identity or recognize themselves as belonging to a group because of such activities, and (ii) that as a diasporic and non-heterosexual metaminority (a kind of hyphenated identity), there are "shared and supported" community links thought which sexual identity and activities can be negotiated. How do we account for people who do not have such identities and/or such associations? Therefore, in such instances, I suspect that abandoning the notion and label of MSM might be premature, and I wonder what we will fill the gap with.[1]

Therefore, dilemmas abound when considering how masculinity and sexuality are linked because of issues related to how sexuality is coded as a distinct identity that accompanies sexual practices or not labelled as an identity. The project of intersectionality offers a way of unpacking these dilemmas, without offering simple or straightforward answers, but permits us to acknowledge difference and diversity within a seemingly homogenous construct.

In the next section I explore some of these dilemmas further from an Indian and Indian diasporic context, through the use of data from an open access, publically available blog.[2] I believe blogs are a good source of information to understand and unpick some of the issues related to contemporary Indian masculinities because they not only highlight some of the dilemmas, distinctions, and discourses that people use to frame these masculinities, but also provide us with the language used to define, describe, and debate various positions. While the topics in such blogs are initiated by one individual, they often get taken up by others who then become participants and commentators of the topic being discussed. This multiplicity of authorial voice and intent offers exciting possibilities for the analysis of discursive practices in public domains. Such discursive analyses are important in the exploration of social constructs and can offer new insights into understanding *intersectionality in action*.

Assessing Sexuality by Reading Masculinity

From a purposefully selected blog I inspected two topics[3] and the discussions that ensued that related to Indian men. Ravi (the blogger) presents his readers with a conundrum he experiences with regard to an Indian colleague of his: that of mis/reading this man as "not gay" but interested in Ravi, or just being an ("androgynous") Indian man. This challenge Ravi faces is partly due to his (and others') inability to read sexuality from the masculinity portrayed by the object of his desire. Therefore, the "gaydar" that gay men use to identify other gay men, in Ravi's words, "collapses here ... it's quite useless." It is interesting to examine why this gaydar collapses.

There is an indication that by reading non-verbal interactional behavior and gender performance one can assume the sexuality of the other. For such a reading to be accurate, both maleness and gayness need to be coded in ways in which there is minimal blurring of boundaries. From the text in the blog there is a sense that this can be easily achieved in the West (or perhaps more accurately, by Westerners or "Western(ized)-Indians"). Such coding inevitably leads to a homogenizing of genders and sexualities to the extent that the *authenticity* of an individual's gender or sexuality is called into question when the game is not played by the rules (rules, perhaps created by the West). Take for instance this extract from Ravi, where he has referred to homosocial behavior (such as public displays of hand-holding, caressing, etc.) amongst men in India:

> Well, all of this means, it gets awfully hard for *actual* gay men like me to figure out who's in who's "camp"— if you know what I mean. It's incredibly risky to assume someone's gay, or someone has the "hots" for you just by their non-verbal behaviour and displays of intimacy [emphasis in the original].

Ravi creates a distinction between *those men* and "'actual' gay men" (like himself), thereby suggesting a legitimacy of his own gayness vis-à-vis the other.[4] This then, perhaps, is one way of marking out a *hegemonic homosexuality*, one that is consistent with a type of masculinity (in this case, "camp" or effeminate) or one that comes with a sexual identity label (in this case, "gay"). It is also interesting to note the use of the rhetorical pragmatic conditional ("if you know what I mean") in the above extract, which I would argue is an attempt to co-opt the reader into accepting a truth criterion set by the author. It seems to suggest: If you understand what I'm saying, you will agree (with me) that it is difficult to verify *their* membership to *our* club. Perhaps we can retain this proposition, because we notice respondents then being sympathetic to Ravi's position. For instance, one respondent felt that Ravi was "doubly screwed" "not only to be in such a homophobic culture, but a *homosocial* homophobic culture" (italics in the original). The problem is identified as stemming from both the homophobia that gay people face and also the homosocial nature of Indian society.

Ravi advances a proposition that it is the interdependence and collectivistic nature of Indian societies that "probably plays a fuelling factor in the kind of social, non-verbal behaviour Indians exhibit among themselves." This perhaps relates to Dumont's notions of the Indian personhood as being distinct from the idea of the individual, and to Marriott's idea of the Indian "dividual" (in contrast to the "*in*dividual," who in Western thought is indivisible and bounded) in the creation of a multiply authored composite of personhood. "An individual is indivisible, something which cannot be divided; a dividual can. A dividual then is a person who is made up of lots of strands, a person who can be divided, and is able to pass on parts of the self to others" (Osella & Osella, 2006: 11). This line of thinking is in keeping with the spirit of intersectionality (elaborated later), whereby the different strands are woven together to create the fabric of personhood.

Deciphering Male–Male Physical Contact in Homosocial Contexts

The preceding argument about homosexual vs. homosocial intimacy comes back to a problem located in the behavior and performance of masculinity by Indian men because they appear to contravene the standard; again, one that appears to be set in the West. Therefore, maleness and straightness are under threat because some males are performing the tropes of femininity or (camp) gayness in subversive, and ultimately, "confusing" ways. However, as one blogger points out, the problem may be a problem only for those like Ravi (who appears to be of Indian origin living in the West and has subsequently moved [back?] to India) who don't speak the behavioral language or understand the gender/sexual codes used by men in India: "We are a very adaptable race and I'm sure the Indian Gay community has its own ways of distinguishing between straight and gay men."

For another blogger, this confusion:

> highlights the unpredictable predicament of Indian males who enjoy comparatively closer ties and emotional bonds between them even without a sticky label like "gay" or "homosexual." I think it is a unique social phenomenon in the Indian subcontinent...

However, other bloggers contest the assertion that male-male non-sexual intimacy is "uniquely Indian" and challenge the notion that such a (public) display of affection is a feminine trait. Akash says:

> In the Arab Gulf men touch their noses and make a smacking sound with their lips when they greet each other [...] In many other Asian cultures men can be found walking hand in hand. Who is to say that holding hands or lips approaching lips is not masculine, but feminine? [...] I see the camaraderie among Indian men expressed in the ways you mention as a very masculine thing.

And another adds:

> Italian men hold hands in public, walk arm in arm, very common. Kissing to express emotion and in greeting is also common. None of which should ever be indicative of sexuality, ever.

This type of deferring of sexual interpretations of male-male touch and physical contact is also tentatively advised in Indian "cultural etiquette" pages on websites such as eDiplomat,[5] which state that "Indian men may engage in friendly back patting *merely* as a sign of friendship" (emphasis mine).

Some other bloggers report such displays of masculine camaraderie in "the world playing fields of soccer, football, hockey, cricket, baseball, army, construction, card table and many other straight planets. Well hetero-sexually speaking of course." Therefore, masculinity which includes physical contact in specific contexts (such as sport, hazing or "ragging") is not misread as *overtly* (homo)sexual. This is the point that Akash (above) makes when he refers to different types of touch and contact. The argument goes something like this: Straight women can distinguish between a friendly hug and a sexual touch by a man, so it would stand to reason that a gay man would also be able to distinguish different forms of physicality from another man (independent of his sexuality). This observation is echoed in Sumit's viewpoint:

> The way I look at it is that it's no different from the playful physical contact that a male would have with a female friend, sans any sexual undercurrent. This leads me to wonder whether the perpetual physical distance maintained between heterosexual men in the U.S. is *perhaps a conscious choice so that they aren't mistaken for being gay*. The same behaviours that plays out between men and women who have a completely platonic relationship ought to exhibit itself, quite naturally one would assume, between 2 heterosexual men [emphasis mine].

Osella and Osella explore this important aspect of contact — whether "actual or magical" (2006: 192), when referring to the relationship between Indian male fans and male film stars. They suggest that male audiences are perhaps able to slip into multiple positions of appreciation and adoration of these male stars, by imagining themselves as the star, by taking on female subjectship of enjoyment of the male star, or a more frank homoerotic "pull" towards the star (2006: 191).

The patterns of homosocial behavior in India also vary with urban and rural geographies, with some urban areas experiencing what I see as a corrosion of homosocial public behavior and public spaces. There appears to be a growing awareness of the Western coding of practices, such as handholding, as being indicative of a distinct sexual identity (i.e., "gay"), which some people are keen to distance themselves from because of the negative effects it can attract (see Sumit's viewpoint above). Perhaps as a result of the hyper-vigilance of gendered behaviors and expectations, and perhaps due to censuring of gender variant performances (e.g., men showing "feminine" traits), I have heard phrases such as, "What yaar, are you a gay or what?" and "Hey man, I'm not gay" being articulated in public when men have attempted physical homosocial contact. This (hyper)awareness of "gay" signs creates a binary in male sexual codes and conduct, preventing displays of slippage from homosocial to homoerotic to homosexual actions. This is reflected in an observation by Osella and Osella, when they suggest that "homosocial arenas and the quiet intimacy of closed family spaces provide refuges from the demands of public, heterosexual masculinity and may yet offer spaces where same sex relationship of various flavours may flourish" (2006: 205). This binaried notion of homo/ hetero sexuality (imprinted by colonialism, and now through globalization — ostensibly streamed through the medium of Western and Bollywood film and

TV) being embedded in the Indian collective consciousness gives rise to predictions that the "performances of masculinity which will be required of men ... will become more stringent, the self-policing of desire relentless and the self-consciousness about homosocial spaces heavy" (Osella & Osella, 2006: 206).

Homosociality "sometimes mitigate the effects of the tightly drawn matrix of heterosexuality" (Osella & Osella, 2006: 3). However, for one blogger, homosociality:

> ...could possibly lead to a further psychological burial of a gay man's homosexual expression because of the ambiguous nature of homosocial behaviour he observers among the men around him. Moreover, this ambiguity probably leads Indian gay men to try and seek satisfaction and fulfilment of their psychological desires to be intimate with another man in such homosocial relationships (i.e., in safe homosocial intimacies with straight men) thereby repressing a full-blown expression of their *proper sexuality* with other gay men [my italics].

Homosociality, for this author, serves to repress or bury the genuine sexuality of Indian gay men. My reading of this suggests that the author advances an argument that gay male identity cannot be consolidated in a milieu where sexual and gender boundaries are porous, whereby confused men engage in male-male (non-sexual) contact to fulfill their "psychological desires" (not sexual ones), which then leads to a lack of sexual contact with "other gay men." The elision of bisexuality and MSM identities and practices is noteworthy, perhaps because bisexuality poses a problem to the neat and convenient dichotomy of sexuality. This is considered next.

Will the Real *Gay/Bi Men Please Stand Up?*

Foucault, in *The Use of Pleasure*, refers to the "manner in which one ought to 'conduct oneself'— that is, the manner in which one ought to form oneself as an ethical subject acting in reference to the prescriptive elements that make up the code" (1990: 26). For Foucault, there are different ways to conduct oneself morally and different ways for "the acting individual to operate, not just as an agent, but as an ethical subject of this action" (1990: 26). The "mode of subjection" is one way in which "the individual establishes his relation to the rule and recognizes himself as obliged to put into practice" (1990: 27). Foucault illustrates these points by referring to the practice of conjugal fidelity, but it could very well be applied to the practice of performing the (pre)dominant tropes of (hegemonic) masculinity also. To this extent, gender performativity can be seen as a moral code. There is the passive adherence to these rules and codes, but there is also a felt need to assert masculinity through certain performances which serve to preserve, maintain or revive the construct. The latter may be especially the case when masculinity is adjudged to be under threat.

As seen from the blog data, discourses around authenticity of sexuality (the "actual," "true," "real" gay men) and gender (camp vs. masculine) attempt to create neat boundaries between homosexual and heterosexual men. This binary is somewhat problematized by the existence of bisexual activities and/or identities and people who identify as trans/gender. It is beyond the scope of this paper to address trans issues, so I will limit my discussion to male bisexuality.

The authenticity of men's bisexuality is often questioned, with some commentators from this blog suggesting that "some Indian gay men delude themselves into thinking that they are in fact bi-sexual, or maybe even straight! undoubtedly, with terrible consequences for themselves and for those they come in close contact with." Charting through several generalizations, an article from the *Times of India* makes similar assertions such as "In the First World, men see bisexuality as a stepping stone before they eventually and inevitably jump full on into gayness" (*Times of India*, 2 July 2006). Then the author turns to the issue of authenticity: "There are a fair amount of people who regard bisexuals as genuine enough to enjoy both the genders." Notice that there is no hedge in the first part of the sentence, and the author asserts a maxim of quantity ("a fair amount"). Notice also the quality of the authenticity ("genuine *enough*"). Later, the author goes on to say that "counsellors" say that homosexuals who marry "find the touch of the opposite sex uncomfortable and soon suffer from depression. Those who remain are *probably genuine* bisexuals. They are rarer than one thinks. Time and again the 'bisexuals' one encounters are the ones suffering the camouflage of marriage" (italics mine).

The existence of bisexuality as a "phase" for some notwithstanding, such assertions create a climate of suspicion, whereby individuals are called upon to prove the genuineness of their sexuality to themselves and to others. Furthermore, the temporality of bisexuality when viewed as a phase suggests that this is a phase that homosexuals go through to achieve their true homosexual potential, rather than viewing all sexualities as being fluid. Conversely, for one blogger, the process of becoming heterosexual was through bisexuality: "A man moves through homosexuality, bisexuality before becoming a husband and exclusively heterosexual." For this man, because of the unavailability of female contact for sexual exploration in adolescent male life in India, he feels that Indian society considers it "'normal' for boys to maybe explore each other in adolescence." Fluidity, unlike phase theories, defies and disrupts the project of normative categorization.

Sexuality categorization may coerce people, who hitherto had perhaps not considered themselves as having a sexual identity label or belonging to a specific category, to select one label or category and (preferably) stick with it. This then restricts the possibility of a moment to moment feelings and expressions of sexual desires, without an *a priori* defined sexuality. I believe that it is the feeling that there needs to be fixed categories that add to the demands of attaining and maintaining normative masculine gendering. Ideas of fluidity and performativity challenge these norms. As Judith Butler reminds us, "[t]here is no gender identity behind the expressions of gender … identity is performatively constituted by the very 'expressions' that are said to be its results" (2008: 25).

These local performances of gender, however, have increasingly been performed on global stages, and this increases the risk of something being lost in translation or migration. As one commentator on the blog explains:

> I am Indian … my friends & I … we hug each other (in private as well as public) … we kiss on the cheek while greeting … we slap each other's ass (even in public) … we put our hands around each other's shoulders … sometimes we hold hands … we even say "I love you" face to face and even on phone … these are as normal and common to us as saying namaste … please do not misjudge them as sexual … some of my friends are non–Indian … but they understand that it's just out of love and nothing sexual.

Assessing Sexuality by Reading Ethnic Masculinities

The complexities of reading gender and sexuality of immigrants and ethnic minorities in the West have been documented (e.g., Han, 2006; Butler, das Nair, & Thomas, 2010; das Nair & Thomas, 2012; das Nair & Thomas, 2012). Misreading of sexual orientation (i.e., "gay" or "straight") and the type of sexual roles men play (e.g., "top"/active or "bottom"/passive) can occur when people make these assumptions based on ethnic and cultural stereotypes. Such racialized reading of the male body (by other men) and masculinity is locked within a framework of inter-racial desires. The non-white male body in the West is a marked construct, one that is either the object of derision or desire because of race. Colonial and Orientalist notions of the brown man, and who he is, and what his body represents is framed from romanticized transpositions of the man from the *Kamasutra* or the dusky prince skilled in the art of tantric sex. Conversely, he is also the closeted man with a small penis, who will one day get married to a girl his parents choose for him. There is little by way of a middle ground, or average, when it comes to reading the non-white body.

Unfortunately, for some South Asian men in the West, the White male body also represents the ideal; an ideal to be achieved for themselves and/or an ideal represented in their partners. Poon et al. (2005) have observed this in a study of gay Internet chatrooms, where Asian men report a preference for White men/bodies to Asian men/bodies for sex and/or relationships. A cursory glance at some such gay social networking websites shows South Asian members explicitly describe their ideal partners. What is interesting here is how in these statements of preference are couched explanations for the lack of desire for other South Asian men. For instance, one says: "no Asians/brown ppl (just a preference, sorry.... I don't even know why ... probably some bad experience"); and another young South Asian man who describes himself as "toffee coloured skin, black eyes and internally beautiful" is "looking for a white guy aged between 18–27, he must be caring, loving and passionate"; and yet another, "I usually go for Caucasian boys, just a preference (no offence to others)." These explanations attempt to explain away a desire and/or lack of desire so as to not cause "offence." Similar expressions of desire and attempts to explain these have been reported by McKeown et al. (2010).

When considering desire in Western gay spaces, we need to also focus on the notion of the ideal gay body (shape). Body satisfaction amongst gay men in the West has been related to upper body strength, being slim and/or muscular (Atkins, 1998), and has resulted in increased incidents of eating disorders, and gay men engaging in activities to increase muscularity, such as exercise and steroid use (Yelland & Tiggemann, 2003). This hegemonic masculine body aesthetic has come to be seen as the ideal that all gay men, independent of their race, have come to be judged against.

This body aesthetic is highlighted in the blog previously mentioned, wherein Ravi's portrayal of his love object (the Indian co-worker), who he has described as being "handsome," is disputed by his friends/colleagues who also know the Indian man being discussed. Mary replies, "And no, he is NOT 'this handsome, Indian boy ... tall, has broad shoulders, a sharp face' [referring to Ravi's description] ... he is so NOTTTT! He's barely 5'5" and really non-muscular and skinny." This is followed up by another retort by another person:

> emmm ... listen up. I'm agreeing with Mary on this one. I KNOW who u talking about! What kind of taste do you have ya? [...] "he's tall, has broad shoulders, a sharp face.... As I said, he's quite handsome." ... umm ... HOW?

Both these disputations seem to question the presence of the features in the Indian man that Ravi describes, and in doing so they also collude in suggesting that it is a combination of these very features that makes a man "handsome." In fact, Mary's assertion that the Indian man is "barely 5'5" and really non-muscular and skinny" drives home this point. Barely 5'5" is barely handsome. Interestingly, this is about the average height of Indian males. Ravi's response to these two detractors brings in the issue of standards:

> Listen, he's quite attractive, okay ... going by Indian standards! I mean, he does have a square jaw, a broad smile, proportionate body (which includes the broad shoulders), and he is CERTAINLY NOT "skinny"!

The phrase "going by Indian standards" stands out as marking a certain quality threshold that is somehow different from the wider (White) male body aesthetic. The list of attractive qualities is expanded here to include a square jaw, a broad smile, proportionate body. Based on the "objectification theory" (Fredrickson & Roberts [1997] originally formulated this theory on women's bodies, but it has subsequently been applied to gay male bodies also), where the body becomes an object of desire for the consumption and pleasure of others (men) and the individual's self-worth (or internalized gaze) is dependent upon how closely their body approximates the dominant standards of attractiveness. Although this ideal may have stemmed from the West, "Bollywood buff" has helped enshrine this ideal in India also, particularly in urban India where there has been a proliferation of local/independent and multinational gyms and fitness centers (Jain Nair, 2009).

The Power of the (Imagined) Phallus

For Luce Irigaray, "Female sexuality has always been conceptualised on the basis of masculine parameters" (1985: 23). If we were to take this assertion further to incorporate race and ethnicity, we could view South Asian male sexuality (and masculinity) as being conceptualized on the basis of *Western* masculine parameters. Whether it is in relation to the Freudian concept of "penis envy" or neo–Freudian notions of the *symbolism* of such constructs, the associations between gender and genitalia are constantly invoked through our socio-cultural landscapes via science, the media, the arts, etc. Classical psychoanalysis itself does not engage with race. Brian Carr has queried, "if 'race' constitutes a fundamental repression in the inaugural gestures of psychoanalytic theory, how can we read the symptomatic presence of race in psychoanalysis?" (1998: 119). This elision of race, possibly caused by a "profoundly dehistoricized narrative of individual subject formation" (1998: 121), has been expertly explored by theorists such as Christopher Lane, Kalpana Sheshadri-Crooks, Kate White, among others. Therefore, what follows are only a few cursory ideas connecting psychoanalysis, race, and masculinity, to help theorize the experience of non-heterosexual masculinities amongst racial minorities in the West.

Recent news stories in the BBC for instance, with headlines such as "Condoms 'too big' for Indian men," have reported a study conducted by the Indian Council of Medical Research which found that "more than half of the men measured had penises that were shorter than international standards for condoms" (Grammaticus, 2006). The notion of an "international standard" is interesting, and may not be solely based on a global numerical formulation given that Indians account for a sixth of the world's population. For Han, "the white man's penis becomes the invisible standard by which we measure racialised non-white queer men's penises, and hence, their non-white queer male desirability" (2006: 7). What these observations suggest is that a more literal version of the psychoanalytic concept of "penis envy" is constructed in phallocentric worlds and dialectics.

For Freud, gender was both a psychological and physical construction, and the masculine/feminine binary was apparent in his description of the boy child and the girl child and their attributes and their differentiation, particularly in the phallic stage of development. Pleasurable stimulation was garnered through the boy's penis, while for the girl this was through her clitoris (or small penis, or penis equivalent or substitute; Freud, 1990: 347). Size here defines the activity. The presence of the "real" penis indicates activity (masculinity), whereas the absence of the (large or "imperfect") penis, suggests passivity (femininity). I would argue that the same dialectic can be applied when considering how hegemonic masculinity, when globally considered, is a highly racialized construct.

Richard Fung (1991), in his paper *Looking for My Penis: The Eroticized Asian in Gay Video Porn*, articulates the racialized reading of masculinity in North America. Although referring mainly to East and South East Asian men, we can generalize some of these experiences to some Indian men also. He states how Black men are eclipsed by their penises (quoting Fanon), but how Asian men, by virtue of their smaller penises are seen to have "no sexuality." He therefore queries: "if Asian men have no sexuality, how can we have homosexuality?" (Fung, 1991: no page number). Although this reference is now dated, it still holds sway in the contemporary Western world, as reflected in some of my own and my clients' experiences (das Nair and Thomas, 2012). Such "arrested representations" create static images of identities for Asian masculinity and sexuality: being read and misread as feminine, emasculated, camp, asexual, submissive, or powerless; and on whom non–Asian "phallic power" (to quote Patricia Meyer Spacks, 1990) can be imposed. In fact, Peter Jackson suggests that "[t]he dominant de-eroticisation of Asian men within White gay cultures occurs by an effeminisation of Asian men's bodies and the privileging of a model of masculinity based on the idealised attributes of a Caucasian male" (2000: 183).

Perhaps then, it is a symbolic form of penis envy (psychoanalytically speaking) that makes White males the object of some Asian gay men's desire, like the classical Freudian analysis of woman's desire for a penis being repressed and later substituted through the Oedipus complex. Such desire can also be conceived of as capital (e.g., Han, 2006), or even "phallic power," which when felt to be unattainable in the self can be acquired through the other. In Freudian terms, this could be exemplified by the girl child desiring her father, and later finding a male partner who in some respects represents the father. In a lateral shift, the desire for whiteness can also be observed in the Indian context in relation to the fetishization of white skin and the use of "fairness creams" for men (and women) of "wheatish complexions." Recent advertisements have capitalized on Bollywood actors Shah Rukh Khan, John Abraham, and Shahid Kapoor endorsing such products. In such instances, masculinity is no longer threatened by the use of cosmetics (which was hitherto seen as a feminine preoccupation), because of the hegemonic maleness of the actors who endorse these products. From their elevated status, they *are* the standards, and can define the standards, by which other men are measured. Perhaps as a result of recent campaigns about the ill-effects of these creams to the individual's skin and to the "collective skin" of those with darker complexions, there is a heightened awareness amongst these brand ambassadors of the polemics of wanting to become white or propagating whiteness as the ideal. They attempt to distance themselves from the "fairness" element of these creams, but instead insist on other virtues of these products to help develop "a balanced skin tone," "remove blemishes," etc. Despite what people call the cream (or try not to call the cream), the common tropes in Indian visual media commercials of men's use of the products include an element of phallic power: fairness gets you the desired object (women, jobs, roles in film, etc.), which in turn makes men more masculine.

In this era of "liquid modernity" (a term introduced by Zygmunt Bauman), which broadly relates to a fluid, capitalist, global, technological, nomadic zeitgeist; singular, intransigent and static classifications of gender performance fail to capture the complexities of different stands of individual identities that make up this performance. Using intersectionality as a framework permits us to identify some of these stands and examine how they interact with each other and the external interactional space (the environment) to create versions of masculinity. There is a certain "intertextuality" in the reading of gender performance, in that meaning is not only derived from the index performance itself, but is also produced by the reader from a matrix of extant meanings associated with the notions of gender.

Conclusions

I have argued thus far that masculinity, in the singular, is a limited construct that only serves to essentialize gender without taking into account the multiplicity of its experience and expression. In defining personhood it only serves as a single strand in a complex weave of multiple identities.

Expanding the metaphor of woven fabric, the quality or type of this single strand of masculinity will undoubtedly be influenced by a host of other variables, and also be influenced by its position and relational configurations amongst other strands in that weave. Therefore, *a* masculinity (for me) is a moment-to-moment developmental performance brought about by historical and cultural interplay of factors such as age, sexuality, skin color, race, body shape and movement, social class, etc., and what these factors have come to mean in/for a given society. Therefore, meaning making of a masculinity is contingent upon adjacent signifiers (which can be a string of signifiers, e.g., gay, Indian, urban, English-speaking, etc.) or by constant comparison (e.g., with femininity). Intersectionality offers us a way of seeing, or reading, the multiplicity of these signifiers.

Using blog data, I have shown how the notion of an Indian masculinity is problematized by the interactions between gender, sexuality and ethnicity. The blog used for this essay offered rich sources of such interactions. In fact, one commentator on the blog observed that the discussions were "very interesting, sounds like dissertation material, grant possibilities." There is an honesty about this kind of data which is perhaps naturalistic in that it emerges over time and is not influenced by the guidance or gaze of any one specific observer or facilitator; but there is also an element of impression management that needs to be considered. It could be argued, however, that impression management akin to performance occurs in almost all interactions.

Intersectionality has the hallmarks of a postmodern (or post-structural) conceptual framework. It is at once globally conceived and applicable, and locally (even individually) produced and experienced. Subject positions are seen as incomplete, fluid, relational, plural and contested sites. This of course creates problems but it also creates opportunities. Intersectionality is not a meta-narrative or grand theory, but a way of seeing and challenging orthodoxies that are created through categories and hierarchies that create and maintain power differentials. Intersectionality does not deny the existence (or use of) categories such as "gay," "male," etc., but problematizes these categories. Ultimately, the "triumph of intersectionality ... is its potential to resist the complacency of accepting categories as predetermined, static, and objective truths, and its ability to proactively challenge the composition and limits of these categories" (das Nair and Butler, 2012: 3). In the final analysis, masculinity in the singular *is* a problem, and while intersectionality itself is not a solution, it creates the climate for various solutions to emerge which account for the myriad forms of Indian masculinities.

Notes

1. An anonymous reviewer suggested the gap could be filled by "MLM, Men who Love Men." While this is an interesting possibility (particularly for asexual men), it further muddies the waters by confusing *sex* with *love* (which can be independent of each other), and therefore not a perfect solution.

2. The ethics of using such public domain web blogs has been debated by many and there is no clear consensus about how to strike a balance between striving to protect the anonymity of the bloggers and attempting to provide as much information as possible to enable the reader to make an independent decision about the interpretations of these blogs by the researcher. In the spirit of "fair use" of this material, I have chosen not to provide the web-address of the blog and have also changed the names/pseudonyms of the bloggers, but have largely preserved the words/phrases used, because some of my interpretations are based on the specifics of language use. The interested reader may consult Hookway (2008) for more details about the use of blogs in social research.

3. The blog and the topics were found by searching the Internet for blogs which examined the topics relevant to this essay.

4. Perhaps the emphasis is made ironically, but from other entries made by Ravi in the blog, this does not appear to be the case.

5. http://www.ediplomat.com/np/cultural_etiquette/ce_in.htm.

References

Atkins, Dawn (Ed.) (1998). *Looking Queer: Body Image and Identity in Lesbian, Bisexual, Gay, and Transgender Communities.* New York: Harrington Park Press.

Butler, Catherine, Roshan das Nair, and Sonya Thomas (2010). "The Colour of Queer." *Counselling Ideologies: Queer Challenges to Heteronormativity.* Ed. Lyndesy Moon. Surrey: Ashgate.

Butler, Judith (2008). *Gender Trouble.* New York: Routledge Classics.

Carr, Brian (1998). "At the Thresholds of the 'Human': Race, Psychoanalysis, and the Replication of Imperial Memory." *Cultural Critique* 39 119–150.

Connell, Raewyn (1995). *Masculinities.* Cambridge: Polity

_____ (2000). *The Men and the Boys.* Berkeley: University of California Press.

"Could You Be Bisexual?" *Times of India* 2 July 2006. Web. http://timesofindia.indiatimes.com/home/sunday-toi/Could-you-be-bisexual/articleshow/1696456.cms?flstry=1 26 Apr. 12.

Crenshaw, Kimberle (1991). "Mapping the Margins: Intersectionality, Identity Politics, and Violence Against Women of Color." *Stanford Law Review* 43: 1241–99.

das Nair, Roshan, and Catherine Butler (2012a). *Intersectionality, Sexuality, and Psychological Therapies: Working with Lesbian, Gay and Bisexual Diversity.* West Sussex: BPS-Blackwell.

_____, and _____ (2012b). Introduction. In R. das Nair and C. Butler (Eds.). *Intersectionality, Sexuality, and Psychological Therapies: Working with Lesbian, Gay and Bisexual Diversity.* West Sussex: BPS-Blackwell.

das Nair, Roshan and Shirley Thomas. (2012). "Politics of Desire: Exploring the Ethnicity/Sexuality Intersectionality in South Asian and East Asian Men Who Have Sex with Men (MSM)." *Psychology of Sexualities Review* 3(1): 8–21.

das Nair, Roshan, and Sonya Thomas (2012). "Race & Ethnicity." In R. das Nair and C. Butler

(Eds.). *Intersectionality, Sexuality, and Psychological Therapies: Working with Lesbian, Gay and Bisexual Diversity.* West Sussex: BPS-Blackwell, 59–88.

Epstein, Steven (1987). "Gay Politics, Ethnic Identity: The Limits of Social Constructionism." *Socialist Review* 17.

Fisher, Diana (2003). "Immigration Closets: Tactical-Micro-Practices-in-the-Hypen." *Journal of Homosexuality* 45.2/3/4: 171–92.

Foucault, Michel (1990). *The Use of Pleasure: The History of Sexuality,* Vol. 2. Trans. Robert Hurley. New York: Vintage Books.

Fredrickson, Barbara, and Tomi-Ann Roberts (1997). "Objectification Theory: Toward Understanding Women's Lived Experiences and Mental Health Risks." *Psychology of Women Quarterly* 21: 173–206.

Freud, Sigmund (1990). "Femininity." *Freud on Women: A Reader.* Ed. Elizabeth Young-Bruehl. New York and London: W. W. Norton, 342–362.

Fung, Richard (1991). "Looking for My Penis." Web. http://www.richardfung.ca/index.php?/ articles/looking-for-my-penis-1991/ 26 Apr. 12.

Grammaticus, Damian. "Condoms 'Too Big' for Indian Men." *BBC News Online* 8 Dec. 2006. Web. http://news.bbc.co.uk/1/hi/6161691.stm. 26 Apr. 12.

Gramsci, Antonio (1971). *Selections from Prison Notebooks.* London: Lawrence and Wishart.

Han, Alan (2006). "I Think You're the Smartest Race I've Ever Met: Racialised Economies of Queer Male Desire." *ACRAWSA e-journal* 2.2. Web. http://www.acrawsa.org.au/files/ejour nalfiles/82AlanHan.pdf 26 Apr. 12.

Han, Chong-suk (2006). "Geisha of a Different Kind: Gay Asian Men and the Gendering of Sexual Identity." *Sexuality & Culture* 10.3: 3–28.

Hookway, Nicolas (2008). "'Entering the Blogosphere': Some Strategies for Using Blogs in Social Research." *Qualitative Research* 8.1: 91–113.

Irigaray, Luce (1985). *This Sex Which Is Not One.* Trans. Catherine Porter with Carolyn Burke. New York : Cornell University Press.

Jackson, Peter (2000). "'That's What Rice Queen's Study!': White Gay Desire and Representing Asian Homosexualities." *Journal of Australian Studies* 65: 181–188.

Jain Nair, Rupam. "India's Pot-Bellied Males Hit Gym for Bollywood Buff Look." *The Telegraph* 9 Nov. 09. Web. http://www.telegraph.co.uk/expat/expatnews/6513661/Indias-pot-bellied-males-hit-gym-for-Bollywood-buff-look.html 26 Apr. 12.

Jowett, Adam (2010). "'Just a Regular Guy': A Discursive Analysis of Gay Masculinities." *Psychology of Sexualities Review* 1.1: 19–28.

Marriott, McKim (1976). "Hindu Transactions: Diversity without Dualism." *Transaction and Meaning.* Ed. Bruce Kapferer. Philadelphia: ISHI, 109-II.

McKeown, Eamonn, Simon Nelson, Jane Anderson, Nicola Low, and Jonathan Elford (2010). "Disclosure, Discrimination and Desire: Experiences of Black and South Asian Gay Men in Britain." *Culture, Health & Sexuality: An International Journal for Research Intervention and Care* 12.7: 843–856.

Meyer Spacks, Patricia (1990). *Desire and Truth: Functions of Plot in Eighteenth-Century English Novels.* Chicago: University of Chicago Press.

Monro, Surya (2010). "Sexuality, Space and Intersectionality: The Case of Lesbian, Gay and Bisexual Equalities Initiative in UK Local Government." *Sociology* 44.5: 996–1010.

Osella, Caroline, and Filippo Osella (2006). *Men and Masculinities in South Asia.* London: Anthem Press.

Poon, Maurice Kwong-Lai, Peter Trung-Thu Ho, Josephine Pui-Hing Wong, Gabriel Wong, and Ruthan Lee (2005). "Psychosocial Experiences of East and Southeast Asian Men Who Use Gay Internet Chat Rooms in Toronto: An Implication for HIV/AIDS Prevention." *Ethnicity & Health* 10.2: 145–167.

Wetherell, Margaret, and Nigel Edley (1999). "Negotiating Hegemonic Masculinity: Imaginary Positions and Psycho-Discursive Practices." *Feminism and Psychology* 9: 335–56. Print.

"What Are the 78 Differences Between Women and Men?" *BBC Online* 19 June 2003. Web. http://news.bbc.co.uk/1/hi/uk/3002946.stm 2 Feb. 12.

Yelland, Christine, and Marika Tiggemann (2003). "Muscularity and the Gay Ideal: Body Dissatisfaction and Disordered Eating in Homosexual Men." *Eating Behaviors* 4.2: 107–16.

Young, Rebecca, and Ilan Meyer (2005). "The Trouble with 'MSM' and 'WSW': Erasure of the Sexual-Minority Person in Public Health Discourse." *American Journal of Public Health* 95: 1144–49.

Bearly Indian

"Fat" Gay Men's Negotiation of Embodiment, Culture, and Masculinity

Pranta Pratik Patnaik

Drawing on interviews with twelve Indian gay men, this essay explores the ways in which men talk about their own bodies and bodily practices, and how they negotiate their masculinity and sexuality via their body weight. The specific focus is around discourses of desirability, fatness and gay men's concern and anxiety with fitness and body shape. Shilling (1993) points out that the human body is portrayed as a project which needs continual work and development if it is not to revert to its "natural" state. Many of our everyday practices include personal grooming, hygiene and presenting ourselves in certain "acceptable" ways to other people.[1] In recent years the internet has provided a platform for examining some of the issues surrounding desirability, body image and sexual exploration. The internet allows the user to indulge in the production of imagined spaces, which Anderson (1983) and Taylor (2002) consider to be "social imaginaries."[2]

This essay examines a website for gay men, a place which is regulated by its own rules, and which primarily considers and upholds the notion of the "fair, fit and healthy body" as the ideal. The body is a central point around which gay men display their masculinity to others as well as develop a personal sense of masculine identity. I attempt to answer certain questions, such as: Where does the fat gay fit in such sites? How do they cope with the space that demands strict disciplining of bodies? What are the strategies through which they negotiate these virtual as well as real spaces? How do they perceive fatness? How does the fat body intersect with other aspects of identities like caste, class, age, education, occupation, sexual position, region and religion in India?

"Welcome to our community" is displayed on the login page of Pinksite. com (pseudonym). The word "community" makes one feel comfortable, offering the possibility of sharing commonness among the members. It provides a space for the sexually "marginalized"[3] to connect and interact with each other beyond one's territorial boundaries. Such "deterritorialization," a term borrowed from Appadurai (1996), disrupts the definition of community in terms of its boundaries.[4] However, the notion of a homogeneous gay community needs to be questioned.

A study of queer blogging by Mitra and Gajjala (2008) considers queer bloggers and blogs as individual nodes of connection and a form of community. They argue that blogs enable the production of marginalized subjectivities as scattered individuals and also subsume them into a larger hegemony where they find themselves "placed." It is obvious that those who have access to this website have their own preferences or choices, which ultimately confines them to their, what I call, "mental boundaries" thereby perpetuating or re-establishing the structured hierarchies, discrimination and inequalities in the virtual space.[5] Possible matches are searched for using keywords like "good looking," "muscular and tall," "brahmin," and "delhite," which potentially excludes many from the community. It seemingly develops along the lines of middle-to-upper class values and propagates a youth gay culture. In this site where only specific gay identities have negotiating power, the *hijra* (eunuch) remains outside this *legitimate* virtual gay space.[6] This is the paradoxical function of the webspace — it both enables people to connect with each other and, and also becomes a site of difference.

Sergios and Cody (1985) note that when it comes to dating, physical attractiveness is frequently the most important criterion for gay men. In a culture that idealizes tall, masculine, young male bodies while pathologizing other types of bodies as unattractive and abnormal, it becomes essential to understand the coping strategies of the fat gay men in such a culture. This study, a result of my interest in the issues of gender, "virtual" space and place, began in October 2010 and continued until January 2011. The Internet, for fat gay men, provides an interesting space to enact core values, practices and identities. It is these spaces which are modified by them to culturally specific shapes and purposes. To look at Internet as a virtual space is to suggest that it can provide both means of interaction and modes of representation which can be treated by the participants as real. I take into consideration "virtual" space as providing a kind of space or place where multiple realities and identities are made, unmade and even transcended. It follows Jenna Burrell (2009:187) who considered the field site as a place where social processes occur. It therefore becomes essential to understand how ideas about fat masculinities are constructed and projected in these "virtual" spaces.

Research Process

I posted in the website that I was looking for "fat" people confined only to the Delhi region, the capital of India. Though there are several other websites for gay men, Pinksite.com was chosen for its popularity among the participants of Delhi. Only the users from Delhi were chosen as it has a vibrant gay culture which has recently witnessed gay parades, the triumphant high court order that decriminalized same sex with mutual consent in 2009 and the opening of gay clubs and bars.[7] The responses, which poured in from different parts of the city, averaged fifty responses per day. Questions posed by the users included: What are you going to do with us? and Why are you after the fat guys? The users had profile names like: "Fatty guy for u," "Bear to Bare," "Only4chubbies," "Cuddly Bear," "Fat Men4young Slim Guys," "Fat_bottom with place" and "Cute Indian Bear."

After an overwhelming response to my post, I revised my status line[8] in my profile to "I am looking for 'fat' people who would be interested in an interview about their lives." The responses and visits to my profile immediately declined. My profile was not visited by those who were earlier interested to meet me. There were twelve users left who were interested in "pouring out their lives," as one put it, and to be a part of this academic study.

The respondents' age group ranged from 30 to 52 years old. Three participants belonged to the age group of 30 to 34 years old; three from 35 to 40 years old; three from 41 to 44 years old; two from 45 to 50 years old and one participant was 52 years old. Information about their class, caste, occupation, religion and region were recorded. Seven participants were born in Delhi and the remaining five were migrants from other states.[9] Five participants were Hindus, five were Muslims, and two were Sikhs. Among the five participants from the Hindu community, three identified their caste as Brahmin.[10] The other two did not mention their caste saying that caste status is not important to them but they did say that they did not belong to Scheduled Castes.[11]

Their occupations included bank employee, school teacher, self-employed (business), customer care executive, government employee and doctor. All the participants were married except two — one Hindu and one Sikh — who were unmarried. Of these twelve participants, five identified themselves to be "bottom" in terms of sexual position, four identified themselves to be "versatile" (i.e., they can be both top and bottom) and three identified themselves to be "purely top." The question of a proper sampling method was tricky as the participants volunteered and it was not at the discretion of the researcher to choose the samples for the study.

The data was collected through both online and offline interviews. Three participants from the Muslim community were not ready for an offline interview whereas the rest preferred to meet in person as they had "found a friend in me," as one participant mentioned. It is worth mentioning that Davis et al. (2003) consider online interviews to be impersonal and distancing and impossible for facilitating a detailed exploration of meaning, narrative and discourse. They believe that the quality of data depends on the rapport between the researchers and participants rather than the medium itself.

The interviews, which included open-ended, semi-structured questions, lasted from an hour to an hour and a half. The questions were limited as the goal was to allow each participant to choose what he wanted to talk about. This ultimately led to narratives related to their fatness, an intrinsic part of their identity. The conversation took place both in Hindi[12] and in English. The interviews were not recorded as the respondents were not comfortable with this. Therefore, I took notes at the time of the interview and expanded upon them later. The offline interviews took place in public spaces such as parks, malls, restaurants, and universities. The names of the interviewees have been changed in order to protect their identity. My plan to have a group discussion with these twelve participants was denied because they were not comfortable sharing their views in front of others. Also, those who were not "out of the closet" were afraid of being revealed as gay, despite being told other members of the group would also be gay/queer identified. The interview questions were initially open-ended but at a later stage, when certain common elements were identified in all the interviews, they became the themes for the study. This was pursued further by confining the participants" answers related to those themes.

The study identified four categories of users accessing this website:

a. Users seeking sex — These users prefer to only have fun including sexual relations with the same person or other persons several times with no strings attached (NSA).
b. Users exchanging money — These users include both those who are willing to pay for sex as well as "professionals" — those who actively seek money for sex. They identify as top, bottom and versatile.
c. Users seeking one-night stands — These users have one-night stands with several persons but not with the same person twice. They seek instant pleasure and no money is exchanged.
d. Users seeking a long term relationship (LTR) — These users aim to find a suitable partner to settle down with. Sex is important in this case but what counts more is compatibility between partners, which they confirm through frequent meetings and conversations.

Apart from these well-identified four categories, there were two other kinds of users:

e. Users seeking foreigners — These users, though few, have a special attraction to white men and prefer to have sexual relation only with them.[13] However, when they cannot find foreigners, they look for Indians who are extremely fair-skinned.

f. Users with fake profiles — These users create fake profiles by using pictures of models, celebrities, and other users. They frequently make and delete numerous profiles using different names with various pictures or no pictures at all.

It should be noted that these categories are not exclusive but rather they intersect in many cases.[14] Such categories, one can say, are based upon desires. The desires are influenced by the body, gender, age, religion, caste and class. It therefore becomes essential to understand the body, in phenomenological terms, as a "lived body" through the categories of class, age, caste and religion.

Understanding Fatness as a Lived Experience

In order to understand fatness as a lived experience, I do not make a distinction between the participants' offline and online lives as it assumes that communication through the Internet is not a disjuncture, but is in fact rather quite integral to the social structure. In other words, the Internet is a part of everyday life and its users are not "distanced from embodied social relations" (Miller and Slater, 2000: 7). Bodies need to be seen as lived entities and the perceptions around fat bodies are constructed through societal discourses. The first thing that I wanted to know from the participants was their perception of fatness; what is "being fat" according to them; and if fatness was an enabling experience in the context of their sexual identities. Most of them derived their notion of "fatness" from media, peer groups and family members.[15] The sole category through which they defined their fatness was the disproportion of the weight of their body to their height. While creating an account in at the website, they could clearly see the categories of body types and identified mostly with "Belly" or "Stocky." The weight of the participants ranged between 192 lbs. to 254 lbs. The body's shape along with the social construction of fatness has produced a hegemonical notion of fat masculinity.

When the respondents were asked, how they defined fatness as part of their identity, the following responses were given:

"I know I am fat as I carry a huge body. My belly has come out; my thighs are double of yours (pointing at the researcher)," said Ramesh, a 35-year-old bank employee who has lived in Delhi for twelve years.

Another participant, Yousuf, a 42-year-old government employee born in Delhi, put it as follows: "Can't you see my cheeks are hanging? I weigh 192 lbs. with a height of 5' 4". Last year it was 198 lbs. I have reduced. We *Delhites*[16] indulge in all types of food rich in oil. See in this park there are so many fat people. I have seen them for years. They do exercise over here and after that they go outside to have street food which makes them fat. They never lose weight rather become fat."

Food and exercise were the two necessary things that were identified as factors associated with fatness. The yardsticks set by society makes one accept that s/he is necessarily fat, and at times becomes an issue of ridicule, humor and low self-esteem.

Harjeet Singh, 34 years old, works as a customer care executive for a telecom company. His experience is as follows: "My friends call me '*motu.*'[17] Some even tease me '*Dekho Haathi aa gaya*' (See the elephant has come!). I was fat as a child. I remember my parents taking me to doctors. I took all kinds of precautions but nothing helped. I think it was in my genes as my father was also quite fat. I work in an office where everyone is quite fit. The guys have slim waist and the girls, slimmer. I am not muscular like other guys in the office and therefore become an object of fun. They make fun of me by saying that I should be given a large cubicle in the office to fit in; one burger is not enough for me; and I need two chairs to keep that huge bump. I have never retaliated. It somehow pinches me a lot and the worst part is I cannot do anything about it. In fact I don't want to do anything about it now. I am used to hearing it."

In a society inundated with representations of "fit" bodies in media; fat bodies are highly ridiculed. There is a strong negative component associated with fat bodies. For example, fatness is associated with health problems like obesity and diabetes. This is not to deny that there are certain spaces where positive assessments are structured around fat masculinities, as the Pinksite.com demonstrates.

Perception and Projection of Fatness in the Virtual Space

The cult of male beauty has always revolved round fit, fair and young male bodies on gay websites. The profile images of the research participants in this study included usually headless huge bodies wearing underwear or almost nude.[18] Monaghan (2005) identifies three types of fat bodies — bears, chubbies, and foodies/gluttons though he also mentions that these categories are constructions that are not necessarily mutually exclusive indicating the existence of multiple experiences of fat masculinities. The Indian men who participated in this study, did not know how to differentiate between these terms.

The participants mentioned categories such as "chubs" and "bear" which are often used in gay websites to describe fat gay men. They chose such categorizations after seeing how other men with similar body features identified.

PERSONAL NARRATIVES

Anubhav, a 45-year-old teacher in an English Medium School in Delhi, clarifies his doubt by asking: "I think I am a mixture of all the categories. I cannot specify where I fit in. You tell me what describes me the best. Aren't fat and chubby the same thing? Aren't these unnecessary categories?"

Amandeep, a 37-year-old who works in a private company, seems to have identified which category he belongs to when he says: "I am a bear, a cute bear in fact. I am cute because I am fair and not black like a bear (the animal) though I have got raw instincts like the animal."

Ramesh tries to understand the difference between fat and chubby on his own terms: "Fat is understandable. One who has more weight than the normal. But what is chubby? I have heard about the poem which has a line chubby cheeks but I don't remember it now. Is it for those who have got fleshy cheeks only?"

Tracing the roots of such categories, Soumendhu, a 49-year-old government employee says: "Bear, I think is a western concept. Even if I have plenty of body hair I don't call myself a bear. Why should I associate myself with a wild animal which is unclean, walks on four legs and lives in a jungle? These English educated people, influenced by the foreign culture label themselves as bear. If we translate bear into Hindi it's called 'Bhallu' and we call 'Bhallu' generally to those who are dumb generally in every aspect and I am not dumb!"

UNDERSTANDING THE PERSONAL NARRATIVES

It is clear that fat men on the gay website might have their own way of labeling themselves or may use the site's pre-established categories to describe themselves without actually knowing their meanings, assuming those labels to be the best definers for their bodies. It brings home the fact that these categories and sub-categories that Monaghan (2005) talks about vary in different contexts being subjected to modification, replacement and at times rejection altogether.

It should be noted that the meaning of fatness intersects with other aspects of identity like class, religion and region. The lived experience of being a fat gay man is complicated, contradictory and crosscut by multiple factors.

As Rehaan, a 40-year-old freelance journalist puts it: "Earlier it bothered me a lot. I kept myself confined to my own world. I was not open about my sexuality and it was also quite disturbing. Body weight and sexuality kept hovering over my mind. Subsequently, I accepted the reality and started interacting with only people who knew about me and accepted me as I am. Fatness is something which is visible but being a gay is invisible to others. My parents knew that I was disturbed due to my body weight but they could never know that I was equally disturbed with the 'gay' issue as well."

Faraaz, 44, recounts: "My wife recently told me that she was not sexually satisfied by me owing to my fatness. My manhood (penis) seems to be hidden under my layers of fat making me feel emasculated."

Jerry Mosher (2001) argues that this feminizing aspect of fatness can become acute in extremely overweight males, as the penis is reduced in proportion to body size, or is rendered invisible by the stomach. Gilman (2004) considers this to be what he terms "hobbled masculinity" which surrounds the image of the fat man.

Anurag adds: "I am happy to be an older fat gay man. My age is not an obstacle anymore neither is my body weight. What matters is my class. I have a lot of younger gay men who come to me because they know I can take them out on expensive dates. I don't think that's a problem at all."

Slevin and Linneman (2009) claim that older gay men need to be understood not only in terms of their age and sexuality but also through other markers such as class.[19] Unlike Monaghan (2005) whose study looked at the uneasy relationship between "chubbies" and "slim chasers," and commented on the suspicious nature of their uneasy alliance (slim chasers were often seen as predatory type men looking to exploit fat men lacking self-esteem), the men interviewed in this study, are aware of this and they see it more as a mutual reciprocity rather than an unequal relationship.

Nafis also speaks along the same lines debunking the negative stereotypes associated with fat gay men: "We are thought to be more effeminate, taking bottom position whilst sexual intercourse, and at times impotent. Whatever people might say about us but the truth is we have our own group of admirers."

THINKING THROUGH A DIFFERENT LENS

The pre-occupation with the body might not be the sole concern in these websites when fat masculinities are associated with religion of the user.

As Harjeet, a fat gay man of Sikh origin shares his experience about looking for a potential partner on the website: "Being fat is not an issue with me or my partner(s) but most of the time what turns them off is me being a

Sikh, wearing a turban. I have put my headless body pictures in the website. The hair on my body is a great turn on for many of the users but the moment they know that I am a Sikh, the first question they ask is — do you wear a (pagdi) turban? Are you a pagadi wala sardar? When I answer them 'yes,' the communication ends there. They hate the idea of sleeping with a man who has long hair on his head though they might like hair on other parts of the body. Long hair being associated with female they perceive us to be more feminine or effeminate."

I am therefore challenged to wonder if fat masculinity can be problematized at all? Often an intersectional lens is required to delve through these various markers where the body shape might just be one of the many other layers (See Dasgupta and Gokulsing; das Nair, this volume). Fat masculinity needs to be understood within the contexts of religion, class, skin color, as well as economic indicators. Another thing that would merit further examination is how fat gay men (especially these research participants) celebrate their body weight alongside their sexuality. A fat body also has got something to do with the religious symbols of an individual. Here, the turban of the Sikh, which hides their the long hair in a way "de-masculinizes" them in the eyes of the seeker. This adds a further layer in understanding fat masculinity. While the research participants agree that fat gay men do not lack partners and are comfortably placed within a subgroup of gay desires; it is also true that there is an uneasy body anxiety exacerbated with their motivation striving for a "perfect" body.

Dilemmas of Fatness: Striving for "Perfection"

One cannot deny the role of media in promoting an "ideal male body" which requires a disciplined exercise regime, diet (See Gill, Kenwood, McLean, 2005). Many fat men also are trapped in such hegemonic images of masculinity. Fatness is not always a matter of enjoyment and celebration. There is a deep pressure for fat gay men to be "accepted" by other users. Most profiles would have texts asking fat gay men to stay away — "No fat men will be entertained," "Fat men stay away," "Fatty uncles are a big NO-NO."[20]

Anurag, argues: "You know being fat is both cute and ugly. On one hand we have admirers in the gay website and on the other we are perceived as effeminate male with breasts — impotent or nonsexual. They want a teddy bear to cuddle, to play with. It hurts when someone you like, rejects you because you are fat. Then you develop the urge to reduce your weight, hit a gym and try to look good and to be in shape."

Talking about his married life and sexuality, Faraaz too strives for a perfect body: "I feel sad when my wife looks at other men who are in proper shape. She admires John Abraham the most as he is one of the fittest Bollywood actors. What is lacking in me, she finds that in other men and stares at them. Now I have joined a gym, which I believe will reduce my belly a bit. That's all I want. She wants to see a 'new me.' Moreover it will also increase my value in the pink site."

According to Featherstone (1982), the importance attached to looks in a consumer culture has led to body maintenance and a disciplining of bodies through diet and exercise regimes. He adds further that within consumer culture, the body is proclaimed as a vehicle of pleasure: it is desirable and desiring and the closer the actual body approximates to the idealized images of youth, health, fitness and beauty, the higher is its exchange value. The emphasis on body appearance has also led to the emergence of a narcissistic type of individual where a new self emerges that places greater emphasis upon appearance, display and impression management.[21] In a similar vein, Bourdieu (1984) argues that the body has become a fundamental feature of taste and distinction in which the management of the human form becomes part of the major aspect of cultural or physical capital.

I began with the assumption that the Internet in general and Pinksite. com in particular, provides a site for the performance of one's sexuality. In India where homosexuality is not approved and continues to be stigmatized (for other arguments see Datta, this volume), this website proves to be a "savior" for those caught in between Indian family values and their desire to express their sexuality or to come "out of the closet."[22] In other words, the Internet works as a liberator for oppressed populations and proves to be a safe space for Indian gay men. At the same time it also creates several little enclaves which systematically keep certain people out (See Dasgupta, 2012; Dasgupta and Baker, 2012). The users function on the basis of the stereotypes they have formed. These stereotypes are not merely viewpoints or attitudes rather are a form of social knowledge or, in Anthony Gidden's terms, "practical consciousness knowledge" that constitutes their social worlds through social interaction. In case of the Internet or gay websites, it is not only the fat body of the gay men that matters but also the stereotypes and the ascribed identities associated with it. Even though fat gay men are accepted, admired and found sexually desirable (by certain sub groups), the other side where they are ridiculed and despised is equally true. It would be wrong to assume that they are completely immune to body concerns. While they enjoy admiration, they are also trapped within the market idea of a perfect body and are willing to regulate their bodies. They are trapped between the external problem of representation of their bodies in social spaces, and the internal problem of restraint and control of desire and passion. This should not suggest a denial of human agency. This can be understood using the term "normative freedom" which seeks to capture the apparent paradox by which no notion of freedom is really absolute, but necessarily takes the form of a normative structure, a social order. What the Internet produces cannot be understood in terms of the liberation of new and fluid identities rather a shift and playing of offline identities to the online arena. Despite the stigma associated with fat gay men, one need not conclude that the cultural domination is complete. Those who are stigmatized may elect in various ways to resist such messages and to create alternative notions of manhood. Fat gay masculinity, thus hints at a collection of ideas, attitudes and assumptions which culturally determine the way gay men view themselves as men. It is not something which is fixed or absolute across time and space but rather varies in duration, durability and dominance.

Acknowledgment

I would like to thank Daniel Farr, University of Albany, SUNY who has contributed in many ways towards writing this piece including, suggesting the title of this essay. My heartfelt gratitude goes to the participants, who made my understanding about fat gay masculinity more enriching.

Notes

1. This is what Marcel Mauss (1979) called "body techniques" where certain bodily activities like handshakes, winks, salutes, attention, bending and walking "correctly" forms the foundation of one's social life.

2. Such imagined spaces constructed by people through social interactions may not be physically inhabitable thereby problematizing the notion of "space."

3. I have put the word in quotes because one should also look at what Jeffrey Isaac (1992) has to say—even the most marginalized groups in our society are not completely powerless or do not simply respond to the behavior of the powerful. The reproduction of the relationship always involves their agency, which can be mobilized as well as transform the relationship itself.

4. Appadurai (1996:188–9) has suggested that we increasingly live in a world that has become deterritorialized ... diasporic, and transnational ... a world where electronic media is transforming the relationships between information and mediation.

5. What I mean by mental boundaries is the taste, preference, habits, attitudes and prejudices that subconsciously become a part of influencing our judgment about someone or something in our day-to-day activities. This is how unequal power relations shift from offline to online.

6. It needs to be mentioned here that even though the "Hijras" are outside this virtual space they have their own strong network communities in real spaces.

7. Other parts of the country also have numerous gay clubs and events, particularly Mumbai. Since the researcher is based in Delhi, it becomes easier to access participants from the city.

8. The status line is the first sentence that is written at the top of a profile stating one's likes, dislikes, purpose for being on the site or even a quotation.

9. Two participants were from Bangalore (a city in Southern India); One participant was

from Bhubaneshwar (a city in the coastal part of eastern India); two participants were from Jaipur (Northern India).

10. One of the users had written on his profile — "Looking for *Brahmins* (a higher caste in Hindu Varna Scheme) only."

11. Scheduled castes include Indian population groupings who were previously classed as untouchables and as such were deprived of social, economic, political and cultural rights in India.

12. Hindi is one of the official languages recognized by the Indian Constitution.

13. This preference for white men within the Indian gay community is an indication of embedded or inherent racism which simply maintains the binary structure of racial stereotyping that (re)produces the "other," rather than challenging it.

14. "Being gay" is a learned behavior that involves induction into specific narratives and strategies for interpreting and expressing one's felt desires — desires that are not amenable to being fixed or reduced to a few identity labels. (McLelland, 2002:392).

15. Frank (1991:49) suggests that bodies exist between discourses and institutions, where discourses map the body's possibilities and limitations and institutions ensure the practice of bodily activities as per the discourse.

16. This informally means the inhabitants of Delhi.

17. This is the Hindi word for fat people.

18. Some fat men, being unsatisfied with their bodies, used "fit body" pictures in their profiles. This is what is termed as "screen work" by Monaghan (2005).

19. Bodies, for Bourdieu (1984), bear the imprint of class in three main ways — through the individual's social location, the formation of their habitus and the development of their tastes.

20. Monaghan (2005) points out that desire is an important dimension in the constitution of acting bodies.

21. It should be noted that the desire to have a perfect body and working to get a perfect body reveals those excluded from this culture because of their poverty. The poor, the disabled and other marginalized sections of the society cannot afford this activity.

22. Laurent (2005) notes that Asian values put an emphasis on family and social harmony, which often stand in contradiction to "lesbian and gay rights."

References

Anderson, B. (1983). *Imagined Communities: Reflection on the Origin and Spread of Nationalism.* London: Verso.

Appadurai, A. (1996). *Modernity at Large: Cultural Dimensions of Globalisation.* Minneapolis: University of Minnesota Press.

Bell, K., and D. McNaughton (2007). "Feminism and the Invisible Fat Man." *Body & Society* 13(1): 107–131.

Bourdieu, P. (1984) *Distinction: A Social Critique of the Judgement of Taste.* London: Routledge & Kegan Paul.

Burrell, Jenna (2009). "The Fieldsite as a Network: A Strategy for Locating Ethnographic Research." *Field Methods* Vol. 21 (2):181–199.

Dasgupta, R. K. (2012). "Digital Media and the Internet for HIV Prevention, Capacity Building and Advocacy Among Gay, Other Men Who Have Sex with Men (MSM), and Transgenders: Perspectives from Kolkata, India." *Digital Culture & Education,* 4:1, 88–109.

_____, and S. Baker (Eds.) (2012). *Popular Masculine Cultures in India.* Kolkata: Setu Prakashani.

Gill, R., K. Henwood, and C. McLean (2005). "Body Projects and the Regulation of Normative Masculinity." London: *LSE Research Articles Online.* Available at: http://eprints.lse.ac.uk/archive/00000371/.

Featherstone, Mike (1982). The Body in Consumer Culture. *Theory, Culture and Society* Vol. 1 (2):18–33.

Foucault, M. (1981). *The History of Sexuality. Volume 1: An Introduction.* Harmondsworth: Penguin.

Frank, A. (1991). "For a Sociology of the Body, an Analytical Review," pp. 36–102 in *The Body, Social Process and Cultural Theory*, M. Featherstone et al. (Eds.). London: Sage.

Gilman, Sander L. (2004). *Fat Boys: A Slim Book.* Lincoln: University of Nebraska Press.

Isaac, Jeffrey C. (1992). "Beyond the Three Faces of Power: A Realist Critique" in Thomas E. Wartenberg (Ed.). *Rethinking Power*, pp. 32–55, New York: State University of New York Press.

Laurent, E. (2005). Sexuality and Human Rights: An Asian Perspective. *Journal of Homosexuality* Vol. 48:163–225.

McLelland, M. J. (2002). Virtual Ethnography: Using the Internet to Study Gay Culture in Japan. *Sexualities* Vol. 5 (4): 387–406.

Miller, D., and D. Slater (2000). *The Internet. An Ethnographic Approach.* Oxford & New York: Berg.

Mitra, Rahul, and Radhika Gajjala (2008). "Queer Blogging in Indian Digital Diaspora: A Dialogic Encounter." *Journal of Communication Inquiry* Vol. 32 (4): 400–23.

Monaghan, Lee F. (2005). "Big Handsome Men, Bears and Others: Virtual Constructions of 'Fat Male Embodiment.'" *Body & Society* 11(2): 81–111.

_____ (2007). "McDonaldizing Men's Bodies? Slimming, Associated (Ir) Rationalities and Resistances." *Body & Society* 13(2): 67–93.

Moon, D., and J. Gamson (2004). "The Sociology of Sexualities: Queer and Beyond." *Annual Review of Sociology*, Vol. 30: 47–64.

Mosher, Jerry (2001). "Setting Free the Bears: Refiguring Fat Men on Television," pp. 166–93 in J. E. Braziel and K. LeBesco (Eds.). *Bodies Out of Bounds: Fatness and Transgression.* Berkeley: University of California Press.

Reddy, Vasu (1998). "Negotiating Gay Masculinities." *Agenda*, No. 37: 65–70.

Sergios, Paul A., and James Cody (1985). "Physical Attractiveness and Social Assertiveness Skills in Male Homosexual Dating Behavior and Partner Selection," *Journal of Social Psychology* Vol. 125 (4):505–14.

Shilling, C. (1993). *The Body and Social Theory.* London: Sage.

Slevin, K. F., and Thonmas J. Linneman (2009). "Old Gay Men's Bodies and Masculinities." *Men and Masculinities.* 1–25.

Taylor, C. (2002). Modern Social Imaginaries. *Public Culture* Vol. 14 (1):91–124.

Turner, B. S. (1992). *Regulating Bodies. Essays in Medical Sociology.* London: Routledge.

The Nation as Mimicry
The (Mis)reading of Colonial Masculinities in India

KAMA MAUREEMOOTOO

Postcolonial Residues: The Clash Between "Tradition"
and "Modernity" at Aligarh Muslim University

On April 6, 2010, Dr. Srinivas Ramachandra Siras, aged 64, Reader and Chair of Modern Indian Languages at Aligarh Muslim University (AMU), Uttar Pradesh, India, was found dead in his home. According to numerous news reports, Dr. Siras' body was found "in mysterious circumstances," and it is believed that Dr. Siras might have killed himself.[1] The series of events leading up to Dr. Siras' death were highly controversial: on February 8, 2010, Dr. Siras was in his home in the company of a male rickshaw driver of legal age with whom he had been maintaining an intimate relationship. Unbeknownst to them, three people, two of whom were from the press, surreptitiously entered Dr. Siras's residence and filmed Dr. Siras during a sexual encounter with the rickshaw driver. Dr. Siras was then blackmailed and following the circulation of some pictures to the university administration the next day,[2] Dr. Siras was suspended from the university on grounds of "gross misconduct."[3]

The breach of Dr. Siras' privacy and his suspension antagonized a significant segment of the Indian population, particularly the LGBTQ (Lesbian, Gay, Bisexual, Transgendered, Queer) communities and human rights activists who were still celebrating the "reading down" of Section 377 of the Indian Penal Code (IPC).[4] In "Whose Morality Is This?" an open letter published in the *Hindustan Times* on February 18, 2010, a group of eighteen university teachers and academics across India denounce the actions of the AMU administration as a violation of human liberty: they appeal to the judgment of Chief Justice Shah and Justice Moralidhar in holding Section 377 inapplicable to consenting adults in private (Kidwai et al.). In "Policing Morality at AMU," Narrain et al. argue that though the suspension of Dr. Siras polarized a debate about whether homosexuality is an acceptable "Indian" behavior or not,[5] "the underlying issue [was] really one of various illegal actions perpetrated by the University Authorities whereby they deprived their own faculty of the basic right to be free of intrusion in the sphere of his home and nurture his beliefs, thoughts, emotions and sensations without interference" (Sect. 7). Narrain et al. emphasize that, in *Naz Foundation v. Govt. of India*,[6] the Supreme Court of India established that the right to privacy is inherent to the notion of autonomy and the right to live with dignity.

On the other hand, Dr. Rahat Abrar, public relations officer of the AMU, stated on behalf of the university that "[t]he quarters where he [Dr. Siras] was staying is university property.... [A] teacher has a role of responsibility [*sic*] and should be a figure to be looked up to. AMU has a history of culture and traditions and such things cannot be overlooked" (Sarkar, "AMU Professor"). When an Independent Fact Finding Team set up by a number of lawyers and activists later interviewed Dr. Abrar, he reiterated that "homosexuality even in the privacy of the home is immoral.... [T]his 133-year-old institution has its moral values and they [the university administration, the teachers and the students] must uphold them" (Narrain et al., Sect. 2). Dr. Shakeel Samdani, AMU Faculty of Law Associate, argued that "Part III of the Indian Constitution dealing with Fundamental Rights guarantees certain rights subject to public order, morality and health. A teacher cannot act in such a manner as it violates public order, is a threat to tradition and such acts give rise to AIDS" (Sarkar, "AMU Professor"). In the formal charge sheet that the AMU administration dispatched to Dr. Siras on February 24, 2010, the reason for his suspension was framed as such:

> [Dr. Siras] has committed act of misconduct in as much as he indulged himself into immoral sexual activity and in contravention of basic moral ethics while residing in Quarter No. 21-C, Medical College, AMU, Aligarh thereby undermined pious image of the teacher community and as a whole tarnishing the image of the University [*sic*] [Narrain et al., Sect 1].

Writing for *The Hindu*, Urvashi Sarkar contends that the suspension of Dr. Siras is the result of a clash between conflicting notions of privacy and tradition ("AMU professor"). The rhetoric of "threat to tradition" is pitted against the constitutional rights of citizens, in an attempt to legitimize "public morality" over "fundamental rights." AMU's appeal to "a history of culture" and "moral values" as the aegis under which Dr. Siras was suspended lies in direct opposition to the judgment of the Delhi High Court in *Naz v. Govt.*, which establishes that "[m]oral indignation, howsoever strong, is not a valid basis for overriding individuals' [*sic*] fundamental rights of dignity and privacy

... [and] constitutional morality must outweigh the argument of public morality, even if it be the majoritarian view" (72).

The case of Dr. Siras' suspension and death serves as a preamble to the discussions that follow in this paper: it demonstrates one of the ways in which narratives of sexuality speak to the idea of the nation in India. I argue that the concerns and debates that caused and succeeded the Siras case are, in effect, postcolonial residues that haunt India's contemporary cultural and political scapes: the clash between "tradition" and "modernity," as outlined above, is characteristic of a tension that has been present in India since the late nineteenth- and early twentieth-century. This period marked the shift from colonial to postcolonial India, leading to the country's independence in 1947. This period also brought to the fore questions regarding the space that precolonial traditions could or would occupy within the modern nation India was about to become: amongst these many questions, "acceptable" sexual behavior absorbed a significant part of the nationalist political imagination. In what follows, I examine how the regulation of sexuality shaped aesthetic and political discourses in precolonial and postcolonial India. Through a discussion of literary representations of same-sex desire and through an analysis of the debates that accompanied the decriminalization of Section 377 of the Indian Penal Code, I theorize the discursive change regarding sexual mores in (post)colonial India as a form of colonial mimicry of masculinity that was entrenched in early twentieth-century nationalist movements.

Same-Sex Love, Friendship and Gender Fluidity in Literary Representations in Ancient, Medieval and Modern India

In *Same-Sex Love in India*, Ruth Vanita and Saleem Kidwai map the presence of same-sex love in ancient, Medieval and modern Indian culture as expressed in written forms.[7] In the "Preface," Vanita explains that the anthology "traces the history of ideas in Indian written traditions about love between women and love between men who are not biologically related." Love, in this context, does not necessarily imply sexual encounter: "[a] primary and passionate attachment between two persons, even between a man and a woman, may or may not be acted upon sexually" (xiii). In Ancient and Medieval Indian texts, certain tropes and patterns emerge as sites of representation of same-sex attachment: "friendship as life-defining, often expressed in a same-sex celibate community; sex change and cross-dressing; moving beyond gender; and rebirth as the explanation for all forms of love, including same-sex love" (2). These patterns acquire different dimensions in Hindu, Buddhist and Jain texts, and, in some cases, they remain influential in a number of ways even today.[8]

The sacredness of non-biological and non-marital relationships between persons of the same-sex is expressed as early as 1500 B.C., in the *Rig Veda Samhita*: "[the text] represents the man-woman relation as oriented toward procreation [and] it constructs friendship not as reproductive but as creative" (Vanita 2). Arguably, the most celebrated ideal of same-sex friendship in Indian culture is the relationship between Krishna and Arjuna in the epic, *Mahabharata* (circa 400 B.C.). Vanita argues that "[a]lthough both the main story and many supporting stories celebrate filial, parental, and marital love and fidelity, a persistent strain in the *Mahabharata* represents conjugality and parenthood as obstacles to the love of friends which, for men, may symbolize the path to perfection" (8).[9]

As opposed to the selfless love of friends, the love of parents for children is seen as self-seeking. In the Hindu wedding rite, the *saptapadi* (seven steps), the bride and groom perform seven circumambulations around the sacred fire, during which they recite seven verses that exalt a particular dimension of marriage. While the couple prays for wealth, good health, a long life together etc., "[c]hildren are not mentioned in these seven verses, which focus on marriage as an end in itself, not [as] a means to procreation." (Vanita, *Love's Rite* 129). The seventh step of the *saptapadi* is taken for *sakhya* or "friendship." Vanita argues that the *saptapadi* equates the sanctity of marriage to that of friendship, and in many ways, "no sharp line is drawn between the friendship of conjugality and that of same-sex bonding" (*Same-Sex Love* 7n17).

Ancient and Medieval Indian texts also delineate tropes of gender change, miraculous birth and the undoing of gender. Vanita argues that "[i]n most mythologies, divine, heroic, and semi divine beings are of miraculous origin. Their birth from virgins, from human-divine intercourse, or from a single parent, male or female, signals their difference from ordinary mortals" (12).[10] Miraculous births can also arise out of the interaction between two persons of the same sex. These "miraculous births" validate non-heteronormative possibilities of procreation and restructure the biological human sexual reproductive order. In Ancient Hindu texts, most of the cases of sex-change are involuntary, while in Medieval literature, they are voluntary. The most oft-quoted story of involuntary sex change from Ancient India is that of King Ila in the *Ramayana*: King Ila turns into a female as he encounters Shiva and Parvati making love in a forest.[11]

The prominence of voluntary sex-change in Medieval Indian literature and culture was tightly knit to the prevailing religious contexts of the time. The Medieval period extended approximately from the eighth to the eighteenth centuries A.D. During this period, Islamic cultures established themselves in India, while concurrently interacting, influencing and being influenced by other religious cultures such as Buddhism, Jainism, and Hinduism. Religious texts were produced in Sanskrit and Sanskrit-based languages, southern Indian languages, and in Perso-Arabic and Urdu traditions. In the Sanskrit and Sanskrit-based languages, the *Puranas* were very influential: the later *Puranas* were particularly eminent in representing patterns of voluntary sex change.

This period witnessed a surge in devotional literature, much of which is attributed to the Bhakti movement. Beginning around the seventh century A.D. in South India, and subsequently spreading throughout the subcontinent, Bhakti ("devotion") philosophy influenced numerous schools of Hinduism. Bhakti centers on spiritual practices of mystical loving devotion to a chosen god. During the Medieval period, the intimacy that a devotee held with a deity could be expressed in different forms: many women mystics rejected conventional marriage and claimed to be married to a god; *devdasis* were women dedicated to a deity (male or female) in temples and lived outside the conventional space of marriage; certain male mystics rejected husbandhood since "they [saw] conjugality and parenthood as selfish preoccupations that obstruct[ed] devotion to god and all god's creatures" (Vanita and Kidwai 63).[12]

Bridal mysticism was one of the highly ritualized ways through which devotees expressed their faith in a god. In bridal mysticism, a deity was positioned as the husband or male lover of the devotee and the latter was regarded as a subordinate wife or female lover. In some schools of Hinduism, such as Vaishnavism, for example, *all* devotees, independent of their own sex and gender identification, identified with a female who desired union with a male deity. For male devotees seeking union with a deity, this entailed developing an androgynous religious ideal. In certain schools such as the Vaishnava-Sahajiyas, *kama*, or "desire," was seen as male, while *prema*, or "selfless love," was perceived as female; hence, devotees actively sought to position themselves as female lovers to a chosen deity. Vanita argues that the trope of bridal mysticism is present in the poetry of Medieval male mystics such as Surdas and Kabir (*Same-Sex Love* 64–65). In such poetry, she contends, "a male mystic typically uses feminine verbs for himself, even though his name, used in the poem's signature line, is male" (65). Within this genre of poetry, feminine expressions and female signifiers, such as *sindoor, matki* and *ghunghat* were extensively used.

Within Puranic philosophy, gender is seen "as a garment, a disguise, which is assumed at birth and shed at death" (Vanita and Kidwai 65). In other words, gender is a performance (not an essence), and it holds no importance within the cycle of death and rebirth.[13] This conception of gender fluidity is also echoed in Buddhist and Jain philosophy and Vanita contends that the conception of gender within these traditions "closely resembles the decon-struction of gender in our own times" (*Same-Sex Love* 22).[14] While contem-porary theories of the social construction of gender argue that gender is only performatively and discursively reiterated as "natural," Ancient and Medieval Indian philosophy regard gender as an "illusion" that only appears to be "real." Since gender is not rigid, since it is assumed at birth and shed at death, it does not fully determine the self, and it can be altered during the course of one's life if one is prepared for such a change.

Homoerotic love was also widely represented in Medieval Muslim cul-tures, particularly in the body of literature from the later Medieval period. This period witnessed significant migration of Perso-Turko-Arabic popula-tions to the Indian subcontinent, leading to an increased cosmopolitan atmos-phere. Kidwai argues that the visibility of same-sex love in Muslim Medieval culture is largely attributed to the urban cosmopolitan culture of the time, which was a marked feature from the thirteenth century onwards. Kidwai con-tends that within the urban setting, public spaces grew in importance, as seen in the spread of marketplaces and bazaars, for example. Since these spaces were essentially frequented by males, they became fraught with homosocial and homosexual interactions. In these towns and markets, men of different castes, classes and communities mingled and "communal eating, drinking and social intercourse gradually eroded class distinctions" and created a context where homoerotically inclined men could meet other men (Vanita and Kidwai 108).

The advent of Islam in Medieval India also instituted the development of harems and slavery. Young boys and eunuchs comprised the majority of slaves.[15] In "Alienation, Intimacy, and Gender: Problems for a History of Love in South Asia," Indrani Chatterjee argues that examining sexual relations through the lens of slavery significantly contributes to the understanding of same-sex relationships in premodern India.[16] Slave trading and slave-keeping were common practices in elite households that patronized and produced poetry; in Perso-Urdu poetry, the trope of slavery was used to denote the poet personae as a slave of love and as a slave of his male lover.[17] The language of desire used to express male-male love, as articulated through the trope of slav-ery, was considered appropriate at the time. Chatterjee argues that European observers were insensitive to the slave/master norms prevailing at the time and they misinterpreted these acts as "homosexual," and thus "the latter lens (gender) displace[d] the former (slavery) in the language of the colonized" (61).

The representation of same-sex love in Medieval Muslim India was also influenced by Sufism. Coming into contact with mystics of other religions and influenced by devotional philosophy, "Islamic mysticism had developed a full-fledged institutional structure and become a movement by the time it spread in India" (Vanita and Kidwai 114). Love occupied the core of Sufi music and poetry. Kidwai argues that "[e]arly mystical poetry in west Asia addressed God directly as the beloved. By the twelfth century the notion had gained ground that God's essence was unfathomable and his beauty could be realized only by contemplating his creations who were the witnesses (*shahid*) of his magnificence" (Vanita and Kidwai 115). In Sufi literature, this "contemplation" was expressed in homoerotic metaphors. While Kidwai argues that "[m]any Sufis insisted that only same-gender love could transcend sex and therefore not distract the seeker from his ultimate aim of gnosis" (115), in "Persian Sufism in Its Historical Perspective," Zarrinkoob argues that the object of love represented in Sufi poetry was generally male "because the Sufis pictured the supreme beauty with rather virile characteristics" (169).

Vanita and Kidwai argue that from the beginning of the twentieth century onwards, the representation of same-sex desire in literary works changed as "the minor homophobic voice that was largely ignored by mainstream society in precolonial India [became] a dominant voice" (191). Indeed, the 1920s saw the first public debates around homosexuality, debates triggered after Pandey Bechan Sharma, known as "Ugra" (meaning "fierce" or "extreme"), published a collection of short stories in the leftist nationalist newspaper *Matavala*. Ugra's short stories deal with "the path of chocolate," or the "hellish vice" of homosexuality in Indian society (Ugra, "Foreword" 5). The underlying tenet of Ugra's stories is that if one does not denounce homosexual practices and attempt to eradicate them, "[Indian] culture and civilization will be totally destroyed, which is not permissible" (3).

In the first story published by Ugra, "Chocolate," Manohar, one of the characters, defines the term "chocolate" as such: "'[c]hocolate is a name for those innocent, tender, and beautiful boys of our country, whom society's demons push into the mouth of destruction to quench their own desires" (13). In a radical move away from the representation of same-sex desire in precolonial Indian literature, Ugra's stories depict the "path of chocolate" as an evil one against which young males should protect themselves in order to uphold their integrity and "traditional" values. Most of the tales imply that homosexual practices ultimately lead to suicide, death, social ostracization or diseases such as tuberculosis — a belief widely held at the time. In "Chocolate," the chocolate-lover, Dinkar, disappears by the end of the narrative; in "Kept Boy," Hari dies of tuberculosis; in "Dissolute Love," Kalyanchandra is ostracized from society and ends up killing himself; and in "We Are in Love with Lucknow," Prasad Babu flees Lucknow to Calcutta, where he is imprisoned.

Despite Ugra's moralistic intentions and despite his pejorative representations of "chocolate," his stories created an uproar when they were first published because many believed that the depiction of homosexual desire in literature would be celebrated by "chocolate lovers." For Ugra's opponents, such depictions would not deter homosexual practices, but would instead encourage them, particularly because their representation in literary fiction made them more attractive. Vanita argues that in Ugra's stories "[t]he men ... acquire a local habitation and a name — the stories depict their language, social interactions, even their self-views and self-defense" ("Introduction" xviii). Vanita contends that it is this "naming" that caused the backlash over Ugra's stories when they were first published. For Ugra's narrators, on the other hand, the fact that "society is silent" with regards to young men "destroying their characters, virility, and strength in a terrible way" is unacceptable (28). In the short story "Discussing Chocolate," Ugra defends his point of view through the voice of the narrator who supports the stance of the newspaper *Matvala* in which Ugra's stories were published. While the "guardian of orthodoxy" who represents Ugra's critics asks "[w]hat's the use of shedding light on the wrong acts that society does secretly?" (49), Ugra's narrator and alter-ego replies that:

> [o]ur society itself is degraded. It knows well that many wicked beings are burdening its chest everyday with the rocks of chocolate-love. Every child in this society knows what the practice of chocolate is. In every part of society there are wicked people who are predatory tigers by nature but appear to be mild cows. What is poor *Matvala* doing but exposing such people? It should be thanked for doing so [48–49].

In his stories, Ugra posits an already cosmopolitan and hybrid India: the male lovers are Hindus who cite *ghazals* and other forms of Urdu poetry from memory while showing fair knowledge of French and English literatures. As he draws attention to an already hybrid Indianness, Ugra also holds homosexual practices to be the result of foreign imports. In most of his stories, Ugra accuses the Western education system, with its residential schools and universities, responsible for fostering same-sex desire and same-sex practices. In "Chocolate," for example, the narrator wonders how "[c]an an educated person like Dinkar Babu fall into such a swamp of sin?" (14); in "O Beautiful Young Man!" the character portrayed as the chocolate-lover is described as a "Westernized man" (54); in "Kept Boy," the narrator explicitly states that "[he] can say with certainty that boys should not be sent to modern schools and colleges even if it means their remaining uneducated" (28); and in "Dissolute Love," traditional Indian education is pitted against modern education as one of the young man states that "[m]odern education draws people to such sins.... Our ancient education didn't make us so impure. These days, after fueling the fire for twelve years in an English school in Delhi, educated young men set out to try all the shops of sin" (61). In other narratives, Ugra depicts the love between young men as an evil imported from Islam. In "Dissolute Love," for example, Kalyan the poet is considered disgraced because "the shadow of Muslim poets has fallen on the Hindi poet. The idiot ignores his own culture and pure religion" (61).

Vanita contends that many in India believe that the idea and practice of same-sex love were imported by foreigners — whether Muslim invaders, European conquerors or American capitalists (*Same-Sex Love* xxiii). Vanita and Kidwai further argue that Indian nationalists reacted in two ways against allegations of indecency made by British educators and missionaries who saw India as a primitive place characterized by polygamy, polyandry, child marriage, decadent hedonism, and licentious Hindu beliefs. On the one hand, Indian nationalists responded through counterclaims that practices such as masturbation and male-male sex were unknown to India and Hinduism; on the other hand, if they acknowledged the presence of such "vices" in twentieth-century India, they blamed their presence on foreign interlopers (*Same-Sex Love* 194–197). A century later, during the legal hearings regarding the decriminalization of Section 377 IPC, echoes from the same debates were heard as lawyers and politicians argued that the decriminalization of sodomy is a legal stance that comes from the West and cannot be adopted in India.

Section 377 of the Indian Penal Code: Tradition or Colonial Intervention?

The Indian Penal Code (IPC) was drafted by Lord Macaulay and was introduced in British India in 1861. In *For the Record: On Sexuality and the Colonial Archive in India*, Anjali Arondekar discusses the difficulties that Macaulay faced while attempting to draft the Indian Penal Code in 1835. Arondekar argues that "[f]or Macaulay, none of the presidencies or territories of British India provide[d] any models of criminal codes relevant or impartial enough to work as foundations for a viable form of criminal code" (77). For Macaulay, the major challenge lay in the fact that, in the colonial era, the geographical space that came to be known as India had never been a unified space with homogeneous "national" laws, histories and political structures. In Macaulay's words:

> [a]ll existing systems of law in India are foreign. All were introduced by conquerors differing in race, manners, language, and religion from the great mass of people. The criminal law of the Hindoos was long ago superseded by that of the Mahomedans, and the Mahomedan criminal has in its turn been superseded, to a great extent, by British Regulations [Macaulay quoted in Arondekar 77].

In "The Politics of Penetration: Section 377 of the Indian Penal Code," Suparna Bhaskaran argues that during the nineteenth-century, the drafting of the IPC led to the "colonial homogenizing of the Indian Law" (18–20). According to Bhaskaran, though colonialists intended to "carefully" consult scholars about religious scriptures to determine how the existing heterogeneous laws could be codified in the IPC, the British law remained the basis for the codification of a uniform law for the whole of India.[18] Macaulay was well aware that certain laws applied to a section of society such as a religious community or a caste and not to others. He was also aware that codes of conduct were heavily regulated and solidified through different religious texts. Consequently, Macaulay's attempt at drafting the Indian Penal Code implied a secular codification of the laws of the country.[19]

Roughly 150 years since the introduction of Section 377, the debates surrounding the decriminalization of sodomy still carry traces of the conflicts Macaulay faced in drafting the Indian Penal Code. While these debates occupied the imagination of Indian nationalists in the late nineteenth — and early twentieth-century, they now occupy the contemporary Indian cultural and political scapes: tensions between tradition and modernity, Indianness and Westernization, and the religious and the secular still foreground the composition of the Indian identity. The case of Dr. Siras, for example, captures this tension as an ambivalence with regards to "proper" sexual and gendered behavior within a nationalist structure — as do the grounds for challenging Section 377 which are discussed below.

In 2001, Naz Foundation, a Delhi-based HIV/AIDS-prevention NGO, and the Lawyers' Collective, a legal reform group, filed a petition challenging Section 377 as violative of Article 14 (the right to equality), Article 19 (the right to freedom), and Article 21 (the right to life and liberty) of the Constitution of India. The petition mapped the legal history of Section 377 by tracing the development of sodomy as a crime in England, "categorically prescribed for the burning alive of the sodomite" as early as 1290, to the decriminalization of homosexuality and acts of sodomy between consenting adults in 1967 (Sect. I.A). The petition also sketched the minor punishments that were prescribed for the crime of sodomy in precolonial Indian texts such as the Arthashastra, the Kamasutra, the Manusmriti and the Mahabharata and the Quran (Sect. I.B). In addition, the petition minutely orchestrated the growing discourse of LGBT rights in a global context while simultaneously bringing local instantiations of homosexuality as a crime in postcolonial India. Arondekar notes that unlike Western gay civil rights legal activism, which is articulated through the rhetoric of discrimination and identity, the petition by Naz Foundation "relied ... on the relationality between sexual acts and civil rights, developing its defense of a citizen-subject's privacy as the organizing constitutional right for the repealing of section 377" (172; emphasis added).[20] Arondekar further argues that:

[d]espite such carefully staged shifts in legal strategy, the central challenge for the petition lay in breaking the stranglehold of the Westernization narrative: the familiar argument (not unique to India in many ways) that "unnatural acts" (more specifically sodomy) and/or homosexuality were not part of an Indian past and were mimetic by-products, remaindered through the onslaught of an aberrant and contaminating Western temporality and spatiality. To break such a stranglehold meant providing the state with convincing evidence of sodomy's indigeneity in the Indian context [172].

Through such an attempt, the petition turned to available historical evidence and presented an array of material ranging from literature to art history and medicine in order to "queer" the Indian past and (re)build an archive of same-sex desire and practices that could be traced back to precolonial India. Consequently, the petition turned the criminalization of sodomy into a Christian colonial intervention and ironically presented precolonial India as already modern in its acceptance of sodomy. Countering the Ministry of Home Affairs" claim that "[i]n our country, homosexuality is abhorrent" (*Naz v. Govt. 23*), the petitioners argued that "abundant material has been placed on record which shows that the Indian society is vibrant, diverse and democratic and homosexuals have significant support in the Indian population [*sic*]" (*Naz v. Govt* 22–23). The petitioners thus appealed to modern notions of Indian identity grounded in a liberal framework imported from the West while simultaneously tracing modernity back to precolonial India — a strategy that staged India's past into the present and, at large, functioned as a revisionist history of same-sex desire to be carried into the future.

On the other hand, during the legal proceedings to demonstrate the unconstitutionality of Section 377,[21] the Ministry of Home Affairs (MHA) justified the retention of Section 377 on the grounds that: Section 377 serves to protect minors against abuse and hampers "delinquent behavior" that includes homosexuality (*Naz v. Govt.* 10–11); "Indian society by and large disapprove[s] of homosexuality, which disapproval [is] strong enough to justify it being treated as a criminal offence even where the adults indulge in it in private [*sic*]" (11); and the decriminalization of consensual same-sex acts would cause a decline in public health and foster the spread of HIV/AIDS in India (24).[22]

The differences between representations of same-sex desire in precolonial and postcolonial India demonstrate a shift that occurs during the colonial period, from the late nineteenth- and early twentieth-century onwards. The colonial intervention triggered a significant body of political and aesthetic discourses that spoke in the name of the nation. Homophobia was one such discourse, functioning as a characteristic of modernity that placed the nation as a "moral" and "pure" space. Such an address was necessary to legitimize a nationalist project that mirrored itself in the image of colonial authority. Colonial homophobia, then, was adopted as "tradition," as the originary point that always framed the nation, as seen in Ugra's depiction of homosexuality as a threat to Indian culture, for example. Nowadays, such homophobia still expresses itself politically, as in the arguments put forward by the MHA during the court hearings about the decriminalization of Section 377. Such a standpoint erases precolonial archives of sexuality from contemporary cultural and political scapes and places colonial homophobia as an originary tradition.

Nationalism and the (Mis)reading of Masculinities in Colonial India

Early twentieth-century India witnessed numerous social, political and legal campaigns that centered on the struggle for independence, the abolition of caste and untouchability practices and women's civil rights with special reference to widow remarriage and dowry exchange. These debates were characterized by increasing tensions between Hindus and Muslims and such issues acted as the playground upon which nationalists debated (and were often divided over) the desire to preserve prevailing Indian practices and traditions while embracing modern change and reforms.[23] The proposed reforms were fraught with ambivalence as to how the nationalist movement would reconcile laying claim to an original, indigenous culture and politics while the grounds upon which the need for such a vindication was felt were themselves premised on British colonial assumptions. In *Postcolonial Insecurities: India, Sri Lanka and the Question of Nationhood*, Sankaran Krishna argues that this resulted in "a paradoxical notion of decolonization ... [since] national redemption was impossible without independence from the British, but ... the tasks the postcolonial state set itself mirrored all that the west already was" (4).

The need to legitimize Indian tradition as politically pertinent was accompanied by a desire to assert that India was "already civilized" and "already enlightened," where the terms of civilization and enlightenment were defined by Western, Victorian standards. Vanita argues that "[t]his contradiction is endemic to Indian nationalism and is evident even today throughout the political and literary spectrum. Modern Indian identity remains permeated by *anxieties* regarding its Hindu, Muslim and Western components" ("Introduction" xvii; emphasis added). For Krishna, postcolonial *anxieties* "refer to the fact that the social construction of the past, present, and future for state elites and educated middle classes in the third world are mimetic constructions of what has supposedly happened elsewhere: namely, Europe or the west" (xix). The anticolonial and nationalist projects thus relied on what Bhabha calls a form of "mimicry."[24] Krishna argues that:

> [p]remised on [the] narrative of what once happened "out there," postcolonial elites attempt to remake the recalcitrant clay of plural civilizations into lean, uniform, hypermasculine, and disciplined nation-states.... [P]ostcolonial anxiety [is] this attempt at replicating historical originals that are ersatz to begin with [xix].

This "lean, uniform, hypermasculine and disciplined" representation of the nation proved to be an object of contention in the anticolonial movement, particularly because Indian men felt the need to reshape themselves, their religions and their nationalist ideals to match the "lean, uniform, hypermasculine" Victorian ideal. It is out of this colonial anxiety, this attempt at mimicry that modern homophobia in India emerged.

In *Love's Rite*, Vanita argues that "[m]odern homophobia is deeply intertwined with modern nationalism" (12). As demonstrated earlier, at most times and in most places in pre-colonial India, love and desire between males and between females, even though it may have been disapproved of and/or ignored, was never actively persecuted. In late nineteenth — and early twentieth-century India, the minor homophobic voice that was largely ignored by mainstream society became a dominant voice. For Vanita:

> [a] homophobia that was marginalized and ineffective in precolonial society became dominant in the course of the nineteenth century, especially among the educated classes. This new homophobia was one manifestation of a modern Puritanism imported from Victorian England. Reacting defensively to British administrators' and missionaries' assaults on Indian sexual mores as promiscuous and idolatrous, and on Indian men as effeminate, Indian social reformers and nationalists claimed that Indian society was and always had been sexually purer than British Victorian society itself ["Introduction" xxxi].

During this period, Section 377 IPC was introduced. Vanita and Kidwai argue that "the crushing of the 1857 rebellion, followed by the official incorporation of India into the British Empire with Queen Victoria replacing the East India Company, signaled the violent end of medieval India. For same-sex love, that end was signaled by the 1861 law that criminalized homosexuality" (194). The British anti-sodomy statute of 1860 was progressive for Britain insofar as it reduced the maximum penalty for sodomy from death by hanging to ten years' imprisonment. However, when introduced in India in 1861 as Section 377, the provision was regressive.

The new Puritanism from which emerged a "new homophobia" was well entrenched in the nationalist movement. The manifestation of this newly adopted Puritanism expressed itself in censorship, in silence with regards to sex-related issues, in the advocacy of premarital celibacy, and also in larger social reforms for sex-workers, courtesans and *devadasis*. Vanita argues that "reform, in this context, referred not to improving the working conditions of these women but to [the] moral reform of the women themselves" ("Introduction" xxxiii). The moral concerns regarding sex were part of a larger puritanical nationalism that shared censorious beliefs with regards to fashion (particularly women's fashion), non-didactic fiction, dance, theatre and practices oriented towards pleasure for its own sake.[25] As a result, from the late nineteenth century onwards, there was a movement that insisted that Hinduism had always been a monotheistic religion that professed monogamy.[26] Indian men, as subjects of colonial rule, became particularly vulnerable to the charge of deficient masculinity — a charge of which they tried to acquit themselves by prescribing homophobic discourses.

In "The Economy of Colonial Desire," Revathi Krishnasawmy studies the role that masculinity played within the colonial context in India. She argues that:

> [m]asculinity is not only a foundational notion of modernity, but it is also the cornerstone of ideology in the ideology of moral imperialism that prevailed in British India from the late nineteenth century onward. The cult of masculinity rationalized imperial rule by equating an aggressive, muscular, chivalric model of manliness with racial, cultural, and moral superiority [292].

Modern masculinity was not only elaborated through a strict demarcation between the sexes, but also through an "unmanning" of racial and ethnic minorities within and outside of Europe. The ideal model of masculinity was epitomized in the appearance of the Englishman as tall, clean-cut, strong, and this model served to exclude as deficient people who were narrow-chested, excitable, inefficient — negative qualities attached to women, Jews, the lower classes and colored peoples. This physical ideal of masculine beauty was also equated with higher moral worth through associations between body and soul, outer and inner beauty, physical appearance and morality.[27] In *Gender, Religion, and Nationalism: The Trope of the Ascetic Nationalist in Indian Literature*, Chandrima Chakraborty argues that "[i]mperial masculinity as hegemonic masculinity was not merely an 'ideal'; it appeared to be the 'natural' masculinity of a superior and virile race. Indians were thus convinced of their subordinate masculinity" (26).

Krishnaswamy argues that by the end of the nineteenth century, effeminacy had become the most powerful signifier of India's cultural decline. Within the structure of colonial homosociality, "[e]ffeminacy represent[ed] a critical and contentious idiom through which the racial and sexual ideologies of empire [were] mediated" (294). Effeminacy served to discriminate the colonized Indian by rendering him weak and demonstrating his inability to skillfully concede to reason and mental (hence social and political) control:

[i]f masculine beauty was an expression of white European racial, moral and cultural superiority, ugliness was evidence of nonwhite, non–European inferiority. The disorderly appearance attributed to diverse groups of foreigners and social misfits referred not only to physical deformity, but it also implied lack of mental discipline and emotional moderation [Krishnaswamy 293].

In no other realm was this "disorderly appearance" more obvious than in Hinduism. From a colonialist's perspective, effeminacy as degeneracy permeated the open-ended, unorganized, polytheistic and matrifocal character of Hinduism. In contrast, Judeo-Christian monotheism seemed robust, reasonable, ordered and properly masculine.[28]

Krishnaswamy argues that Indian effeminacy was not a false construct or a stereotype, but instead "a misvalued and distorted recognition of something real in Indian culture" (295). Krishnaswamy contends that what colonizers categorized as effeminacy functioned in Medieval Hindu mysticism as an androgynous ideal (as demonstrated earlier in this essay) whereby a man posited himself as an ideal female devotee: effeminacy signified a heightened state of humility and devotion.[29] The civilizing moment weakened the ideal of Hindu effeminacy-in-masculinity by reinscribing androgyny as Victorian effeminacy, to which Hindu men reacted with the need to reshape themselves and their religion in the image of a robust, monotheistic, heterosexual and masculine ideal regulated by Victorian standards.[30]

The Victorian trope of chivalry as manly ideal was a privileged locus of the colonial self-image and the interaction between colonizer and colonized structured and destabilized both British and Indian masculinity as a threat to each other. In *Colonial Masculinity: The Manly Englishman and the Effeminate Bengali in the Late Nineteenth Century*, Mrinalini Sinha sheds lights on the complexities of masculinity as a battle-ground for the Imperial project. Sinha argues that the relations between colonizer and colonized were constantly articulated and rearticulated in relation to changing political, social and economic imperatives in Victorian England:

[t]he figures of the "manly Englishman" and the "effeminate Bengali" were ... constituted in relation to colonial Indian society as well as to some of the following aspects of late nineteenth-century British society: the emergence of the "New Woman"; the "remaking of the working class"; the legacy of "internal colonialism"; and the anti-feminist backlash of the 1880s and 1890s [2].

Sinha further argues that by the late nineteenth century, the politics of colonial masculinity were structured along a descending scale where on top were British officials who were part of the administrative and military establishment, followed by British officials not directly related to the colonial administration. Last in this ladder were the politically self-conscious Indian intellectuals who represented "an 'unnatural' or 'perverted' form of masculinity" that was referred to as the odious category of the effeminate Bengali *babus* (2). The Bengali *babus* mimicked the British intellectuals, making them a threat to the colonial power. In *The Location of Culture*, Homi Bhabha argues that in instances of colonial imitation, "[the] civilizing mission is threatened by the displacing gaze of its disciplinary double" and to counter this threat, the colonizer marks the colonial subject as a "partial presence" (123). I argue that, to mark the Bengali *babu* as a "partial presence," the colonizer *had to* turn him into an effeminate figure: the *babu*'s effeminacy is what made him "almost the same [as], *but not quite*" the Englishman (Bhabha *Location*, 123; emphasis original).

Although the legitimating discourse of colonial legislation was enacted on behalf of Indian women as hapless victims of barbaric Indian patriarchy, Krishnaswamy argues that the British, while projecting themselves as champions of women, were in fact far more concerned with emasculating or effeminizing Indian men than with the emancipation of women (310). Perceived injustices experienced by Indian women were used by the colonizer as a tool to demonstrate the inferiority of indigenous masculinity. The British Raj functioned as a homosocial space for contending male fears, desires, frustrations and fascinations, much like the homosocial structure developed by Eve Kosofky Sedgwick in *Between Men: English Literature and Male Homosocial Desire*. Sedgwick argues that in Victorian England, women served as objects of exchange in transactions that served primarily to promote the interests of male rivalry and/or solidarity. Since male homosocial desire operated through a homophobically inflected heterosexuality in colonial India, homophobia was not most immediately about oppressing male subjects of same-sex desire but rather, a means of fashioning conventional masculinity for the Englishmen deployed in the colonies, and for controlling the natives through emasculation. Nonetheless, the figure of the effeminate Bengali disrupted the colonial discourse, because, though effeminate, rarely do we find any cases of homosexual Bengalis. Arondekar argues that "most of the native men with the predilection for sodomy are Afghans, Punjabis and Sikhs: all clans of native men characterized for their bravery and prowess in martial arts" (121). Krishnaswamy echoes Arondekar and contends that "[h]omosexual yet manly, heterosexual yet effeminate, Indian masculinity injects a fearful indeterminacy into the economy of colonial desire" (302).

The redefinition of masculinity and the emergence of homophobia in late-nineteenth and early–twentieth century India point to different forms of ambivalence at play in the colonial context. Homi Bhabha theorizes this ambivalence in *The Location of Culture* as the ambivalence on the part of the colonizer in trying to civilize the natives, while simultaneously holding them sufficiently uncivilized so that they are incapable of questioning the civilizing process imposed on them. Bhabha argues that "colonial mimicry is the desire for a reformed recognizable Other, *as a subject of a difference that is almost the same, but not quite*" (Bhabha 122; emphasis original). For the colonizer, the threat of colonial mimicry expresses itself in the displacement of the gaze of its disciplinary double. The menace emerges in moments of slippages or excesses when the subject that is *almost the same but not quite* adopts the colonizer's terms and mimics the colonizing discourse in such a way that the colonial authority is disrupted.

In the case of the effeminate Indian, I argue that androgyny could only be misread as effeminacy and/or deficient masculinity in the colonialist imaginary. As argued earlier, indigenous effeminacy is what made the Indian intellectual "almost the same, but not quite" the Englishman. However, in the nationalist attempt to reclaim Victorian masculinity as Indian, there ensued a dissemination of homophobic discourses that sought to negate the precolonial Indian past by positing modern history as tradition. Homophobia expressed itself not only in the depiction of same-sex desire in literary representations of the early twentieth century, but it continued (and continues) to articulate itself throughout the cultural and political spectrum, as indicated in the legal debates around the decriminalization of Section 377 and the Siras case. The suspension of Dr. Siras and the nationwide debates caused by his suspension demonstrate instances where homophobic discourses, as a characteristic of modernity and postcoloniality, still have (the potential for) real life impacts — beyond just discursive effects — onto the everyday life of citizens.

Notes

1. See "Aligarh gay professor"; Khan and Siddiqui; Kidwai, et al.; Sarkar; Saxena; and Sharma et al.

2. According to various reports, the university administration was aware of the presence of the journalists in Dr. Siras' residence and it has been suggested that they might even have initiated the sting operation themselves. See Dasgupta; Khan and Siddiqui; Narrain et al.; and Saxena.

3. See "Aligarh gay professor"; Kidwai et al.; Maddox and Edmond; and Sharma et al.

4. Section 377 IPC was the anti-sodomy law of India, which, on July 2, 2009, had been "read down" to criminalize only "non-consensual non-vaginal sex and penile non-vaginal sex involving minors" (*Naz Foundation v. Govt. of India* 105).

5. Throughout this paper, unless otherwise stated, I use the term "homosexuality" to refer solely to the sexual *act* between two persons of the same sex, and not to a homosexual *identity*.

6. Thereafter referred to as *Naz v. Govt.*

7. Vanita and Kidwai's use of "India" as a geographical location is arbitrary in nature and they acknowledge that other scholars might have chosen the term "South Asia" instead (xv).

8. In "Transsexualism, Gender, and Anxiety in Traditional India," Robert P. Goldman echoes Vanita in claiming that "a certain strand of hermeneutical continuity is provided by the fact that the contemporary groups and individuals who articulate and/or perform texts of transsexualism, [gender-performance, and same-sex love] seem invariably to derive their sense of the

phenomenon from the ancient sources which they use as sources of inspiration and validation" (375n4).

9. For more about asceticism and same-sex friendship as expressed in the *Mahabharata*, see Vanita and Kidwai 8–10.

10. See Vanita and Kidwai, 12–13.

11. For more details on this tale and its variants, see Goldman 379–80, 393 and Vanita and Kidwai, *Same-Sex Love* 17–19.

12. For more on the types of intimacies between devotees and deities during the Medieval period, see Vanita and Kidwai, "Medieval Materials in the Sanskritic Tradition" in *Same-Sex Love* 55–68.

13. In "Vices, Gods, and Virtues: Cosmology as a Mediating Factor in Attitudes toward Male Homosexuality," Richard J. Hoffman argues that in monotheistic cosmology, the godhead is unborn and does not father any generations. The universe is hence desexualized and the conception of gender rigidified. On the other hand, in polytheistic cosmologies, continuity of creation and gender blurring in the realm of the supernatural offer the conditions for a wide variety of sexual expression and sex-role behavior that include the crossing of gender lines. See Hoffman 27–44.

14. Here, Vanita refers primarily to the work of Judith Butler on gender performativity. Vanita sees correlations between gender performativity (as a discursive "performance" of gender) in Butler's work and gender as an illusion that is taken on and performed in Puranic, Buddhist and Jain traditions. For more on Butler, see *Gender Trouble* 9–18, 163–80 and *Bodies That Matter* 1–55, 223–42.

15. Kidwai argues that eunuchs were highly respected and "[they] were a prized commodity because they were considered the most reliable slaves." Since eunuchs had no progeny, their closest relationship and allegiance was to their owners who in turn entrusted them with positions of high responsibility (Vanita and Kidwai 109).

16. According to Chatterjee, slavery in the context of Medieval India, "would need to be carefully separated from the institution identified with eighteenth- and nineteenth-century plantation economies so that it would not be conflated with issues of *violence* but with a dialectic of *alienation and intimacy* originating in peaceful sales and commerce characteristic of South Asian evidence" (61; emphasis original).

17. Chatterjee contends that though it is widely believed that the male-male love poem was addressed from the perspective of an adult male to a "boy," this belief is erroneous for the term "boy" itself (*launda* or *larka*) could denote a male slave of any age (63).

18. Bhaskaran further argues that "[d]isregarding the numerous complex variations of customary law and practice prevailing among Hindus and Muslims in different parts of the country, Macaulay decided that all Muslims were governed by the Quran and all Hindus by the *Manusmriti*" (20).

19. Arondekar notes that in addition to the near-impossible task of translating English legal codes into Indian vernaculars, colonialists had to face the challenge of understanding and adjusting to Indian legal and forensic epistemologies which were a priori incompatible with that of Victorian standards (79–81). The Islamic law of evidence, for example, did not recognize written documents as proof for a crime, unlike British law.

20. In *The History of Sexuality I: The Will to Knowledge*, Michel Foucault argues that, in the West, before the nineteenth century, sodomy was a forbidden act. It is only by the end of the nineteenth century that the homosexual became a full-fledged character, an identity: "The sodomite had been a temporary aberration; the homosexual was now a species" (43). This in turn allowed the proliferation of "reverse discourses": the homosexual became an identity to be claimed and reclaimed: "homosexuality began to speak in its own behalf, to demand that its legitimacy or 'naturality' be acknowledged" (101). In similar fashion, Arondekar argues that while the rhetoric around the legal status of homosexuals in the West is grounded in acknowledging the identity of LGBTQ individuals (through civil rights aimed at rendering them equal to the rest of the population) the grounds for decriminalizing sodomy in India relied on rendering the *act* legitimate as a choice by consenting adults in private.

21. The unconstitutionality of Section 377 IPC was disputed through two contradictory affidavits filed by two different wings of the Union of India: the Ministry of Health and Family (MHF) demanded that the Section 377 be repealed because it hampered HIV/AIDS prevention interventions, while the Ministry of Home Affairs (MHA) sought to justify the retention of Section 377 based on concerns regarding public morality.

22. For more on the rhetoric adopted by the MHA, see *Naz v. Govt.* 12, 23–24.

23. One such debate was over what would be the national language of India: right-wing Muslim and Hindu leaders insisted that Hindi was the language of Hindus and Urdu the language of Muslims and yet both groups had "West-phobic" tendencies.

24. Bhabha's concept of colonial mimicry and its implications in the postcolonial context are further discussed later in this paper.

25. Interestingly, Vanita argues that the term *Westernization* "often functioned, and continues to function even today, among both right-wing and left-wing nationalists, as a code for selfish sensuality and self-indulgence" ("Introduction" xxxiii).

26. Around the same time, reformers attempted "purification" campaigns aimed at "cleaning" precolonial literature. For example, Muslim reformers tried to remove tropes of love and wine from Urdu poetry, and attempted to heterosexualize the *ghazal*, a form of poetry that celebrated male-male love.

27. These beliefs were firmly grounded in new eighteenth century sciences such as physiognomy, anthropology and modern medicine that used aesthetic and physical criteria to distinguish between races, both physically and morally.

28. English as a language was also considered hard, energetic, rational and masculine while Persian and other oriental languages were deemed soft, voluptuous and effeminate (Krishnaswamy 296–97).

29. Krishnaswamy also argues that this view of femininity "[does not imply] a pro-woman or feminist stance, because Hinduism generally devalued female activity to male stasis, while androgyny was held out as a liberating ideal primarily for men rather than for women" (295).

30. However, Chandrima Chakraborty argues that while mimicking imperial ideals of masculinity, Indian nationalists also formulated their own version of masculinity as an anticolonial strategy, namely through the Hindu ascetic figure.

References

"Aligarh Gay Professor Found Dead, May Have Killed Self." *Times of India* 8 Apr. 2010. India times.com. Web. 23 Jan. 2011. http://timesofindia.indiatimes.com/india/Aligarh-gay-professor-found-dead-may-have-killed-self/articleshow/5771916.cms.

Appadurai, Arjun (1996). *Modernity at Large*. Minneapolis: University of Minnesota Press.

Arondekar, Anjali (2009). *For the Record: On Sexuality and the Colonial Archive in India*. Durham, NC: Duke University Press.

Bhabha, Homi K. (2004). *The Location of Culture*. Oxford: Routledge.

_____ (Ed.) (1990). *Nation and Narration*. London: Routledge.

Bhaskaran, Suparna (2002). "The Politics of Penetration: Section 377 of the Indian Penal Code." Vanita, *Queering India* 15–29.

Butler, Judith (1999). *Gender Trouble: Feminism and the Subversion of Identity*. London: Routledge.

_____ (1993). *Bodies That Matter: On the Discursive Limits of "Sex."* London: Routledge.

Chakraborty, Chandrima (2004). *Gender, Religion, and Nationalism: The Trope of the Ascetic Nationalist in Indian Literature*. Diss. York University.

Chatterjee, Indrani (2002). "Alienation, Intimacy, and Gender: Problems for a History of Love in South Asia." Vanita, *Queering India* 61–76.

Dasgupta, Debarshi (2010). "These Walls Have Ears." *Outlook India* 08 Mar. 2010. OutlookIndia.com. Web. 23 Jan. 2011. http://www.outlookindia.com/article.aspx?264462.

Foucault, Michel (1990). *The History of Sexuality*. Vol. 1. Trans. Robert Hurley. New York: Vintage.

Goldman, Robert P. (1993). "Transsexualism, Gender, and Anxiety in Traditional India." *Journal of the American Oriental Society*, 113.3: 374–401.

Hoffman, Richard J. (1983–84). "Vices, Gods, and Virtues: Cosmology as a Mediating Factor in Attitudes Toward Male Homosexuality." *Journal of Homosexuality*, 9.2–3: 27–44.

Khan, Ashhar, and Maha Siddiqui (2010). "AMU VC Had Ordered Sting Operation on Dr. Siras." *India Today* 12 Apr. 2010. *IndiaToday.in*. Web. 23 Jan. 2011. http://indiatoday.into day.in/site/Story/92557/LATEST%20HEADLINES/'AMU+VC+had+ordered+sting+oper ation+on+Dr+Siras.'html.

Kidwai et al. (2010). "Whose Morality Is This?" *Hindustan Times* 18 Feb. 2010. HindustanTimes. Web. 23 Jan. 2011. http://www.hindustantimes.com/Whose-morality-is-this/Articlel-510 347.aspx.

Krishna, Sankaran (1999). *Postcolonial Insecurities: India, Sri Lanka, and the Question of Nationhood*. Minneapolis: University of Minnesota Press.

Krishnaswamy, Revathi (2002). "The Economy of Colonial Desire." *The Masculinity Studies Reader*. Eds. Rachel Adams and David Savran. Oxford: Blackwell, 292–317.

Maddox, Georgina, and Deepu Sebastian Edmond (2010). "AMU Action Against 'Gay' Professor Condemned." *Indian Express* 19 Feb. 2010. Indianexpress.com. Web. 23 Jan. 2011. http:// www.indianexpress.com/news/amu-action-against-gay-professor-condemned/581756/.

Narrain et al. *Policing Morality at AMU: An Independent Fact Finding Report. Alternate Law Forum*. Alternate Law Forum. Web. 23 Jan. 2011. http://altlawforum.org/news/Amumoral policingfinal10.03.pdf.

Naz Foundation v. Government of NCT of Delhi and Others. WP(C) No. 7455/2001. High Court of Delhi at New Delhi. 2009. *Judgment Information System*. District Courts of India. 2 July 2009. Web. 23 Jan. 2011. http://lobis.nic.in/dhc/APS/judgement/02-07-2009/APS 02072009CW74552001.pdf.

Sarkar, Urvashi. "Mystery Shrouds Death of AMU Professor." *The Hindu* 8 Apr. 2010. *The Hindu*. Web. 23 Jan. 2011. http://www.thehindu.com/news/national/article391265.ece.

_____. "AMU Professor a Victim of Clash Between 'Tradition,' Privacy." *Hindu* 25 Feb. 2010. *The Hindu*. Web. 23 Jan. 2011. http://www.hindu.com/2010/02/25/stories/20100225623 72200.htm.

Saxena, Pradeep. "AMU Administration Behind Siras' Death: Teachers." *Hindustan Times* 13 Apr. 2010. Hindustantimes. Web. 23 Jan. 2011. http://www.hindustantimes.com/AMU-administration-behind-Siras-death-Teachers/Articlel-530888.aspx.

Sedgwick, Eve Kosofsky (1985). *Between Men: English Literature and Male Homosocial Desire*. New York: Columbia University Press.

Sharma et al. "In Mysterious Circumstances." *Outlook India* 07 Apr. 2010. OutlookIndia.com. Web. 23 Jan. 2011. http://www.outlookindia.com/article.aspx?264986.

Sinha, Mrinalini (1995). *Colonial Masculinity: The Manly Englishman and the Effeminate Bengali*. Manchester: Manchester University Press.

"Ugra," Pandey Bechan Sharma (2009). *Chocolate and Other Writings on Male Homoeroticism*. Trans. Ruth Vanita. Durham, NC: Duke University Press.

Vanita, Ruth (2005). *Love's Rite: Same-Sex Marriage in India and the West*. New York: Palgrave.

_____ (Ed.) (2002). *Queering India: Same-Sex Love and Eroticism in Indian Culture and Society*. New York: Routledge.

_____ (2009). Introduction. *Chocolate and Other Writings on Male Homoeroticism*. By Pandey Bechan Sharma "Ugra." Trans. Vanita. Durham, NC: Duke University Press, xv–lxviii.

_____, and Saleem Kidwai (Eds.) (2001). *Same-Sex Love in India: Readings from Literature and History*. New York: Palgrave.

Writ Petition, Naz Foundation v. Government of NCT, Delhi and Others. WP(C) No. 7455/ 2001. 2001. Made available by the Lawyers' Collective, Bangalore, India.

Zarrinkoob, Abdol-Hosein (1970). "Persian Sufism in Its Historical Perspective." *Iranian Studies*, 3.3/4: 139–220.

Mobilizing for Sexual Health

The Experience of Queer Indian Men in London

DAVID A. ANSARI

Introduction

This study aims to understand how queer men from Indian backgrounds integrate their cultural and sexual identities. By exploring the experiences of men from first- and second-generation immigrant communities in England, this study considers how men from these backgrounds may face additional familial and social pressure with regard to queer identities, in comparison with queer men from the dominant White British community. Previous research in the UK (Bhugra, 1997a), Canada (Gosine, 2008), Australia (Abraham, 2009), Pakistan (Badruddin, 1997) and India (Khan, 2001) has described the fluid nature of men's expressions of sexuality and has found that sexual identity tends to be subsumed by family and community identities. Gosine (2008) describes how queer youth from diaspora communities may constantly feel like outsiders. That is, in their nation of origin, they may be marginalized because of deviant sexual expression and in their "host" nation, they are considered on the margins of both the mainstream, white-centred lesbian and gay scene and in heterosexual milieux. Similarly, Gopinath (1997) explores how members of the queer diaspora explore their "threat" to structures of the home, family and the nation, thereby developing a resistance to "disciplinary mechanisms" within these structures (p. 470). Lastly, Desai (2002) explains how the relationship between diasporic communities and the homeland may be queer in that queerness may be a form of displacement. Thus, the foundations of home, citizenship and the nation are called into question. The concepts proposed in these studies provide an understanding for how queer young people make sense of their identities and how potentially divergent cultural influences impact their sexual expression.

The term "community" refers to a realm of family, religion, marriage, language, tradition, relationships and social values interact, which may be challenging for men as their sexual behavior and desires run contrary to the dominant social fabric (Khan, 2001: 107). The concept of the South Asian family and the corresponding identities that develop among young people has been described in detail elsewhere (Mehta, 1998). However, I intend to adopt Badruddin's (1997) conceptualization of the family as a practical platform into economic and social life among young people. Further, as stated by Boyce and Khanna (2011: 97), queer men do not forego marriage or parenthood since these are inherently linked to "successful social roles." Khan (1996: 165) has described that the denial of homosexual activity and homosexuality among men, from communities as well as from the men themselves, may perhaps be more aptly characterized as "maasti," or "mischief," since sexual activity outside of the marital context is perceived as indulgent rather than a substantive component of men's sexual identities.

Previous research in South Asian cultures focuses on how sexual activity has less of a bearing on a man's identity than other roles such as being a husband or a father. Many young men find themselves shaped by familial obligations. Personal identities are often absorbed by family and community identities (Khan, 1996, Badruddin, 1997). Badruddin (1997) states that the focus on families may be practical as entry into economic and social life depend on how people identify themselves through their families. This focus on kinship becomes relevant here, as these men may not necessarily have the privacy to explore their sexualities. Moreover, sex outside of marriage may be seen as indulgent rather than as a substantive component of a man's sexual identity (Khan, 1996).

Empirical work on the experiences of "coming out" among gay men from South Asian backgrounds in the UK has described the notion of "Asian insularity" (Bhugra, 1997, p. 555), in which young gay men from these communities experience isolation from mainstream gay communities. Other research on the experiences of disclosure of these men has also highlighted similar experiences of discrimination from White British gay men (McKeown et al., 2010) and has introduced the notion of "erotic capital" (p. 853), in which these men see themselves placed in a hierarchy of desirability based on their ethnicity. As such, those from certain minority communities may be perceived to be more desirable than others, potentially introducing additional fodder for exclusion.

This essay arises out of a larger study that sought to understand the experiences of South Asian men accessing sexual health services in London. By focusing on the experiences of queer men from these backgrounds, I aim to better understand how sexual and cultural identities overlap and impact decision-making in sexual health. Queer men from black and minority ethnic (BME) communities may face additional cultural and linguistic barriers to sexual health services than White-British men. Research undertaken on the sexual health of BME communities has suggested that sexual health services are often culturally inappropriate and that there is a lack of effort to incorporate the needs of these communities into services (Elam et al., 1991). While the prevalence of health conditions may be lower amongst ethnic minority communities, the rate of service uptake is also lower (Weston, 2003).

In addition, the culural heritage of service users may have a profound effect on sexual attitudes and lifestyles since it influences how people learn about and experience sex, shapes the development of sexual behaviors, and affects sexual health service use (Elam et al., 1999). Numerous studies conducted on sexual health amongst members of ethnic minority communities have found that sexual health service messages and services are culturally inappropriate (O'Brien and Khan, 1996; Elam et al., 1999; Beck et al., 2005). However, growing up in the UK provided more opportunities for learning about sex through peers from different ethnic groups and that religious influence on sexual behavior was weakened (French et al., 2005).

This denial drives sexual encounters underground, potentially increasing risky sexual behavior. An understanding of the process of stigma may provide additional insight into aetiology of this denial. Moving beyond the seminal work of Goffman (1963) in which individuals are identified based on attributes, more recent conceptualizations of stigma focus on the process of devaluation (Link and Phelan, 2001), view it as centred at power, culture and difference (Parker and Aggleton, 2003), and explore it in terms of individual and macro-social components (Campbell and Deacon, 2006). For many of these men, elements of their cultural background such as religious beliefs, family structures, social reputation and tradition make non-heterosexual desire and behavior seem impossible. This notion of impossibility necessitates an exploration of the identity of these men to appreciate how sexual and cultural identities are reconciled. An understanding of identity also introduces the possibility of resistance to stigma (Howarth, 2006).

Parker and Gagnon (1995) emphasize a need to shift attention from sexual behavior alone to the social and cultural contexts that govern it. As such, one must understand the realities of queer Indian men to understand their considerations when making use of sexual health services. The present study seeks to address these issues by incorporating our current understanding of sexual health and sexualities amongst these men with empirical work that assesses the needs of queer men from ethnic minority communities.

Methodology

This study was undertaken a London-based sexual health organisation that aims to mobilize BME communities for better sexual health. Research respondents were members of the organisation's social groups geared towards queer men from South Asian backgrounds. Interviews were conducted with 15 men from Indian backgrounds living in London who identified as queer. Interview guides were developed based on findings from previous research undertaken amongst queer men from South Asian backgrounds (Bhugra, 1997a, Bhugra, 1997b, Minwalla et al., 2005; Boyce, 2006; Boyce, 2007; Elford et al., 2010; McKeown et al., 2010; Boyce and Hajra, 2011).

Findings and Discussion

This study identifies the relevant aspects of sexual and cultural identities as they affect the experience of sexual health services of queer men from Indian backgrounds. Another aim of this study was to investigate how a London-based community support network could help mobilize these men to address factors that undermine their sexual health and promote the use of sexual health services amongst this group of men.

CONTEXTS IN WHICH THESE MEN LIVE

This section explores how the cultural identity of queer men from Indian backgrounds has impacted their expression of sexuality, drawing on five principal themes: (a) attitudes of and stigma towards same-sex activity within the Indian and South Asian communities, (b) familial pressure and expectations of these men, (c) religion and spirituality, and (d) experiences on the mainstream gay scene.

Stigma of Same-Sex Activity Within the Indian and South Asian Communities

Most of the men I spoke with believed that they experience more stigma than queer White-British men. One man from India who moved to the UK to undertake his studies described an incident at work:

There's this guy from Pakistan who works [with me] and he was like, "you're Indian and you're gay, how can that be?" it was just like, "you just can't be Indian and you can't be gay" [Yash, 22].

This perception that homosexuality does not exist in Indian societies is widespread in literature on ethnicity and sexuality and came up in many of the discussions I had with my interviewees. Yash further stated that many people consider homosexuality to be a Western import without looking within Indian societies. He stated that Indian society is much more "homosocial" than Western societies because, for example, it is not uncommon to see two men walking hand in hand in public without ever being considered homosexual. Participants echoed the findings in the literature of the fluidity of sexuality and stated that same-sex behavior and relationships have existed in Indian societies for a long time. Only is it relatively recently that the Western notion of homosexuality and the response to it have been imposed on these societies through legislation:

> And then the cultural response in India to homosexuality is not indigenous, it's the section 377 of the [Indian] Penal Code, 19th century penal code that outlaws unnatural carnal acts, including sodomy [Vikram, 28].

Since Section 377 has been declared unconstitutional (Misra, 2009), will stigma disappear over the course of a few generations? What implications does this have for queer Indian men living in the UK? One respondent described how the Indian and South Asian communities perceive same sex relationships:

> [It's] Completely homophobic.... It's just the universal background that South Asians come from. It's just, there's no such thing as a gay identity [Ajay, 29].

Thus, one may surmise that stigmatising views towards homosexuality do not only hinge upon imposed legal frameworks. However, same-sex behavior is tolerated if it does not reflect the blossoming of a personal identity which conflicts with a larger community identity. Khan (1996) has described how individual identities are subsumed by community identities. One must consider the position of queer men within familial and social structures and how the desires and behaviors of these men do not reflect what is expected of them.

Familial Pressure and Expectations

During the interviews, the men spoke of how being gay or having sexual relationships with men runs contrary to what their families and communities expect of them as young males. One man described an internal struggle reflecting tension between personal attractions and cultural values:

> There's a constant battle going on in their head, they've got their cultural values and then what they're brought up with, is very much about you're a man, you're going to get married, you're going to have kids, you're there to bring a baby home, you're there to support your family, and that is life, really [Saif, 24].

Men from this background who do wish to disclose their sexuality to their families are presented with the additional challenge of explaining the nature of their same-sex relationships. So it is not just a question of whether one's family will accept his sexuality; it also refers to whether being gay fits in with a family's existing socio-cultural schema. Badruddin (1997) states that identifying as gay in South Asian cultures legitimizes a relationship that is inconsistent with the central institution of the family, meaning that the concept of being gay does not exist. In addition to being concerned about how their parents would react, the men in this study were also concerned about how their parents would be viewed by others. One man described his father's reaction upon learning that he was gay:

> Initially when I first came out, my dad said, well if you're gay, what will happen when your sister wants to get married? It will look bad. My sister's potential in-laws won't let them marry because she has a gay brother, and that goes back to the shame bit and appearances [Vinod, 24].

Previous research has described how familial and community expectations revolve around heterosexual norms, resulting in an effort to protect the family from potential shameful perceptions of homosexuality or bisexuality (Parker, Khan, and Aggleton, 1998). As in many communities, protecting the public honor of one's family and community is paramount in Indian and South Asian communities. Honor acts as a principal framework for social control, thus hiding stigmatized behaviors to avoid incurring shame and reinforcing normative identities (Weston, 2003; see also Butler, 1990).

Religion and Spirituality

Much of the stigma of same-sex attraction and behavior draws on religious influences. Yet it is important to highlight the religious diversity within this region of the world, as well as across generations. The men interviewed in this study told me about how religious beliefs have been used to justify criticism but have also provided support in difficult times. Each man shared his experience with the role of religion in culture and how this role impacts sexuality. A few respondents stated that negative perceptions of same-sex activity amongst the Muslim community were rooted in religious beliefs, whereas stigma of male-to-male sex amongst the Hindu and Sikh communities was due to familial expectations. One man from Indian and Pakistani backgrounds described his experience:

> You pray five times a day ... you fast thirty days a year. Yeah and I think the gay thing it completely contradicts that lifestyle.... I find my Indians to be a lot more sympathetic to my situation. I think they wouldn't, I think they'd understand it a lot more than my Pakistani side [Saif, 24].

Another made a firm distinction between religion and culture:

> What I really like about the [Sikh] religion, apparently the first human rights-oriented religion in the world. It believes in equality and respecting one another. There's nothing written about, against homosexuality. I don't like the narrow mindedness that seems to come with the culture and the fact that some things are hidden and kept away and homosexuality is just not discussed [Dharam, 24].

For many communities, religion is an essential element in the concept of ethnicity (Elam et al., 1999) that affects the discussion and manifestation of sexuality and sexual behavior. As stated by O'Brien and Khan (1996), religion and family structure are closely linked to community identity and the religions practiced in South Asian cultures are an essential element of community and public life (Khan, 1996). As noted by another respondent, the separation of religion from culture is perhaps not so simple, suggesting that the lack of acceptance of same-sex behavior and relationships in Indian and South Asian societies is complex and multidimensional. Thus, the realities of these men differ significantly from those of their White-British counterparts. But the fact that most of these men live in the UK and most grew up in the UK means that they adopt a unique blend of identities: on one hand they move within Indian and South Asian milieux. On the other hand, they are living in a country in which the expression of sexualities outside of the mainstream is not restrained by any particular legal doctrine or cultural value system.

Experiences on the Mainstream Gay Scene

These men may also face additional isolation and at times, racism, while on the mainstream gay scene in the UK. Several respondents mentioned instances in which they were identified and discriminated against by other queer men solely based on their ethnicity. One man told me about his experience at a bar in the north of England:

> I've been out in the north lots of times where people on the door of clubs have said to me, "Are you gay? This is a gay only place" and I've said "yeah I'm gay" ... what I take it to mean is, "you don't look gay" and what they mean by that is "you're Asian" [Aftab, 30].

This example of being singled out demonstrates that gay white men are capable of reinforcing the stereotype that there are no gay South Asian men. The fact that some men have described specific instances in which they faced discrimination by other gay men because of their ethnicity illustrates that there is a need to address additional stigma. What is certainly missing from gay bars, clubs, and bathhouses is a platform to address the specific challenges faced by queer Indian men. As one of my respondents summarized quite aptly:

> Many South Asian MSM do not feel part of the scene and they feel that they would be further isolated if they were on the scene ... for some, they go to a club and they really want a supportive environment but you know, a club is really not a place where you can go to get support [Bilal, 27].

Bilal's perspective here illustrates both the challenges faced by queer men from Indian and South Asian backgrounds on the mainstream gay scene and introduces the challenges faced by those who avoid the scene altogether. The fact that these men may face a co-occurrence of racism and a lack of support necessitates a community-driven effort to address the adversity faced by these men.

The realities of these men gives us a much broader insight into "cultural barriers" that are mentioned with little explanation in ongoing research undertaken amongst ethnic minority communities and sexual health service access. Is the concept of "MSM" even appropriate in this context? Much of the public health and development discourse concerning the SA community uses this term rather than gay or bisexual to capture the multitude of identities possessed by the men who share one common trait: that they have sex with other men. This term arose from debates of the conceptualization of sexuality and was a way to refuse the dominant narratives about sexuality and behavior (Roberts, 1995; Gosine, 2006) and sheds all emotional and psychological connotations, and characterizes behavior instead of identity. In this paper, I use the term "queer" in favour of others, such as non-heterosexual, homosexual or men who have sex with men (MSM). Consistent with the approach of Yep et al. (2001), queer allows us to potentially include individuals from lesbian, gay, bisexual and transgender backgrounds. However, on the ground, most of these men describe themselves as gay or homosexual, though some identified as queer or stated that they do not have a sexual identity. This may be due to the fact that living in Britain allows for immersion in a multi-ethnic society in which there are more relaxed attitudes towards sexual relationships (French et al., 2005). Does this suggest that these men can be open about their sexuality in different contexts, such as at home or within their community? Eight out of fifteen men I spoke with had disclosed their sexuality to their parents, and far fewer had come out to relatives beyond their immediate family. One man I spoke with described how he was open in most contexts aside from when he is at home:

> I kind of sometimes feel like I live a double life. I go to work and I'm out at work. Everybody knows about me. But when I'm at home, it's like I have to be a man (laughs), not be a man but just, I can't be myself [Shashi, 25].

The position of these men illustrates the juxtaposition between India and British cultures. Unlike queer Indian men living in India, these men live within a context in which their realities are affected by their relationships with White-British gay peers and experiences they have with the mainstream, predominantly White-British gay scene.

COLLECTIVE ACTION AND MOBILIZATION FOR SEXUAL WELLBEING

This highlights how social groups of queer men from Indian backgrounds may help bridge the gap in sexual health service use. These groups aim to bring these men together to form friendships and to discuss issues that are relevant to their sexual health. I asked my interviewees about their general perceptions of these social groups. Their responses resembled the concept of health-enabling communities (HEC) presented by Campbell et al. (2007) as six principle themes emerged from the data: (a) a social space for dialogue, (b) a sense of common identity and ownership of the issues that affect this group, (c) access to up-to-date and accurate information about sexual health, (d) the ability to form friendships and develop solidarity within the group, (e) exploring and developing the strengths of the group, and (f) links with external organizations and resources.

Social Space for Dialogue

The monthly meetings of the social groups are a space in which men can assemble to discuss relevant issues. One of the men I interviewed described the need for a social space because issues that are relevant to queer men, especially from Indian and South Asian communities, are rarely discussed in mainstream gay settings. In fact, he told me how the mainstream gay scene hides the realities faced by many who frequent it:

> There are certain issues, identity issues, internalised homophobia ... we create spaces away from the scene so that people can talk about what's really going on [Bilal, 27].

One of the key factors of a public space is the opportunity for members to share their views and be heard. One interviewee felt that these social groups are a venue in which one's opinions could be shared and respected:

> The whole point ... is that you can go and share your opinion and that's it and not have judgment [Madhav, 30].

Theorists have described the necessity for a public sphere to be open to all members to contribute their opinions, allowing for a plurality in perspectives (Arendt, 1958; Habermas, 1989). Further it is the diversity in perspectives that allows for identities to be negotiated and renegotiated in a manner that allows group members to develop an understanding of their circumstances and mobilize for collective action.

A Sense of Common Identity

The men in this study attend these social groups because they identify as gay, bisexual or queer and are from Indian backgrounds. As stated previously by respondents and in the literature, same-sex behavior and homosexuality are often denied or are subjugated by heterosexual normative attitudes and behavior in the Indian communities. Therefore, the fact that social groups for these men exist is quite remarkable:

I felt that I was by myself, alone in this country and I thought I was the only Indian guy who was gay [Sunil, 26].

Another man described the similarities between himself and the other members of the group:

There are people my age, people my generation who have also gone through a similar, not the same, but a similar journey and I think that's there's that connection there [Dilip, 27].

Many of the respondents described subgroups and cliques that form. In fact, some of the men I interviewed stated that at times they felt alienated from the group. One man stated that the majority of men from the social groups did not share his view of sexuality:

From a personal level, it made me feel slightly alienated ... so I was going in ... with the expectation that terms like gay would be problematised and that sexuality would be thought of outside of those categories [Amitav, 23].

Amitav's perspective appears to be in the minority, but the fact his opinions are not shared by all illustrates the heterogeneity in such social groups. Mizrahi and Rosenthal (1993) state that conflict is inherent for any social space as they describe "dynamic tensions" that account for such conflict. In this context, this tension is inherently necessary for the formation of identities, allowing differences to manifest themselves in the form of dialogue.

Access to Relevant Information and Resources to Develop Skills

These social groups present information on issues such as negotiating safe sex, sexual health screening, coming out, dating and racism. These topics are proposed and voted on by members of the groups. The discussions bring together factual information with group members' experiences.

In this environment, the theories underlying peer education are drawn upon in order to ensure that knowledge is acceptable and accessible. As stated by Jovchelovich (2007), the knowledge shared in local contexts hinges upon the social and cultural elements that affect individuals and groups. Respondents in this study felt that the information shared was serious, progressive and entertaining. However, some of the respondents stated that they do not intend to attend these social groups forever. This is due to the fact that topics are repeated as old members leave and new members arrive. Still, these groups provide a venue in which members can meet and build long-term friendships and discuss relevant issues.

Friendship and Solidarity

One of the vital aspects of a HEC is a sense of partnership and mutual dependence amongst the members (Campbell, Nair, & Maimane, 2007). A key feature of the social groups is the promotion of friendship among members. The men that I interviewed often stated that these relationships were a primary reason for their continued attendance. For many of these men, social networks that support their cultural and sexual identities do not exist outside of these groups: "I know for a fact that at home no one's there to support me about being gay" (Shashi, 24). These social groups provide vital connections amongst individuals with similar experiences of adversity. These connections can be empowering for members as individuals provide mutual support to one another to address adversity and enact resilience (Wexler, DiFluvio, & Burke, 2009). Aggleton and Campbell (2000) note the increase in empowerment of people if they are recognized as partners in problem-solving. In this context, the relationships that are formed are more than just friendships. They are alliances that allow these men to draw upon collective strengths to face the challenges that they may be unable to face alone.

Exploring and Developing Strengths

Most of the men in this group stated that they had very positive experiences with the social groups and many wanted to get more involved. Within these social groups, there is room for members to express their individual needs and talents, allowing members to learn from one another: "You learn and it builds your character as well because you learn about other people's experiences and show they deal with them" (Karam, 29). These quotations illustrate the sense of mutual learning and growth that occurs in the context of these social groups. This learning and growth illustrate the concept of "critical consciousness" proposed by Paulo Friere (1970, 1973), which states that individual can develop the behaviors and attitudes beneficial to health when provided with the opportunity to engage in collective dialogue. What ensues is a sense of confidence in individual and group agency and the ability to mobilize.

Links to External Resources

The concept of health enabling communities must be considered carefully as initiatives geared towards improving the conditions of marginalized groups may prove ineffective if larger societal hindrances are not addressed. One must examine efforts to build a receptive environment in which those with power will listen to the needs and the concerns of marginalized groups and take them seriously. These social groups, as well as the organisation as a whole, are working to develop bridges between this marginalized group and Indian communities.

There are opportunities to draw upon power relations in order to challenge some of the negative perceptions that these men face. One respondent discussed his use of disclosure to challenge existing stereotypes of homosexuality within the Indian Hindu community:

> They're a bit surprised and I'm hoping partly by me coming out is it does establish that you don't have to be a, because you are gay doesn't mean that you don't have self respect, it doesn't mean you can't be spiritual [Madhav, 30].

Madhav is referring to the community at his temple as well as with a Hindu community organization. In this context, he is drawing upon social networks and using his position within the community to serve as an example of a gay Indian man. By doing so, he is challenging existing beliefs, promoting discourse around queerness and maintaining links between communities.

I asked many of my respondents what they thought would be an ideal way to sexual health and wellbeing. One man stated that outreach is needed in order to get more people to get tested. But outreach was only a short-term solution; what was needed was a more widespread effort to combat stigma against same sex activity in the wider Indian and South Asian communities:

> That's a quick fix, generally what we need is a cultural shift. And what I mean by that is for me, the situation, where these men are open and don't feel closeted and don't feel that they can't go to a GUM clinic [Aftab, 30].

Outreach is the most effective method to reach out to these men because it draws on the benefits of peer-education and social networks (Khan, 1996). However, Khan also states that outreach needs a process of empowerment by which queer men can discuss their realities with peers and their families. Therefore, additional effort must be undertaken to promote dialogue not just within the queer community, but also in other milieux. But one needs to take a sensitive approach to community activism in this context. A marginalized group may possess nearly all of the elements to form a HEC, but if they are unable to engage with the wider community, they will not succeed. Similarly, Seckinelgin (2009) states that the political identity of marginalized communities may provide access to services in a specific context but does not improve the position of such groups in the wider community. Therefore, what is needed to move beyond short-term activities such as outreach is a concerted, thoughtful and sustained engagement with the wider Indian and South Asian communities.

Conclusion

Based on the findings of this study, it is clear that queer men from Indian backgrounds face numerous socio-cultural challenges to their sexual health that may not exist for queer men from other cultural backgrounds. These challenges arise from negative stereotypes of same-sex activity from within Indian communities, familial and societal expectations of young men, as well as religious prescriptions concerning sexuality. In addition, this research problematizes the issue of culture and sexuality further as it considers the experiences of men who live in London. The realities faced by the men in this study are different than those faced by queer men living in India and other parts of South Asia because the former experience juxtaposition between Indian and British cultures. Such a mix of cultures may provide additional opportunities for sexual expression but may also further alienate those who find their White-British peers are unable to relate. The exploration of these cultural factors was not intended to be exhaustive. Rather, the realities faced by these men impact their sexual health since sexual expression may be driven underground, increasing their sexual risk, and these factors may serve as hindrances to accessing sexual health services.

The men in this study discussed their experiences and perceptions of their involvement in one of two social support groups for queer men from Indian backgrounds. The findings suggest that groups such as these may bridge the gap in a lack of sexual health service use amongst this group of queer men. Specifically, the respondents' perceptions of the groups suggest that these groups demonstrate the qualities of HEC (Campbell et al., 2007) and community coalitions (Butterfoss et al., 1993). Specifically, these groups of men from similar backgrounds provide a social space in which accurate information is presented in an accessible way, members develop their skills based on the mutual process of learning, and long-term connections are fostered within and outside of the groups. The efforts that members of the group, its organizing sponsor, and allies put forth to engage with British Indian communities will gradually pave the way to better sexual health and reduced marginalization of these men.

Although the perspectives of the men in this study allow us to gain a broader understanding of the nexus of cultural and sexual identities in the context of sexual health, it is important to note that these men have made use of sexual health services and are actively working to address issues of stigma in their community. Much of the research focusing on sexualities of queer men from Indian backgrounds in the UK, with the exception of a few studies (e.g., Jaspal & Cinnirella, 2010), has considered the perspectives of men who actively participate in lesbian, gay, bisexual, transgender, and queer (LGBTQ) organisations. Therefore, one can only surmise about the lived realities of queer Indian men who never get tested or know there resources are available. In addition, the youth of the men in this study does not provide insight into the experiences of older men who may be married, have children, or have experienced disclosure at an older age. Older men who have not reconciled their cultural and sexual identities will find it more difficult to draw on peer and family support resources than will younger men, as previous research among the general population has found that the benefits of peer and family support may decrease with age (Mustanski, Newcomb, and Garofalo, 2011). Thus, this study does not sufficiently explore the lives of queer men who are less visible. Yet one must never underestimate the efforts of these men whose courage and passion pave the way for others in their community.

As with any group, social inequalities manifest themselves in a number of ways. This study considered the stories of men who are minorities within minorities. Future research should consider how factors such as class, immigration status, regional backgrounds and serostatus add an additional layer of complexity to marginalization. Many respondents in this study highlighted the lack of services catered to queer Indian men outside of London. Therefore, future studies should consider how social groups as well as other community-driven initiatives might flourish in different geographic areas.

References

Abraham, I. (2009). "'Out to Get Us': Queer Muslims and the Clash of Sexual Civilisations in Australia." *Contemporary Islam* 3: 79–97.

Aggleton, P., and C. Campbell (2000). "Working with Young People — Towards an Agenda for Sexual Health." *Sexual and Relationship Therapy, 15:* 283–297.

Arendt, H. (1958). *The Human Condition.* Chicago: The University of Chicago Press.

Badruddin, K. (1997). "Not-so-gay Life in Pakistan in the 1980s and 1990s." In S. Murray and W. Roscoe (Eds.). *Islamic Homosexualities: Culture, History and Literature* (275–296). New York: New York University Press.

Beck, A., A. Majumdar, C. Estcourt, and J. Petrak (2005). "We Don't Really Have Cause to Discuss These Things, They Don't Affect Us": A Collaborative Model for Developing Culturally Appropriate Sexual Health Services with the Bangladeshi Community of Tower Hamlets. *Sexually Transmitted Infections, 81:* 158–162.

Bhugra, D. (1997a). "Coming Out by South Asian Gay Men in the United Kingdom." *Archives of Sexual Behavior* 26 (5): 547–57.

_____ (1997b). "Experiences of Being a Gay Man in Urban India: A Descriptive Study." *Sexual and Marital Therapy* 12 (4): 371–5.

Boyce, P. (2006). "Moral Ambivalence and Irregular Practices: Contextualizing Male-to-Male Sexualities in Calcutta/India." *Feminist Review* 83: 79–98.

_____ (2007). "'Conceiving Kothis': Men Who Have Sex with Men in India and the Cultural Subject of HIV Prevention." *Medical Anthropology* 26: 175–203.

_____, and A. Khanna (2011). "Rights and Representations: Querying the Male-to-Male Sexual Subject in India." *Culture, Health & Sexuality* 13: 89–100.

Butler, J. (1990). *Gender Trouble: Feminism and the Subversion of Identity.* New York: Routledge.

Butterfoss, F. D., R. M. Goodman, and A. Wandersman (1993). Community Coalitions for Prevention and Health Promotion." *Health Education Research, 8(3):* 315–330.

Campbell, C. (2003). *Letting Them Die: Why HIV/AIDS Program Fail.* Oxford: James Currey.

_____, and H. Deacon (2006). "Unravelling the Contexts of Stigma: From Internalisation to Resistance to Change." *Journal of Community and Applied Social Psychology, 16:* 411–417.

Campbell, C., Y. Nair, and S. Maimane (2007). "Building Contexts That Support Effective

Community Responses to HIV/AIDS: A South African Case Study." *American Journal of Community Psychology, 39*:347–363.

Desai, J. (2002). "Homo on the Range: Mobile and Global Sexualities." *Social Text 73*: 65–89.

Elam, G., K. Fenton, A. Johnson, J. Nazroo, and J. Ritchie (1999). *Exploring Ethnicity and Sexual Health: A Qualitative Study of the Sexual Attitudes and Lifestyles of Five Ethnic Minority Communities in Camden and Islington.* University College London, London.

Elford, J., E. McKeown, R. Doerner, S. Nelson, N. Low, and J. Anderson (2010). "Sexual Health of Ethnic Minority MSM in Britain (MESH Project): Design and Methods." *BMC Public Health* 10: 419–30.

French, R. S., L. Joyce, K. Fenton, P. Kingori, C. Griffiths, V. Stone, H. Patel-Kanwal, R. Power, and J. Stephenson (2005). *Exploring the Attitudes and Behaviors of Bangladeshi, Indian and Jamaican Young People in Relation to Reproductive and Sexual Health: A Report for the Teenage Pregnancy Unit.* London: University College, London and British Market Research Bureau.

Friere, P. (1970). *The Pedagogy of the Oppressed.* London: Penguin.

_____ (1973). *Education for Critical Consciousness.* New York: Continuum.

Goffman, E. (1963). *Stigma: Notes on the Management of a Spoiled Identity.* Englewood Cliffs, NJ: Prentice Hall.

Gopinath, G. (1997). "Nostalgia, Desire, Diaspora: South Asian Sexualities in Motion." *Positions* 5: 467–89.

Gosine, A. (2006). "'Race,' Culture, Power, Sex, Desire, Love: Writing in 'Men Who Have Sex with Men.'" *IDS Bulletin, 37(5)*: 1–9.

_____ (2008). "Fobs, Banana Boy, and the Gay Pretenders: Queer Youth Navigate Sex, 'Race' and Nation in Toronto, Canada." In S. Driver (Ed.), *Queer Youth Cultures* (223–241). Albany, NY: State University of New York.

Habermas, J. (1989). "Public Sphere: An Encyclopedia Article." In S. Bronner and D. Mackay Kellner (Eds.). *Critical Theory and Society: A Reader.* London: Rutledge.

Howarth, C. (2006). "Race as Stigma: Positioning the Stigmatized as Agents, Not Objects." *Journal of Community and Applied Social Psychology, 16*: 442–451.

Jaspal, R., and M. Cinnirella (2010). "Coping with Potentially Incompatible Identities: Accounts of Religious, Ethnic, and Sexual Identities from British Pakistani Men Who Identify as Muslim and Gay." *British Journal of Social Psychology* 49: 849–70.

Jovchelovich, S. (2007). *Knowledge in Context: Representations, Community and Culture.* London: Routledge.

Keogh, P., P. Weatherburn, L. Henderson, D. Reid, C. Dodds, and F. Hickson (2004). *Doctoring Gay Men: Exploring the Contribution of General Practice.* Original Research Report. London: Sigma Research.

Khan, S. (1996). "Under the Blanket: Bisexualities and AIDS in India." In P. Aggleton (Ed.), *Bisexualities and AIDS: International Perspectives* (161–177). Bristol, PA: Taylor and Francis.

_____ (2001). "Culture, Sexualities, and Identities: Men Who Have Sex with Men in India." *Journal of Homosexuality, 40 (3)*: 99–105.

Link, B. G., and J. C. Phelan (2001). "Conceptualizing Stigma." *Annual Review of Sociology, 27*: 363–385.

McKenna, N. (1996). *On the Margins: Men Who Have Sex with Men and HIV in the Developing World.* London: Panos Institute.

McKeown, E., S. Nelson, J. Anderson, N. Low, and J. Elford (2010). "Disclosure, Discrimination and Desire: Experiences of Black and South Asian Gay Men in Britain." *Culture, Health and Sexuality* 12: 843–56.

Mehta, P. (1998). "The Emergence, Conflicts, and Integration of the Bicultural Self." Pp. 129–67 in *The Colors of Childhood.* S. Akhtar and S. Kramer (Eds.). Northvale, NJ: Aronson.

Minwalla, O., B. R. Simon Rosser, J. Feldman, and C. Varga (2005). "Identity Experience Among Progressive Gay Muslims in North America: A Qualitative Study Within Al-Fatiha." *Culture, Health & Sexuality* 7: 113–28.

Misra, G. (2009). "Decriminalising Homosexuality in India." *Reproductive Health Matters, 17 (34)*:20–28.

Mizrahi, T., and B. B. Rosenthal (1993). "Managing Dynamic Tensions in Social Change Coalitions." In T. Mizrahi and J. Morrisson (Eds.). *Community Organization and Social Administration: Advances, Trends and Emerging Principles* (11–40). Binghamton, NY: The Haworth Press.

Mustanski, B., N. Michael, and G. Robert (2011). "Mental Health of Lesbian, Gay, and Bisexual Youths: A Developmental Resiliency Perspective." *Journal of Gay & Lesbian Social Services* 23: 204–25.

O'Brien, O., and S. Khan (1996). "Stigma and Racism as They Affect Minority Ethnic Communities." In M. Haour-Knipe and R. Rector. *Crossing Borders: Migration, Ethnicity and AIDS*. London: Taylor and Francis.

Parker, R. G., and P. Aggleton (2003). "AIDS-related Stigma and Discrimination: A Conceptual Framework and Implications for Action." *Social Science & Medicine, 57:* 13–24.

Parker, R., S. Khan, and P. Aggleton (1998). Conspicuous by Their Absence? Men Who Have Sex with Men (MSM) in Developing Countries: Implications for HIV Prevention. *Critical Public Health, 8(4):* 329–346.

Parker, R. G., and J. H. Gagnon (Eds.) (1995). *Conceiving Sexuality: Approaches to Sex Research in a Postmodern World*. New York: Routledge.

Roberts, M. W. (1995). "Emergence of Gay Identity and Gay Social Movements in Developing Countries: The AIDS Crisis as a Catalyst." *Alternatives, 20:* 243–264.

Seckinelgin, H. (2009). "Global Activism and Sexualities in the Time of HIV/AIDS. *Contemporary Politics, 15(1):* 103–118.

Weston, H. J. (2003). "Public Honor, Private Shame and HIV: Issues Affecting Sexual Health Service Delivery in London's South Asian Communities." *Health and Place, 9:* 109–117.

Wexler, L. M., G. DiFluvio, and T. K. Burke (2009). "Resilience and Marginalized Youth: Making a Case for Personal and Collective Meaning-Making as Part of Resilience Research in Public Health." *Social Science and Medicine, 69:* 565–570.

Yep, G., K. Lovaas, and P. Ho (2001). "Communicating Our Relationships: Communication in 'Asian American Families with Queer Members: A Relational Dialectics Perspective.'" In M. Berstein and R. Reimann (Eds.). *Queer Families, Queer Politics: Challenging Culture and the State* (152–72). New York: Columbia University Press.

Masculinities of Desire, Derision and Defiance

Global Gay Femmephobia and *Kothi-Hijra*-Trans Heterosexualities

ANIRUDDHA DUTTA

Introduction

Over a decade ago, Dennis Altman proposed the thesis that a process of "global queering" was afoot, particularly manifested in the transnational expansion of a "western-style gayness" to create an increasingly visible constituency of "global gays" ("Global Gaze" 420). While some of his early articulations of the argument seemed to suggest that such "global queering" was driven by western (particularly U.S. American) example and influence (Altman, "On Global Queering"), this idea was much critiqued, and rightly so. As Fran Martin pointed out, Altman's thesis missed cultural variation and local agency for a homogenized picture that served the narcissistic gaze of the white gay male (Martin). In response, Altman modified his arguments with a greater recognition of non-western agency in forming and transforming queer identities ("Global Gaze" 419; "Rupture or Continuity" 79), and scholars like Boellstorff and Jackson came up with nuanced descriptions of how transnational gender/sexual identities develop through different cultural trajectories, such that terms like "gay" might evidence multifarious cultural meanings rather than a homogenous western-derived one (Boellstorff 8; Jackson 360). But today, more than fifteen years later after initial articulations of the "global gays" argument, perhaps the time has to reconsider the thesis, but in a less liberatory and celebratory sense than what Altman might have had in mind. In keeping with the emerging body of scholarship that has argued that dominant LGBT politics has taken a "homonormative" turn to assimilate into emerging configurations of power that perpetuate racial, class and gender discrimination, this essay will explore the transnational consolidation of normative "global gay" masculinities that often subordinate relatively feminized subject positions, just as discourses of gay rights overshadow other queer constituencies and forms of politics.[1] Particularly comparing U.S. and Indian contexts of LGBT community formation and activism, I will suggest that there are emergent transnational alignments between dominant discourses of gay identification across western/metropolitan and non–western/postcolonial societies, which assimilate "gay" into a reconfigured complex of gender-normative masculinities spanning vastly different cultural locations. These newer articulations of masculinity may accommodate same-sex desire, but nevertheless exclude and hierarchically subjugate feminized subject-positions, signaling pervasive patterns of male dominance within and without LGBT communities.

Within this globalizing — which is not to say globally homogenous — tendency, "gay" seems to be located at a transitional cusp between gender variance and gender normativity. While male homosexuality has been commonly associated with feminization and *difference* from normative masculinities, the "gay" construct becomes increasingly assimilated into masculinity, even as concurrent alterations to straight masculinity such as "metrosexuality" are increasingly noted in contemporary media across the U.S. and India. Such alterations to hegemonic masculinities increasingly accommodate previously excluded gay identities into the larger category of "men," which may still function as a categorical complex that defines itself against femininity and gender variance, thus exerting the normativizing force of sexual/gender hierarchization through which a desirable gay masculinity is valorized above gender variant subject positions. As I will argue, the construction and policing of a categorical divide between "gay men" and male-born "transgender" identities is crucial to this formation.

To provide a situated critique of the aforementioned phenomena, this essay will analyze normative and counter-normative evocations of masculinity within spaces of gender/sexual variance in the state of West Bengal in eastern India, where I have conducted ethnographic fieldwork since 2007 as a participant observer, both within the organized LGBT movement and in unorganized community networks. Particularly focusing on communities of gay, transgender, and *kothi* or gender variant persons (which might include individuals who go by multiple, one or none of these labels), I will examine their relation to the aforementioned transnational trends. Examining the question of what kinds of masculinities are valorized as objects of desire or ideals for subject-formation, I will interrogate the transnational construction of a liberated metropolitan or urbane gay identity framed around the defiance of stereotypes of effeminacy and assimilation into desirable "good" masculinities, as opposed to lower class and/or non-metropolitan *kothi* and trans communities that are derided for desiring "bad" patriarchal masculinities and for remaining trapped in a victimized femininity. Such analysis also demonstrates how negotiations with masculinity and gender variance often simultaneously involve negotiations with caste/class difference, and more broadly, how constructions of gender/sexuality foundationally intersect with class/caste.

On one hand, I will interrogate the defiance of stereotypes within urbane gay community networks as implicitly "good" or "progressive," and examine how such redefinitions of gayness may reiterate undeconstructed masculine privilege. On the other hand, I will examine the evocation of "patriarchal" gender roles within non-metropolitan lower class subcultures as both potentially conservative and counter-normative. I contend that recognizing how evocations of masculinity might occur in such politically unexpected and unstable ways can help us imagine social change beyond tired binaries such as patriarchy and sexual progress, or rural conservatism and urban liberation, and provide a cartography of gendered power and queer space that is attentive to both normative and counter-normative trends without presuming any pre-defined narrative of progress such as gay liberation, which might perpetuate male and class/caste dominance.

Before moving on to the specifics of this argument, it may be helpful to include a note on categories of identification used in this essay. In keeping with emerging activist usages, I use trans as a broad term for gender variance including and beyond specific identities like transgender, transwoman and transman (Killermann) — in this context, including "vernacular" Indian terms (or more precisely, terms that are vernacularized relative to the dominant status of English-language terms), such as *kothi*, *dhurani*, and *hijra*. *Kothi* and *dhurani* are closely interlinked terms, of which the first is much better known and used in Indian LGBT activist circles (Cohen 270). It signifies feminine-identified gender variant persons assigned male at birth, who may or may not identify as (trans) women, and are usually thought of as desiring relatively masculine men whom they call *parikh* or *panthi* (NACO 13). *Kothis* have been mapped as feminine MSM (men who have sex with men) by the National AIDS Control Organization (NACO 13), and as male-to-female transgender (TG) by a consultation report funded by the United Nations Development Programme (SAATHI 19). Such discrepancies reveal the complexity and diversity of *kothi* identifications that cannot be easily contained within official definitions. *Dhurani* is a term used within lower and lower middle class gender variant community networks in West Bengal, signifying a feminine male who has sex with men, and/or a male sex worker — as I discovered in the course of my ethnographic fieldwork, *dhurani* may be used synonymously with *kothi* within intra-community contexts, even though the term is not correspondingly recorded within official activist discourse. Hijras are a well known community of people assigned male at bith who dress as women but often identify as a separate gender, and who combine their gender variance with specific religious practices and often claim an auspicious status to pursue occupations such as *badhai*, proffering blessings in return for money, though many *hijras* also perform sex work (Reddy 45). As I argue elsewhere, *kothis* may also sometimes identify as *hijra* or transition to being *hijra*, and thus none of these terms (*kothi, dhurani* and *hijra*) should be thought of as rigidly separated or uniformly demarcated identities (Dutta). "Gay" is of course the best known term for male homosexuality — as I argue below, its overlap or distinction from trans identities and/or behaviors is a controversial question and dominant versions of gay identification have increasingly stressed a gay-transgender distinction despite the close historical and cultural association between gender and sexual variance (Valentine 216). In the particular ethnographic context of this essay in eastern India and West Bengal, publicly gay-identified males may privately use terms like *kothi* and *dhurani* (more on this in the third section), but such overlaps are often denied or elided in more public and dominant narratives of gay identity and desire. The term "femmephobia" is sometimes used loosely and colloquially in the U.S. context to signal gay distanciation from feminine (or "femme") males, whether gay or trans ("Douchebags of Grindr"). I borrow this usage, rather than the more academically common "transphobia," to signal patterns of distanciation from and/or discrimination against a wider range of feminized subject positions than just explicitly trans identities, which might be paralleled within increasingly dominant versions of gay identity in the U.S. and India.

Global Gay Femmephobia

Historically, late nineteenth and early twentieth century discourses on both male and female same-sex desire and behavior, which constructed the category of "homosexuality" as a distinct arena of human personhood and identity, closely linked homosexuality with gender variance or "inversion" (effeminacy for males and masculinity for females) (Minton 2; Valentine 216). However, this connection has been increasingly ruptured in the second half of the twentieth century, with the emergence of distinctions between "gay" and "transgender" or "third gender" subcultures and communities, particularly in the west but also in some non-western locations such as Indonesia (Valentine 216; Altman, "Rupture and Continuity" 82). With the emergence of transnationally connected gay rights discourses and attendant forms of identification and community formation in the 1990s and 2000s (Altman, "Global Gaze" 420), these tensions might be intensified, such that male gay identities become located at the juncture of gender variance and gender-normative masculinity across different socio-cultural locations. In this context, I contend that transnational (and aspirationally global) assemblages of gay identification can be negatively evidenced through patterns of distanciation from gender variance that repeat themselves across vastly different socio-cultural contexts. As I describe below, such trends, loosely and colloquially termed "femmephobia" in the U.S. LGBT context, have been noted by some Indian trans activists as well, signaling a transnational tendency or pattern. In as much as such "femmephobia" is evident across vastly different socio-cultural locations, it may be interpreted as a structural feature or symptom of transnationally expansive patterns of gay assimilation into hegemonic forms of masculinity.

Probably the most visible and overt site of global(izing) patterns of femmephobia are male-male dating and sexual networking websites, ranging from Grindr, an Iphone application for sexual networking used primarily in the U.S., and Planetromeo, a dating site with a large following in India. Several recent commentators in the U.S. have noted simultaneous patterns of racism and femmephobia on online dating or sexual networking services (Rowlson; Bielski). The site "Douchebags of Grindr" (www.douchebagsofgrindr.com) keeps a tab on the discriminatory tendencies evidenced through GrinDr. profiles. A range of sample user profiles documented on the site include injunctions like the following: "Only into 101% masculine: Fems dnt fkin mssg me [sic]. 22College athlete (not some pansy sport)"; "Looking for studs: no fats, fems [sic] or anyone above 30"; "If your only personality is gay, move on"; "Be masculine please! I'm gay don't want a girl!"; "Into other white guys only. No Asians, fatties or femmes"; "No Asian, No Indian, No Latino, No Black, No Fat, under 30 years old," and so on. In a recent (2011) article critiquing these systemic tendencies, Alex Rowlson states: "The negative language so prevalent on Craigslist and GrinDr. seems to signal that the culture of sexual liberation has been replaced by sexual segregation." Rowlson quotes Mattilda Bernstein Sycamore, a prominent queer activist and a leading critic of homonormative trends within GLBT communities: "Gay men have forgotten how to have sex (...) Sex should be about opening possibilities, not closing them off (...) these are not neutral terms (but) reinforce dominant systems of power in an unquestioning way" (qtd. in Rowlson). While the racial filtering of "Asians,' "Latinos" or "Blacks" might not directly translate into the Indian context, patterns of femmephobia are repeated on almost identical terms in dating websites like Planetromeo. Witness these sample quotes from three different profiles[2]: "A request to all the pansy ... sissy ... uncles ... quinz [queens] ... as well as "koti" [kothi] guys, pls stay away from me"; "I do not entertain those who are femme men, money seekers, massage boys"; "unfit, uneducated and feminine guys please don't bother." These are of course a small sample size, but may be just the tip of the iceberg. Echoing Rowlson and Sycamore's laments across the oceans, a trans activist posted the following spontaneous critique in 2012 on a closed or private group largely comprising gay men on Facebook, the Kolkata Party Forum[3]:

> The amount of "transphobic" posts and profile texts that are there on Planet Romeo is simply sickening! Some samples (and these aren't even exhaustive!): "Girlish guys plsss stay awaayy," "I am not going to entertain with ant girlish boy.. if u really proud 2 b a man ... then only call me...," "girlies, pansy sort of guys fuck off..." etc.

As the comment indicates, such patterns are transnationally pervasive: while the exact statistical prevalence of these profiles might vary between locations and specific websites, their recurrent appearances across vast distances, and the fact that activists across U.S. and India have felt compelled to register their recurrence, is perhaps more significant than their exact rate of prevalence.

Moreover, these sites evidence a symptomatic tension between contrasting patterns of phobia or hierarchization, which signals a transitional juncture in the gendering of the "gay" category. In one tendency, any overt or public gayness is derided for lacking masculinity and/or for being associated with effeminacy. Witness statements like the following from profiles featured on Douchebags of Grindr: "I want strictly straight acting only"; "If you talk and confetti/feathers/a purse come out ... way too gay for me!"; "Masculine is not subjective. If people can tell you're gay ... you're not masculine," "Masc only: not into gay guys!" etc. In the second tendency, there is a resignification of gay category itself, reclaiming gay as masculine, evident in another set of profiles documented on Douchebags of Grindr: "I am gay don't want a girl!" or "Looks are deceiving. I'm out and proud but I'm no queen with hand bags pouring out of my mouth!" Thus, the defiant reclamation of an "out and proud" gay identity as masculine disavows and redirects the derision directed at effeminacy, which remains the locus of undesirability and distanciation, whether equated with "gay" or not (more on this in the next section).

Similarly contrasting tendencies may be noted In India, too. While "gay" still carries strong connotations of gender variance, re-masculinizing tendencies are also operative within gay-identified individuals and communities. For instance, the television program "Zindagi Live" on IBN7 featured a session on "*samlaingikta*" (homosexuality) on 22nd January 2012, which prominently included stories of gender variance (e.g., growing up as "feminine" children) narrated by gay-identified males. Yet on the other hand, a contemporaneous report in February 2012, published in the Kolkata-based newspaper *The Telegraph* and titled "Gay, Happy and Sad," quoted several gay men to highlight how they aspired to a normative masculinity with attributes like strength, athleticism, and so on: "Gay men are fitness conscious," says Sunil. "It's competitive and you can't let yourself go like any middle-aged heterosexual man," he laughs. Jerry explains: "Unlike women who are less focused on their men's looks, gay men set very high standards for each other — opting for a muscular appearance and style" (Martins 1). Here, "gay" is posited as more, not less, aesthetically masculine than heterosexual men "who let themselves go"; gay desire for masculinity both as object-choice and self-identification narcissistically demands higher standards from both the self and the other. It is not surprising, then, that such competitive masculinist hierarchies turn up in dating sites across U.S. and India. These similarities do not suggest that a masculinized "gay" identity is now homogenously "global," but rather that such masculinization is a powerfully hegemonic transnational pattern that links the postcolony with the metropole.

As the above examples suggest, these hierarchies are not limited to just sexual/dating contexts, and are reflected in broader communities and mainstream media representations. As I will argue, they often inflect spaces of LGBT activism as well. In the U.S., Sycamore argues that "a gay elite has hijacked queer struggle" (2), prioritizing gay marriage, adoption and military service, rather than structural problems affecting working class queers of color like violence and homelessness. In India, there are recurrent forms of phobia against lower class/caste gender variance within activist spaces, which I discuss in the third, fourth and fifth sections.

This masculinization of "gay" can also be related within larger resignifications and alterations of both hetero and homo masculinities, of which the most salient transnational trend seems to be "metrosexuality." As noted by media reports both in the west and India, metrosexuality seems to indicate the relaxation of certain masculinist injunctions — straight and gay men alike can now partake in fashion, grooming, and skin care, consciously fashioning themselves as objects of the desiring gaze rather than just the subject, and participating in forms of consumption that had previously been feminized (Ghosh 12; Drum). While at first sight this may indicate a less heterosexist and more queer-friendly reconfiguration of "masculinity" in general, the metrosexual trend seems to have prompted two reactions, both indicating continuing patterns of heterosexist masculinism. On one hand, "regular guys" or "retro-sexuals" may deride the feminized metrosexual (Barker; Chrisafis; Ghosh 12), while on the other, metrosexuals claim masculinity and machismo for themselves, rather than articulating a publicly feminized maleness (Dodds): as an article headline in *The Economist* states, "Real Men Get Waxed." Of course, there might be resignifications of "metrosexual" that ally it with gender variance and trans identities (as evident in the website www.itspronounced metrosexual.com), but these do not seem to the majoritarian tendencies, to go by media coverage. Rather, the more mainstream tendencies of metrosexual identification parallel femmephobic patterns within gay identification — as noted previously, "straight-acting" guys deride and reject "gay" ones, which parallels the derision of feminized "metrosexuals" by "regular guys" (Barker). On the other hand, "gay" is itself resignified as masculine — as a GrinDr. profile puts it, "I am gay, don't want a girl!" — which parallels the resignification of "metrosexuality" (fashion, consumerism) as masculine. Whether relatively feminized terms like "metrosexual" and "gay" are derided by "regular" or "straight-acting" guys, or resignified and reclaimed as masculine, both cases perpetuate underlying patterns of hierarchization that reinscribe the dominant position of masculinity relative to feminized subject positions. This suggests that even as hegemonic masculinities get altered to allow for same-sex desire, changing lifestyles and ephemeral consumption trends, they assimilate into more continuous and durable patterns of masculine privilege and dominance.

Defying Stereotypes, Desiring Masculinity

Ironically, the gay assimilation into masculinity is often made on the plea of resisting stereotypes of gayness, particularly the cross-cultural perceptions linking male homosexuality with effeminacy. The formation of a masculine gay identity is asserted both through a disdain for stereotyped gender roles (gay as sissy/pansy or feminine/effeminate), and as a rebellion against heteronormativity.

This trend can be illustrated across vastly separated socio-cultural contexts. The Internet, as an iconic medium of transnational communication, is an apt place to start. Davey Wavey is a popular U.S.–based gay-identified video blogger and internet commentator whose videos on Youtube, several of which focus on gay identification and lifestyle, have found an international audience, as evidenced not only through Youtube viewership statistics but also through re-postings of some of his videos on Indian virtual forums, such as the group LGBT-India on Facebook. One of Wavey's videos, titled "Things NOT to Ask a Gay Guy," has more than a million hits on Youtube, with most of the hits concentrated in the U.S. but also scattered across several Asian countries, including India. The video seeks to debunk common misperceptions about gay men by pointing out common questions that one should not ask of gay men (the geographic locus of "gay men" as a category is not defined or delimited in the video and Wavey seems to take on the representational mantle of all gay men everywhere, thus also setting up a an aspirationally globalizing version of male gayness for his audience). The very first question tackles the issue of gendering:

> I get a lot of questions from mostly straight people and sometimes gay people, and so I decided to make a video about things that you should never, ever, *ever* ask a

gay person. So let's get started: here's question number one. "So like, you are in a relationship bro, but like, who's the woman in your relationship?" Hi! I like dick, and so does my boyfriend. As it turns out, we are both the men in our relationship. That's the whole point of being gay. There is no need of trying to fit my relationship into your heteronormative box. That's right, I said it: Keep your heteronormative box away from me and my body, okay? [Wavey].

This supposed debunking of the "heteronormative box" goes only so far as to affirm, contra effeminacy and gender variance, the mirroring of a mutually reinforced manliness between the gay couple: "I like dick, and so does my boyfriend ... we are both the men in our relationship." As Davey Wavey delivers his speech in this video (as in many others) shirtless from the waist up so as to prominently showcase his chiseled muscles, the kind of masculinity espoused here is quite clear. This putative subversion of heteronormativity through the reaffirmation of hetero —*and* homo-normative masculinity also performs a "cultural erasure" of the historical role of drag (cross-dressing) and camp (gendered flamboyance) in queer rebellion and anti-heteronormative politics both in western and non-western contexts (Sycamore 4).

Such tendencies are also evident among gay-identified men in Kolkata and West Bengal, the ethnographic loci of this article, as gleaned through both informal conversations and formal interviews.[4] Nakul, for example, is an activist in his twenties who has worked with a community-based organization in the northern suburbs of Kolkata for several years, and has been actively involved in organizing events that are part of the Rainbow Pride Week. One evening after a fundraising party for the Pride Week in 2011, the organizers, including Nakul and myself, stayed up late chatting, and the conversation turned to feminine-masculine (or *kothi-parikh*) roles among gay and *kothi* males. Nakul opined that "sexuality is fluid," and added, "Actually, the *kothi-parikh* concept is itself gradually going obsolete," a proposition that was met with general approval by the larger crowd. While the discomfort with rigid gender roles is understandable, the easy dismissal of the gendered *kothi*–Parikh framework as "obsolete" (backward, tradition-bound) might perpetuate a simplification of *kothi* negotiations with mainstream masculinity, and of the ways in which *kothi-dhurani-hijra* and other male-born trans persons might both affirm and subvert conventionally "feminine" roles (more on this in the third section). Moreover, the apparent dismissal of stereotyped gender roles often translates into a valorization of the normative gender symmetry of the mutually masculine gay couple (as exemplified in the aforementioned video), and the concurrent public invisibilization and/or disavowal of gender variance by gay-identified males. While working as a participant observer in the Rainbow Pride Week preparations, I noted how in private, Nakul would sometimes identify simultaneously as *kothi* and gay, and would use typical *kothi/hijra* tropes of sisterhood and mother-daughter kinship — boasting on occasion that s/he had mothered many daughters both inside and outside the organization where s/he worked. However, in terms of public activism he was a gay man, entirely masculine-attired, without much reference to the trope of feminine sorority within which he privately placed himself. Nakul was also an eager reader/consumer of the gay lifestyle magazine Pink Pages, which proclaims itself to be "India's national gay and lesbian magazine" even though lesbian representation is marginal, and which mirrors transnationally dominant trends within gay media by featuring prominent displays of buff gay couples in several issues. One of its recent issues features an article critiquing stereotypes of gay people, taking on the common association of gay males with fashion designing, which in turn is a relatively feminized profession (Iyer). The author argues that "apples are not all red," and the article is accompanied by the image of a muscular man holding a green apple — all too predictably, the defiance of stereotyped gayness leads us back into a conventionally valorized masculinity of desire, into which the reader is seductively invited. Perhaps, across these various transnationally separated yet connected instances, the defiance of stereotypes is less about political subversion, and more a sign of a gay male *ressentiment* against the societal withholding of a desired and desirable masculinity, with its attendant privileges, from gay men.

Gay Masculinities: Managing Contradictions

Of course, none of this is strictly speaking new phenomena, and debates and critiques around the gay valorization and appropriation of masculinity have a long academic and activist lineage. While, as noted above, early discourses on homosexuality closely linked sexual deviance with gender inversion for both males and females, the emergence of "macho gay man" and "lipstick lesbian" subcultures in the 1970s marked the public assertion of a sexual orientation separated from gender variance, particularly in the USA (Altman 1996). Dennis Altman and Jeffrey Weeks are among the prominent gay activists and academics who have celebrated the "macho gay man" trend as a challenge to heterosexist machismo: a reappropriation of conventional tropes of masculinity which, according to Weeks, "gnaw(s) at the roots of male heterosexual identity" (191). In his classic 1980s essay "Is the Rectum a Grave?," Leo Bersani prefigures contemporary critiques of gay male homonormatiivity (Sycamore 4), countering the idealization of a liberated, stereotype-defying and apparently radical western gay identity with a critique of its attendant racial and class privileges, and an appreciation of its assimilationist rather than unilaterally subversive potential. Whereas Weeks and Altman saw gay masculinity as both subversive of masculinism and as democratizing and equalizing intra-male relations, Bersani is far more cautious and sees it as often supportive of and desiring conventional heterosexist masculinity, as well as being complicit with hierarchies of race and class:

> On the whole, gay men are no less socially ambitious, and, more often than we like to think, no less reactionary and racist than heterosexuals (...) I do not, for example, find it helpful to suggest, as Dennis Altman has suggested, that gay baths created "a sort of Whitmanesque democracy (...) far removed from the male bondage of rank, hierarchy, and competition that characterize much of the outside world." Anyone who has ever spent one night in a gay bathhouse knows that it is (or was) one of the most ruthlessly ranked, hierarchized, and competitive environments imaginable. Your looks, muscles, hair distribution, size of cock, and shape of ass determined exactly how happy you were going to be during those few hours, and rejection, generally accompanied by two or three words at most, could be swift and brutal, with none of the civilizing hypocrisies with which we get rid of undesirables in the outside world [205–206].

In the larger context of this ranked hierarchy based on hegemonic masculinity, gay desire for masculinity (both as sexual object and as self-identification) need not be parodistic of heterosexual masculinity at all. As Bersani puts it, "the macho-style for gay men ... indicate(s) a profound respect for machismo itself.... If licking someone's leather boots turns you (and him) on, neither of you is making a statement subversive of macho masculinity" (208).

Rather than seeing gay masculinity as transformative in itself, Bersani rather locates the potential for subversion in the contradiction between the desire to identify with hegemonic masculinity and the appeal of having it violated, particularly through the pleasure (and, at the AIDS-inflected historical moment of Bersani's writing, the death risk) of receptive anal sex. "The sexist power that defines maleness in most human cultures can easily survive social revolutions (...) If, as Weeks puts it, gay men "gnaw at the roots of a male heterosexual identity," it is not because of the parodistic distance that they take from that identity, but rather because, from within their nearly mad identification with it, they never cease to feel the appeal of its being violated" (Bersani 209). Historically, perhaps the most salient and recurring site of this "violation" is the receptive position in anal sex, which, as Bersani notes, was associated with loss of masculine privilege and power in societies as widely varied as ancient Greece and the medieval "Muslim world" (212).

However, though it might not have been apparent in the moment of Bersani's writing, even the subversive potential of this contradiction might be increasingly managed and contained through the resignification and/or privatization of any desired "violation" of hegemonic masculinity. Firstly, receptive anal sex or "bottoming" itself, as a historically salient site of such violation

(Bersani 212), has been increasingly resignified in the gay porn industry as an act definitive of masculinity rather than violating it, especially when the "bottom" is a normatively gendered white man with desirable "masculine" attributes such as musculature and penis size: "taking it like a man" is a common simile that masculinizes the receptive act in this context.[5] Moreover, the phrase is sometimes extended from its sexual connotation to masculinize other aspects of gay identification or lifestyle. For example, an article on gay fitness on the online magazine *Realjock*, titled "Bootcamp: Take it like a man," proclaims: "It's not just for porn anymore. Bootcamp workouts, designed and nicknamed after those very same training drills, are all the rage in fitness circles these days. The good news is, you don't have to enlist in the Army or Marine Corps to get in on the action. You just have to know how to take orders like a man. Something tells me most of you have had years of experience" (Toussaint). Here, rather than a site of violation, bottoming functions as an essential training into masculinity ("know how to take orders like a man"), which prepares gay men for militaristic "bootcamp workouts." However, such masculinization might be withheld when the bottom is relatively disempowered in terms of race or class (Fung 233). In porn that focuses on such scenarios of disempowerment, bottoms may be described through terms such as "bitch" or "slut," which — rather than celebrating or reclaiming these terms — more often signifies a devalorization through feminization that reinscribes the hierarchical superiority of the relatively more masculine partner.[6]

Secondly, acts of gender/sexual variance by publicly masculine gay men might occupy a privatized arena that avoids any public subversion. Emerging schisms between private behavior and public gay politics is already noted by Bersani in the 1970s–80s U.S. context — "Many gay men could, in the late '60s and early '70s, begin to feel comfortable about having "unusual" or radical ideas about what's OK in sex without modifying one bit their proud middle-class consciousness or even their racism (...) being gay slumlords during the day and, in San Francisco for example, evicting from the Western Addition black families unable to pay the rents necessary to gentrify that neighborhood" (205–06). More recent essays by Sycamore (4), Handhardt (64) and Joshi (448) note the continuation and increasing consolidation of such trends in the western context.

In my particular ethnographic context of eastern India, I noted how many gay-identified men — including both people who were politically active in organizing events of public activism such as public activism such as the Kolkata pride walk, and those who stayed away from such civic activism — would partake in gender/sexual variance in private intra-community situations, often drawing upon the lower class/caste subcultures of *kothis* and *hijras*, using common idioms, figures of speech and gestures prevalent within these (sub)cultural formations. However, many of them — though by no means all — would also simultaneously distance themselves from such performances of gender/sexual and caste/class difference in more public contexts, and more-over, participate in systemic forms of discrimination and/or exclusion of such difference from LGBT spaces. My initial and tentative observations of these tendencies found support in an interview with Abhirup, a young gay-identified activist who helped with organizing pride week events in 2011. During our conversation, Abhirup, who does not shy away from gendered flamboyance and has often presented hirself as a "diva" and a "queen" in semi-public spaces such as LGBT parties and Facebook, described how "many gays" would have macho pictures and self-descriptions on their profiles on dating websites such as Planetromeo, usually including injunctions like "no feminine guys please." Yet this positioning may be contradicted in more private contexts — as Abhirup put it, "the same people themselves resort to *dhuranipona* when they are just hanging out with friends." Here, "*dhuranipona*" — acting in a *dhurani* mode — signifies not only the camp associated with *kothi/dhurani* (sub)cultural for-mations, but also the lower class/caste inflection of such camp. Gender fluidity, in this context, need not entail a dissociation from the empowered and desir-able position of conventional masculinities, but may be strategically managed in order to preserve gender and caste/class privilege. In addition to injunctions against "feminine guys," Abhirup also spoke of "high class" and "low class" demarcations within dating websites and the party circuit, signaling the rou-tine policing of such spaces from lower class encroachment.

While these tendencies may be more overtly marked in sexual or party spaces, which are by their very nature meant to serve individualized desires and privatized consumption rather than any politically transformative agenda, they are by no means absent in spaces of civic activism. Many politically involved gay men did not seem to share Abhirup's keen consciousness of the ironies and hypocrisies of gay distanciation from *dhuranipona*. Pre-pride meet-ings from at least 2007 onward have evidenced numerous instances where organizers have condemned and sought to discipline the public gendered flam-boyance of relatively lower middle or lower class participants in pride walks, even as a lesser number have spoken up for individual self-expression. For instance, in a meeting preceding the 2007 Kolkata pride walk, one activist spoke out against public acts of gendered assertion and display in earlier walks: "the action of some of the participants such as dressing up during [last year's] walk was indecent and lowered the dignity of the walk. It was also detrimental to the objective of the movement ... establish(ing) the rights of community people."[7] Such complaints prompted an unwritten consensus among organ-izations and activists on the greater surveillance of such "indecent" behavior in subsequent pride walks: in particular, the *thikri*, a loud clap commonly used by *hijras* and some *kothis* that is immediately recognizable as a public gesture of (trans)gendered difference and assertion, came under scrutiny and censure during subsequent walks.[8] Yet, this very same gesture — the clap or *thikri*—turns up in more privatized forms within middle class gay circles, particularly within humorous or parodic exchanges among community members who might be otherwise gay-identified. During the 2011 pride preparations, I would often come across several organizers "giving *thikri*" (*thikri deowa*) to one another by way of humorous sparring — in a typical exchange, someone would playfully insult someone else, and the second person would "give *thikri*" back to the first. At the same time, when some participants in the pride walk spontaneously "gave *thikri*" during the walk itself, particularly in reaction to hostile stares or comments from the onlookers, voices among the crowd cautioned, "no *thikri* here!" Thus, in both activist and non-activist contexts, there may be not only a "dissonance" (Joshi 448) between private deployments of gender/sexual variance and public strategies of gaining acceptance, but more egregiously, a culturally exploitative process of the simultaneous appropriation and disavowal of forms of difference and/or resistance associated with gender/sexual and class/caste marginality.

LGBT Rights and Gay Privilege

In addition to the contradiction between privatized forms of gender variance and dominant versions of gayness, there are contradictions between activist commitments to transgender inclusion and continuing phobic reactions to certain forms of gender/sexual and class/caste difference or dissidence within and without activist communities, which are sought to be managed through the discourse of LGBT rights and inclusive symbols of diversity such as the rainbow flag. But the LGBT discourse may be tokenistic in its inclusions and disguise the privilege of relatively elite groups through the apparent symmetry and equality of "L," "G," "B" and "T" sections, to extrapolate an argument that Sycamore has articulated powerfully in the U.S. context: "LGBT" usually means gay, with lesbian in parentheses, throw out the bisexuals, and put trans on for a little window dressing. Don't even think about queers who don't fit neatly into one of the prevailing categories!" (2). In the context of Indian LGBT community formation and activism, such tokenistic inclusions and substantive exclusions are evident for forms of gender/sexual and class/caste difference that do not "fit neatly" into middle class narratives of LGBT (i.e., predominantly gay) identity and rights. To provide a recent example: on the evening of the 2011 Kolkata pride walk, a group of *kothi* and transgender-identified participants who had traveled to Kolkata from Murshidabad were harassed by some policemen when they went to tour one of the prominent cruising areas of the city. As is typical in such cases, the policemen accused them of public soliciting for sex work and demanded bribes. Several of the senior organizers of the pride walk intervened and actively coordinated the process to extricate them from the abusive and potentially violent situation, which certainly marks a laudable activist commitment against femme — and transphobic violence, in keeping with the desired broad-based inclusions of the LGBT rights discourse. Yet, when I narrated this incident to one of the organizers who had been absent during the event, he expressed a cursory condemnation and added, "But tell me, don't you think that their dress and manner was too *ugra* (garish/extreme/provocative)?," echoing the common imputation of indecency and/or provocation to public assertions of female and feminized sexualities. A senior functionary of the community-based organization to which the victims belonged also opined that the organization should not go out of its way to protect those members who failed to behave responsibly in public.

This unease with *kothi* and trans public visibility and behavior falls within a broader discourse around the "aggressive" or uncivil behavior of lower class trans communities like *kothis* and *hijras* in public during their customary occupations like *badhai* or *chhalla* (proffering ritualized blessings in return for money), which allegedly provoke further violence and discrimination from the mainstream. In a recent comment "thread" on the Facebook group LGBT-India, the initiator of the thread wrote: "I have full respect for LGBTs but wheneva [*sic*] I saw transgenders, I didn't like the way they demand money and stuffs." He cited a case where a "transgender" had allegedly "spat on the face" of someone who refused her money, while other commentators protested the generalization of transgender/*hijra* behavior based on a single incident and defended the occupational choices of *hijras*, pointing out the lack of other economic opportunities. These discussions continue a discursive trend evident in several media reports, which while nominally standing for the constitutional rights of *hijra* communities, simultaneously condemn *hijra* occupational activities such as ritualized demands for money in return for blessings for violating the same liberal model of individual and property rights. This suggests that a model of LGBT rights derived largely from a gay rights discourse, which advocates for individual rights and desires assimilation into mainstream society and economy as similar citizens (Agathangelou, Bassichis and Spira 121), may not really address and accommodate the intersections of gender/sexual and caste/class dissidence across the "LGBT" spectrum, and may justify the continued structural marginalization of lower class trans individuals and communities.

Furthermore, it may be argued that the LGBT rights discourse and the attendant rhetoric of diversity — while countering blatant expressions of transphobia to an extent — serves to preserve the desirability and privilege associated with gay masculinities, and promotes the devalorization of (trans)gender variance. Defenses of gay superiority, privilege and desirability many be based on arguments of individual rights and choices — in which the power hierarchy involved in the relative exclusion and sexual devalorization of feminine, *kothi/ hijra* and trans persons is denied or disavowed with the argument that such exclusions are a matter of personal preferences. For example, in a thread on transphobia in dating websites on the Kolkata Party Forum group on Facebook, many commentators denied that such phobia exists at a structural or systemic level. To cite one comment, "If they don't want to have sex with someone feminine they have a right to mention that on thier [*sic*] profile. "Girlish guys fuck off" is kind of harsh, but even my profile on pr [Planetromeo] says very clearly — unfit, uneducated and feminine guys please don't bother. (...) You have met me and you know that I am neither transphobic nor judgmental about transsexuals or feminine guys or whatever but when I'm looking for sex I have the right to make my own decision about what I want and mention that on my profile." Here, as per the discourse of LGBT diversity and rights, one respects "transsexuals or feminine guys or whatever," just like the aforementioned commentator who condemned *hijra* occupational practices but declared "I have full respect for LGBTs." But the sexual hierarchies in gay dating scenes are dismissed as matters of personal preference that can be justified by the same liberal discourse of individual rights through which gay and LGBT inclusion is claimed, thus denying the systemic relations of power that are reflected within and perpetuated through such individual sexual preferences. Sycamore's critique of U.S. gay scenes seems very extensible to the Indian case: "On the one hand, people are stating their preference, but on the other, these are not neutral terms (...) when sexual preference reinforces dominant systems of power in an unquestioning way, that's when it becomes problematic" (Rowlson). As Green argues, there are "connections between our most inner sexual desires and the sociopolitical landscape" (ibid.), and as we see above, the liberal LGBT rights discourse may fail to interrogate these complicities. To borrow a term from Agathangenlou, Bassichis and Spira (120), this justifies and perpetuates the "intimate investments" of relatively privileged queers in structures of power.

Kothi-Hijra-*Trans Heterosexualities: The Myth of* Kothi *Victimization*

Meanwhile, even as the desires associated with dominant articulations of gay masculinity are celebrated for defying stereotypes of effeminacy and accusations of femme — and transphobia are dismissed for targeting personal preferences, desires associated with lower class trans individuals and communities might be privately and publicly disparaged and seen as regressive by middle class LGBT (predominantly gay) activists. As a particularly visible identity among lower class gender/sexually variant communities, *kothis* seem to be a common and easy target of such critique. My early introduction into community-based organizations in small towns of West Bengal was mediated by Anurag, a middle class activist working with an HIV-AIDS prevention NGO in Kolkata, who accompanied me to the district of Murshidabad to record a survey on local "sexual minorities" in 2007. He described the organization, Sangram, as a collective primarily comprising *kothis*, and presuming that I did not know much about *kothi* communities, gave me a lurid description of the alleged sexual preferences of *kothis* as a collective group. *Kothis* are "*dukkhobilashi*," he explained — they take pleasure (*bilash*) in suffering (*dukkho*). He graphically described how many *kothis* would not only put up with physical and sexual abuse from their macho boyfriends, but come to desire it themselves — for instance, someone had her nipples almost torn off by her boyfriend, and would still assert that she liked getting sexually abused and beaten, instead of protesting the situation. This was seen as symptomatic of the internalized victimization of *kothis*. While Anurag's critical yet voyeuristic description of *kothi* desire and victimization might be seen as a more extreme form of stereotyping undertaken in private, such pejorative tropes occur in more "official" documents that perpetuate large and simplified generalizations about *kothis*, such as this DFID-funded report published in 2007:

> In the kothi context, a biological male who is penetrated becomes "not man enough"; therefore "less than a man"; therefore "like a woman" ... the penetrated man does not perceive himself as a man, and internalises a stereotypical, often highly caricatured image of the woman, and looks upon victimisation and/or violence as an integral part of existence. (...) therefore ... the gay identity, which is closely linked to egalitarian relationships between "men" does not find a very strong footing in India [Bondopadhay and Shah 36].

Not only is the alleged *kothi* desire for victimization vis-à-vis patriarchal masculinity derided in comparison to putatively "egalitarian" gay identities, the gender roles that constrain their desire are also derivative of heterosexuality:

> Same-sex relationships therefore often play out in a heterosexual model. It is characterised by the role play of participants where one plays out the role of the more powerful man and the other the role of the less powerful woman. The sex acts also follow the stereotypical notions of what the specific roles of the man and woman are supposed to be. The penetrator-penetrated dynamic is maintained at all levels of the relationship and this in turn defines the power dynamic of the relationship. It is emphatically not a relationship of equals, and is therefore open to violence on the disempowered [Bondopadhyay and Shah 56–57].

However, there are internal contradictions within official discourses that belie such attempts to construct a homogenized and uniform definition of kothi feminization and victimization due to their alleged fidelity to conventional heterosexuality. For instance, while the national AIDS Control Organization's (NACO) policy document on "high risk groups" for HIV transmission constructs kothis as a particularly vulnerable group due to their receptive position in anal sex, it also notes that there are "varying degrees of femininity" among kothis, and further, that some kothis might even like to take penetrative roles in sex, and are known through intra-community labels such as dupli kothi, signifying "versatile" kothis (NACO 13). These contradictions, which turn up even within hierarchically mediated official representations, expose the impossibility of essentializing kothi desire through statements like "the penetrator-penetrated dynamic is maintained at all levels." However, the supposed inegalitarianism of kothi desire for a patriarchal, and potentially violent, masculinity — the parikh or panthi — is a thesis derisively repeated by several gay activists whom I have met or worked with in West Bengal. During the preparations for the 2009 pride walk, I interacted with Aniket, a gay-identified activist, who during a long conversation described how he preferred "equal" relationships that were not constrained by gender roles. "Gay relations have an equality in them, which is not there in this idea that feminine males will always desire masculine men. I like that idea of equality; both will give each other sexual satisfaction. If you have to be feminine to make a man desire you, then you are stuck in that same social inequality (shamajik boishomyo)." Aniket said he did not understand the desire for "inequality" within same-sex relationships as evidenced in kothi desire, which seemed to replicate the same shamajik boishomyo associated with conventional heterosexuality. These oppressive constructs were overcome by the putative equality of gay identity, desire and relationships — thus in both Aniket's narrative and the more official document quoted above, the kothi-gay contrast defines the teleology or linear progression from a repressive heterosexuality to an egalitarian and authentic homosexuality, aligned with the metropolitan, middle class, educated and implicitly masculine "gay."

In this teleology, equality is equated with symmetry — symmetry in gender roles seems to ensure power equality, whereas gender asymmetry (i.e., differences in gender roles between partners) is conflated with inequality in power. Moreover, there is an automatic, and unconsciously misogynist and transphobic, association between feminization and inequality. There is a certain self-congratulatory gay liberationist affirmation of the masculinized gay model where none of the partners takes on a feminized position relative to the other — thus supposedly indicating relational egalitarianism — as opposed to internalized feminization and victimization of *kothis*, equated with convention, tradition and backwardness. Thus, the straightjacket of mutual masculinity imposed by the gendered symmetry of "gay" is not interrogated, even as *kothi* investments in masculinities are derided as bad.

This is not to say that lower or lower middle class trans communities are necessarily empowered or self-consciously egalitarian, but rather to acknowledge the complexities and contradictions that beset these community and identity formations which are not acknowledged in the aforementioned official and unofficial descriptions, just as dominant narratives of gay identity have to privatize and effectively deny the complexities of gender variance among gay-identified males (recall the discussion on gay *dhuranipona* above). During my fieldwork among lower class gender variant communities in the districts of Murshidabad, Nadia and Kolkata spread over five years since 2007, I have encountered a diversity of individual trajectories of desire, which would be impossible to do justice to within the space of this essay. However, there are dominant intra-community patterns, including a taboo against sex among feminized persons within *kothi, hijra* and transgender circles. Such sex is often described as "*porota bela*" — kneading bread together, like women in a kitchen — and may be often derided relative to the desirable masculinity of the *panthi, parikh* or *giriya* (masculine partner who remains external to the sisterhood within these communities). However, the taboo against or derision of feminine-feminine couplings might vary in its strictness — for example, communities I have interacted in Ranaghat, Nadia have been more willing to recognize *kothi* pairings that do not fall within the logic of sisterhood, even staging a full-blown wedding between a *kothi*-identified community member and her not-so-masculine partner, described as a *dupli kothi* (or "versatile" *kothi*), in the summer of 2011. Moreover, even within the apparently normative rendition of desire expressed in the *kothi-parikh* structure, the metaphors used for negotiating such gender asymmetry often denote forms of erotic consumption in which the relatively feminized partner takes the agential role. For instance, metaphorical phrases like "*parikh khaowa*" (eating *parikhs*) or "*parikh deowa*" (sharing *parikhs*) are commonly used to describe *kothi* and *hijra* desire. In the district of Murshidabad, Bijoy is one of the leaders of the local community-based organization Sangram who describes hirself as a "*swad-hincheta nari*" (independent-willed woman) who cannot be restrained or controlled by hir masculine partners or *parikhs*. Bijoy has a situationally contingent sense of hir gender role — in various occasions, s/he has described hirself both as "*meyeli chhele*" (feminine male) and as "*ontore nari*" (a woman inside), breaching any strict gay-transgender divide. Bijoy often professes a voracious female sexuality for hirself, and attributes it to other *kothi* friends as well: "beware of that one, she catches parikhs and eats them one after the other" ("*o toh kop kop kore Parikh dhore kheye nay*"). Here, the desire for the masculinity of the *parikh* is accompanied by a defiance of the socially/sexually dominant position of masculine men, rather than by assimilation into masculinity. Similar desires of control over their husbands or *giriyas* have been documented in the Bengali literature on *hijra* groups or clans (Majumdar and Basu 74). These forms of sexuality among trans communities are structured around and negotiate heterogeneous gender roles — constructing variable forms of "hetero-sexuality" where the partners are gendered differently, rather than being homogenously masculine — without necessarily conforming to the gendered power dynamic of conventional "heterosexuality" as such.

Here, I do not wish to idealize the subversive potential of *kothi* or *hijra* articulations of desire, neither deny that they sometimes express rigid and constrictive gender roles, even as in other cases they challenge such constrictions. However, I do suggest that the range of trans (specifically *kothi-dhurani* and *hijra*) hetero-sexualities deconstructs "heterosexuality" from within and without through the appropriation, resignification and contestation of mainstream gender roles, rather than claiming a simplistic categorical distinction from (and/or opposition to) heterosexuality, which might end up replicating heterosexist masculinities and masculinist hierarchies even as it proclaims gay liberation.

Conclusion: Generational Normativities

I will end with a question that harkens back to the theme of masculine dominance that links the various discrete sites spanned by the essay. To what extent are transnational "gay" constellations today counter-normative, and to what extent do they represent a newer generation of norms that perpetrate their own forms of masculinist dominance, both within LGBT communities and as a part of broader hegemonic masculinities? As I have endeavored to show through the article, increasing articulations of gay rights are accompanied by attempts to gain social acceptance for gay-identified persons through assimilation into hegemonic forms of masculinity, including such apparently counter-normative trends such as "metrosexuality." In some sense, then, the putative culture war between male homosexual identity construction and societal homophobia might be less a face-off between norm and counter-norm, and more a generational conflict between older constructions of hetero-patriarchy that deride "gay" as feminine, and newer normative constructions of masculinity which resignify gay to accommodate same-sex desire within hegemonic masculinities, largely to the exclusion, elision or privatization of gender variance. The defiant resignification of "gay" into desirable forms of masculinity, evident across locations that are transnationally separated and connected, thus commonly entails the continuing derision and devalorization of gender variance and femininity.

Notes

1. For theorizations and critiques of "homonormativity" see Duggan (175), Murphy (1), Sycamore (4), Puar (8); For activist critiques of gay dominance within LGBT politics and discourse, see Sycamore (2).

2. I have not cited profile names in order to maintain as much confidentiality as possible, and also because personal identity is less important here than metaphors or tropes that are repeated across different personal profiles.

3. As the group is a closed/private one, its name has been changed to protect the confidentiality of individual members.

4. All interviews and conversations mentioned in the context of my fieldwork are translated from the original Bengali. Personal names have been changed to maintain individual confidentiality. Bengali lacks gendered pronouns; I have used variable pronouns in English (including gender neutral ones like "hir") to indicate the varying gender presentations of the different persons; the gender presentation of any one person might be situational and changeable.

5. "Take it like a man" is a common name for gay porn movies featuring anal sex; see, for example, "VCA Gay — Take it Like a Man," www.xvideos.com, Online. Available at http://www.xvideos.com/video1047077/vca_gay_-_take_it_like_a_man_-_scene_1. The metaphor also turns up outside porn, for example, in articles on gay men's fitness (Toussaint).

6. For an entire pornographic site dedicated to class-based tropes of domination-subordination, see www.butterloads.com.

7. Quoted from the minutes circulated in English among the participants after the meeting (e-mail correspondence, May 25, 2007).

8. The "consensus" I mention here was not officially recorded in the meeting minutes; however, it was evident in attempts by senior community members and activists to regulate behaviors such as *thikri* that I observed in the Kolkata Rainbow Pride walks of 2007, 2008 and 2009.

References

Agathangelou, Anna M, Daniel M. Bassichis, and Tamara L. Spira (2008). "Intimate Investments: Homonormativity, Global Lockdown and the Seductions of Empire." *Radical History Review* 100: 120–143.
Altman, Dennis (1996). "On Global Queering." *Australian Humanities Review* 4: n. pag. Web. 5 May 2012. http://www.australianhumanitiesreview.org/archive/Issue-July-1996/altman.html.
_____ (1997). "Global Gaze/Global Gays." *Gay & Lesbian Quarterly* 3: 417–36.
_____ (1996). "Rupture or Continuity? The Internationalization of Gay Identities." *Social Text* 48: 77–94.
Barker, Olivia. "Regular Guys Cast a Jaded Eye at 'Metrosexual' Trend." *USA Today* 21 Jan. 2004: n. pag. Web. 5 May 2012. http://www.usatoday.com/life/lifestyle/2004-01-21-metrosexual-backlash_x.htm.
Bondyopadhyay, Aditya and Vidya Shah (2007). *My Body Is Not Mine: Stories of Violence and Takes of Hope: Voices from the Kothi Community in India*. New Delhi: Naz Foundation International.
Bersani, Leo (1987). "Is the Rectum a Grave?" *October* 43: 197–222.

Bielski, Zosia. "'No Indian, No Asian': Picky Dater or Racist Dater?" *The Globe and Mail* 23 Feb. 2012: n. pag. Web. 5 May 2012. http://www.theglobeandmail.com/life/relationships/love/dating/no-asian-no-indian-picky-dater-or-racist-dater/article2348129/.

Boellstorff, Tom (2007). *A Coincidence of Desires: Anthropology, Queer Studies, Indonesia.* Durham, NC: Duke University Press.

Cohen, Lawrence (2005). "The Kothi Wars: AIDS Cosmopolitanism and the Morality of Classification." *Sex in Development: Science, Sexuality, and Morality in Global Perspective.* Eds. Vincenne Adams and Stacy L. Pigg. Durham, NC: Duke University Press, 269–303.

Chrisafis, Angelique. "Neutered Modern Man to Be Offered Back His Missing Pride in Exchange for His Wallet." *The Guardian* 16 Jun. 2003: 4.

Dodds, Paisley. "Metrosexual Machismo All the Rage." *CBS News* 25 Nov. 2003: n. pag. Web. 5 May 2012. http://www.cbsnews.com/stories/2003/11/25/world/printable585549.htm.

"Douchebags of Grindr." n.p. n.d.: n. pag. Web. www.douchebagsofgrindr.com.

Drum, Gary R. "The Metrosexual: Fashion-conscious Heterosexual or JGE (Just Gay Enough)?" *Hardyboy* n.d.: n. pag. Web. 5 May 2012. http://www.hardyboy.com/metrosexual.html.

Duggan, Lisa (2002). "The New Homonormativity: The Sexual Politics of Neoliberalism." *Materializing Democracy: Toward a Revitalized Cultural Politics.* Eds. Russ Castro novo and Dana D. Nelson. Durham, NC: Duke University Press, 175–194.

Dutta, Aniruddha (forthcoming 2012). "An Epistemology of Collusion: *Hijra, Kothi* and the Historical (Dis)continuity of Gender/Sexual Identities in Eastern India." *Gender & History* 24:3: n. pag.

Fung, Richard (1999). "Looking for My Penis: The Eroticized Asian in Gay Male Porn." *The Columbia Reader on Lesbians & Gay Men in Media*, Society and Politics. Eds. Larry Gross and James Woods. New York: Columbia University Press, 235–253.

Ghosh, Biswadeep. "What Is Metrosexual Anyway?" *Times of India* 20 Oct. 2010: 12. Print.

Hanhardt, Christina B. (2008). "Butterflies, Whistles, and Fists: Gay Safe Streets Patrols and the New Gay Ghetto, 1976–1981." *Radical History Review* 100 : 61–85. Print.

Jackson, Peter (2009). "Capitalism and Global Queering: National Markets, Parallels Among Sexual Cultures, and Multiple Queer Modernities." *GLQ: A Journal of Lesbian and Gay Studies* 15: 357–95.

Joshi, Yuvraj (2012). "Respectable Queerness." *Columbia Human Rights Law Review* 43.2: 415–467.

Killermann, Sam. "What Does the Asterisk in Trans* Stand For?" *It's Pronounced Metrosexual* 1 May 2012: n. pag. http://itspronouncedmetrosexual.com/2012/05/what-does-the-asterisk-in-trans-stand-for/.

Majumdar, Ajay, and Niloy Basu (2005). *Bharoter Hijre Shomaj.* Kolkata: Deep Prakashan.

Martin, Fran (1996). "Response to Dennis Altman." *Australian Humanities Review* 4: n. pag. Web. 5 May 2012. http://www.australianhumanitiesreview.org/archive/Issue-July-1996/altman.html.

Martins, Reena. "Gay, Happy and Sad." *The Telegraph (Calcutta): 7 Days* 26 Feb. 2012: 1. Print.

Minton, H. L. (1986). "Femininity in Men and Masculinity in Women: American Psychiatry and Psychology Portray Homosexuality in the 1930s." *Journal of Homosexuality* 13.1: 1–21.

Murphy, Kevin P., Jason Ruiz, and David Serlin (2008). "Editor's Introduction." *Radical History Review* 100: 1–24.

NACO: National AIDS Control Organization (2007). *Targeted Interventions Under NACP III: Operational Guidelines: Core High Risk Groups.* New Delhi: Government of India.

Puar, Jasbir (2007). *Terrorist Assemblages: Homonationalism in Queer Times.* Durham, NC: Duke University Press.

Toussaint, David. "Bootcamp: Take It Like a Man," *Realjock: Gay Fitness Health and Life* n.d.: n. pag. Web. 5 May 2012. http://www.realjock.com/article/153.

Reddy, Gayatri (2005). *With Respect to Sex: Negotiating Hijra Identity in South India.* Chicago: University of Chicago Press.

"Real Men Get Waxed; Metrosexuality. (We're all metrosexuals now.)" *The Economist (U.S.)* 5 Jul. 2003: 57. Print.

Rowlson, Alex. "Not Just a Preference." *Fab: The Gay Scene Magazine.* 12 Oct. 2011: n. pag. Web.
SAATHII: Solidarity and Action Against the HIV Infection in India. (2009). *Report of the Regional Transgender/Hijra Consultation in Eastern India.* Kolkata: SAATHII.
Sycamore, Mattilda B. (Ed.) (2004). *That's Revolting: Queer Strategies for Resisting Assimilation.* Brooklyn: Soft Skull Press.
Wavey, Davey. "Things NOT to Ask a Gay Guy." *Youtube:* n. pag. Web. 5 May 2012. http://www.youtube.com/watch?v=ehhVv748OOU&list=PLEF743AE7F616F662&index=132&feature=plpp_video.
Weeks, Jeffrey (1985). *Sexuality and Its Discontents: Meanings, Myths and Modern Sexualities.* London: Routledge.

Corporal Punishment

English and Homosocial Tactility in Postcolonial Bengal

NILADRI R. CHATTERJEE

There is a story I once heard about a Western woman visiting Calcutta. This was her second visit. The first visit was in the 1970s when she was a teenager. The next was in the twenty-first century when she was in her late thirties. After going around the city for a few days, on her second visit, she asked her Bengali friends, "Aren't there any gays in Calcutta anymore?" The friends were puzzled and asked her to explain her question. She said, "Well, the last time I was here, I often saw men walking down the street holding hands. Surely they were gay. Why don't I see such gay couples around anymore?" There are several ways in which one can read the story. But its most accessible reading would be as an example of cultural incomprehension or misreading. Since, in her native culture, two men holding hands could univocally mean that they were in a homosexual relationship, she had assumed that manual tactility between men in all societies can mean only one thing. She was the native of a society where English was the most commonly spoken language. The story has stayed with me all these years because somewhere in that story I detected an intriguing relationship between language/culture and the body. Looking at myself I find that my reduced use of English is inversely proportional to the increase in my sense of security. When I was younger I spoke in English far more than I do now. I was also aware of the reason for this. I felt English was a language which was protecting me from visceral emotional self-exposure. I felt English was a mask which would de-emotionalize even an emotional statement that I may make. I felt protected by the language. This protection also brought in its wake a certain emotional frigidity and unavailability that I acquired, which can be used to explain that when I was younger I was far lonelier than I am now, when I do not speak English as much as I used to. This essay is an attempt at exploring how and why the male body in Bengal

165

functions in a certain way when the owner of that body — and that body must be unequivocally male — speaks his native tongue and in quite another way when he speaks English.

I have often noticed that there is a marked difference between the way men in Bengal who speak English think of their bodies and the way those who do not speak English think or do not think of theirs. The holding of hands becomes the touchstone method of telling apart those who do not speak English from those who do. I have repeatedly observed that those men who are obviously employed in blue collar professions, or are even daily wage earners, and therefore almost certainly not in possession of English, show a far greater level of tactility among themselves than those who are white collar workers and are not entirely unlettered in English. Men or boys who do not speak English hold hands in public, embrace each other a lot more, even kiss each other on the cheek far more frequently than those who can speak English. In fact, in my own English-speaking circle of friends I have noticed a particular horror of physical contact among male friends, and an inversely proportional lack of corporeal self-consciousness among those who do not speak English. Is it a mere coincidence? Would it be entirely erroneous to speculate whether the English language in any way straitjackets the male body and prohibits same-sex tactility beyond the "firm" handshake? Is the firmness of the handshake an indicator and a performance of hegemonic masculinity?[1] Is the handshake the only kind of same-sex tactility that has been sanctioned and approved as a physical gesture that carries no risk of endangering the heteronormativity of a patriarchal society?

English was formally introduced as the preferred language of instruction, business and government in Bengal in the later part of the eighteenth century, Calcutta having been settled by the East India Company towards the end of the seventeenth century. Lord Macaulay's notorious Minute on Indian Education was written in 1835. As Gauri Vishwathan says, English education was introduced to solve the conflict between the proselytizing goal of the missionaries and the policy of religious neutrality adopted by the British Government (Vishwanathan, 38). So, as I say elsewhere, English and Christianity were being discreetly conflated by smuggling in Christianity under the cover of English literature (Chatterjee, 38–39). Foucault tells us that in the nineteenth century in the West in general and in England in particular the human body, and especially the male body of the schoolboy, was being pathologized, sexualized, classified and medicojuridically disciplined, with active support from Christianity (Foucault, 28).

There are two famous instances of homosocial tactility in the New Testament of Bible and both carry negative valence. Judas identifies Christ for the Roman police by kissing him. Thomas doubts the reality of Christ's resurrection by inserting a finger into one of the wounds received by Christ on the cross. There is only one instance of homosocial tactility in the Bible with positive valence. This is that of St. John the Beloved — not to be confused with St. John the Baptist — who was in the habit of resting his head on Christ's shoulder. There are statues in Germany dating from 1300 where this instance of homosocial tactility in the Bible is iconized.[2] The fact that these statues are not very well known points to the marginalization of positive homosocial tactility in the New Testament. The only way in which the story of John the Beloved resting his head on Christ's chest has travelled into English literature is through its homosexualization by Christopher Marlowe when he declared that John the Beloved had a homosexual relationship with Christ. According to a late–sixteenth century manuscript, "[Marlowe] affirmed ... [that] St. John the Evangelist was bedfellow to Christ and leaned always in his bosome, that he used him as the sinners of Sodom" (Higgins, 68). So, that apparently asexual and positive instance of Biblical homosocial tactility was appropriated by Marlowe and therefore reinserted into the criminalizing Christian discourse on homosexuality. Therefore all the three instances of Christian homosocial tactility become associative of crime. It is interesting, however, that doubting Thomas was allowed to poke a finger into one of Christ's wounds, but Mary Magdalen was asked not to touch. Titian's painting *Noli Me Tangere* (1508) immortalizes the moment when the resurrected Christ told Magdalen gently but firmly, "Touch me not." The tactility refused in this painting can be seen in contrast to the tactility implied in Michelangelo's *Creation of Adam* (1510) painted two years later. What must be noted is that even in Michelangelo's fresco, the male God and the male Adam are not shown touching each other. Mind the gap between the index fingers of God and Adam! So "Noli me tangere" seems to hover over Christianity like a dictat. I was struck by how uncomfortable men and women standing on either side of me at a church in Austin, Texas, were when at the end of the Midnight Mass on Christmas Day 1996 the congregation was asked to give the person standing next to them the sign of peace. As the sign of peace, I noticed, most men shook each other's hand. By contrast, men embracing each other after prayers is sanctioned in both Islam and Hinduism. In Islam men embrace each other after Eid prayers. In Hinduism men embrace each other on Bijoya Dashami, after Goddess Durga and Her Children have returned back to Their home in the Himalayas after the three-day Durga Puja. Painted a decade or two after *Creation of Adam*, a page from the *Bhagavad Purana* traced to the Delhi-Agra area shows the embrace of Nanda and Vasudeva (1520–30). Such a representation of two male bodies would be unthinkable at that time in Europe.

The pathologization of the male body gets underway in England at the same time that the teaching and dissemination of English becomes public policy for the British Government in Bengal. In order to understand how English was affecting the body of the Bengali male one need not look any further than the bodies of Vivekānanda and his spiritual master Rāmakrishna, two men living in nineteenth century Bengal; one fluent in English, the other completely unlettered in the language. If one looks at the photographs of the two men it becomes obvious that they had almost hygienically opposite attitudes towards their own bodies. While Vivekānanda's most commonly reproduced posture shows him with his arms cross-locked against his chest, Rāmakrishna's hands are either loosely, limply resting on his lap, near his folded feet, fingers loosely meshed into each other or his left hand is at his chest while the right hand is raised in ecstasy, with two fingers pointing heavenward. There are no photographs available of Rāmakrishna where he is in control of his body. His body seems to have no importance to him at all. Vivekānanda, on the other hand, is always conscious of his corporeality. Rāmakrishna was often known to dance with his disciples. There are no recorded instances of Vivekānanda dancing. Vivekānanda's generation was the first in Bengal to be put through an education imparted in the English language. Rāmakrishna did not know English. In his attitude towards the body, nay the gendered male body, Vivekānanda was totally interpellated in the British ontology. Hardly surprising that the privately racist Anglo-American Vedantist and novelist Christopher Isherwood found Vivekānanda far easier to like and understand that he did Rāmakrishna. From Isherwood's published diaries it becomes clear that he often resented the obviously Indian aspects of the Rāmakrishna order and approved of the recognizably Western ones.[3] As said above, Foucault catalogues the ways in which the schoolboy's sexuality started being put under constant surveillance in the nineteenth century, lest it swerves away from the strict path of hegemonic masculinity and thereby endanger Britain's status as an imperial power.

It is this masculinity which gets transmitted to the natives of Bengal when they are educated in the language which discursively produces the imperial master's. With the language come the clothes. It is physically difficult, if not impossible, to be as corporeally mobile in a suit as it is to be when one is wearing only a dhoti or a thin short cotton shirt over the dhoti. The male body has greater freedom in traditional Bengali clothes than it does in severely cut two-piece or three-piece suits. So, language brings with it its own sartorial culture which the learners of the language find themselves subliminally pressured to adopt. The body is clothed in a way which restricts its mobility, the kind of mobility it had when it was garbed in native "Oriental" clothes. If masquerade is an important aspect of acquiring an identity, then there is also the chance of the mask growing into the face, so that the face and the mask become organically inseparable. Such an osmosis happens in the case of the Bengali male's attitude towards his own body once he starts to speak in English. The stronger fluid of English seeps into the evidently weaker fluid of Bengali culture in the nineteenth century, changing the latter so profoundly that its presence can still be detected in the Bengali psyche even today, sixty-six years after Independence. English and its notions of gender and sexuality continue to wield power in contemporary Bengali society where homophobia, for example, can be cited as an obvious result of the Englishing of Bengal. These prejudices regarding gender and sexuality have proven to be so powerful that they have seeped into the consciousness of even those who may have only a passing or tenuous relationship with English.

In our colleges, when we start to learn about the history of the English language and philology, the language is presented to us firmly gendered as masculine. We are told, in no uncertain terms, that English is a masculine language. The text that is still used is Otto Jespersen's *Growth and Structure of the English Language* (1905). In this book, Jespersen regards English as a language that has words with more consonants and therefore requires more energy to speak (Jespersen, 8). He writes, "If briefness, conciseness and terseness are characteristic of the style of men, while women as a rule are not such economizers of speech, English is more masculine than most languages" (Jespersen, 4–5). After setting down some more features of the English language, Jespersen concludes, "All this seems to justify us in setting down the enormous richness of the English vocabulary to the same masculinity of the English nation which we have now encountered in so many fields" (Jespersen, 15–16). We ingest this gendering of English without any feminist contestation or criticism. What we do not realize is that in declaring English a masculine language a few other gendered associations are being smuggled into our consciousness. In receiving English as a masculine language we are also accepting English as a disciplined, ordered, scientific language cleansed of any feminizing emotional contagion. In Jespersen's words, "The English language is a methodical, energetic, business-like and sober language, that does not care much for finery and elegance, but does care for logical consistency..." (Jespersen, 16). Since the patriarchal connotation of finery and elegance is "feminine" or "effeminate," English is summarily constructed as "masculine." Any kind of excess is apparently foreign to the language. Excess is where the feminine lives! Tactility is an indication of that feminizing excess.

Homosocial tactility should be studied in a way that takes into account the site of its performance and the class of subjects performing. If one looks at PDA — Public Display of Affection — one notices that the concept unproblematically conflates affection with erotic or romantic desires. It is as if affection can only be sexual. Is not a mother kissing her child in public a public display of affection? Why is that acceptable and why is not the sight of two lovers or even a married couple kissing acceptable? What kind of affection therefore is heteronormatively assumed to exist between two men holding hands or embracing in public, depending on the site of that performance being Western or Eastern? Here I propose to use English as a verb; to English, to be Englished. In a non–Englished context, the holding of hands, the embracing and even kissing between two men may be assumed to be "brotherly," "friendly," and therefore unproblematically and uncomplicatedly asexual. In an Englished context two men holding hands, embracing and kissing will be assumed to be unproblematically and unequivocally sexual. In Isherwood's novel *A Meeting by the River* (1967) Patrick writes to his American lover Tom, "Perhaps you weren't aware of the eyebrows raised by some of the other passengers when you kissed me smack on the mouth? That's why I made it a point of kissing you right back with equal enthusiasm! But I imagine most of the people who saw us doing it assumed you were my younger brother and we were foreigners of some kind, bidding each other a big Latin-style farewell" (Isherwood, 38). We are aware, that German and English cultures have frequently regarded Southern European societies as being the Orient of the West, as opposed to the real Orient which consists of countries like China, Japan and India. Jespersen does that too. He writes, "An excessive use of this emotional tonic accent is characteristic of many savage nations; in Europe, it is found much more in Italy than in the North" (Jespersen, 8). So, Southern Europe is the East to Northern Europe's West! The geographical location of the homosocial tactility, therefore, needs to be factored into the reading of a performance of homosocial affection in public.

The other variable that needs to be factored in is class. As I have mentioned above, blue-collar professionals tend to be less worried about the dangerous messages their being homosocially tactile may send out.

As in any other construction of the Lacanian Imaginary, the imaginary of homosocial tactility is also produced on the silver screen or on the small screen of television. It would be interesting to see how the hero of a Bengali film, for example, performs his friendship with his male friends. How tactile is he? Has the level and nature of tactility changed post-globalization, where English words have infiltrated into colloquial Bengali and is increasingly audible in Bengali movies? Does the Bengali hero of today touch his male friends more or less than the Bengali hero of the '40s, '50s, '60s, '70s, '80s? Even on the screen does the nature and extent of homosocial tactility depend on whether the hero knows English or not? And even if the hero himself does not know English, does the director's knowledge of English proscribe the hero's homosocial tactility? Is the director excising any possibility of the homoerotic by keeping the hero's hands far away from the bodies of his male friends? These are questions that may be engaged with. It is not surprising that Englished director Anjan Dutta should have a scene in his film *Byomkesh Bakshi* (2010) where he has Byomkesh kiss his assistant Ajit on the cheek. Apparently, it was done to suggest that the relationship between Byomkesh and Anil was not entirely asexual. It is interesting that the presence of the erotic has to be signified by a physical gesture. So a strange binarization seems to be active here. Tactile is equated with sexual, non-tactile with the asexual. This is how the colonial legacy continues to operate in the Bengali consciousness once it has been colonized by the English language.

There is an absence of homosocial tactility in art produced in Bengal. As far Indian art is concerned the only artist who deals with man-to-man tactility is Bhupen Khakhar, but the tactility represented in his paintings are redolent of overt or covert homosexuality, which is the result of his knowledge of English, of course. In *My Dear Friend* (1983) the two male lovers hold hands, but in private. In his most famous painting *Man with a Bouquet of Plastic Flowers* (1976) there are homosocial groups towards the right of the central figure, but even in these groups there is no touching. There is touching in *Seva* (1986).

How and why is rampant, enthusiastic homosocial tactility culturally acceptable in the realm of sport? The uninhibited embracing of a goal-scorer by his teammates is not regarded as being problematic because the football field has been so discursively sanitized and declared innocent of the homoerotic that the post-goal homosocial tactility among the members of a team is not seen as posing any kind of threat to the unimpeachable heterosexual nature of the football field. The football field, or indeed any other sporting site is assumed to be hegemonically and eternally masculine. So homosocial tactility is not seen as a threat to its ontology. But even here it has been noted that non–English teams are much more homosocially tactile than the English team. Irani Chatterjee is a dietitian to sportspersons and she regularly associates with personal trainers across India. She says that she notices a distinct difference between the ways in which English-spoken and non–English-spoken gym trainers interact with their clients. Those who speak in English will only speak out their instructions and they try to keep their physical contact with clients to the bare minimum.[4] Whereas those who instruct in, say Bengali or Hindi, think nothing of establishing repeated physical contact with their clients.

In her book *The Body: The Key Concepts* (2008) Lisa Blackman speaks of two ways in which the body can be theorized in sociology: microperspectives and macroperspectives. According to her, microperspectives concentrate on the way in which the self is identified and invented through talk. Microperspectives reify conversational activity and the body is submerged. Macroperspectives, on the other hand, see the body as the effect of power and discourse, the way in which Michel Foucault theorizes the production of identities by power. But is there that much of a difference between the two ways of examining identity formation? And even if there is, I believe that there can be conjunctures where conversational activity and talk can very well be the way through which power covertly produces the "docile" body as theorized by Foucault in his *Discipline and Punish* (1976). I believe that English exerts a disciplinary power over the male body in Bengal. If, as Foucault says, power produces us by instituting internal forms of self-monitoring and self-regulation and if these forms are inculcated as particular body techniques and practices, then English is one such form.

The English language puts at abeyance the spontaneous tactility of the male in Bengal and institutes itself inside the body of the speaker as a mechanism which ensures that the body is regulated from within, *not* without. So, the language becomes like an electronic tag that prisoners out on parole wear around their ankles. Surveillance of the body is embedded *in* the body. Over time the body gets used to the mechanism and ceases to regard it as anything other than organic to its existence, something "natural." In this case the mechanism is English. It was/is so easy to implant because it promised and continues to promise social, political, cultural and economic empowerment. But it takes away with one hand what it seemingly gives with another. In return for socio-economic empowerment, the body had to lose its spontaneous tactility, its delight in the human touch.

There is, therefore, a certain astringent quality to the English language that not only starches an identity into stiff non-tactility, but it also introduces an element of cold asexuality, even a fear of sexuality. It is often observed that when non-native speakers make love, they prefer the dirty talk to be in a non–English language. It is access to the non–English language which revives the erotic in the verbal. One has heard about the decolonization of the mind. The assumption is that the mind can be decolonized through discourse, just as the body has been decolonized through tangible, concrete political actions. This assumption needs to be complicated, because discourse colonizes the body too. Language can colonize the body, disciplining it in a certain way alien to the body's native culture. Over a period of time the body forgets the physical freedom it had when its verbal expression was in the native language. The body learns to regard as "natural" the restrictions that the imposed or acquired language has sanctioned. The mask grows into the face as it were rendering the two inseparable. It is this inseparability which is regarded as an essential assumption by those who practice the syncretic school of postcolonial theory, such as Bill Ashcroft, Helen Tiffin and Gareth Griffith. I suggest that this syncretically formed postcolonial consciousness effects the way one body touches another, especially when both the bodies in question are intelligibly male and living in Bengal. One does not know whether this inseparability is absolutely impossible. Nor if that separation can be effected only occasionally and is unsustainable indefinitely. But the Englishing of the male body in Bengal seems to have produced anxieties around tactility that may not have been there before.

Notes

1. The concept of "hegemonic masculinity" was put forward by R. W. Connell, S. J. Kessler, D. J. Ashenden, and G. W. Dowsett in 1982, and subsequently systematized in "Towards a New Sociology of Masculinity." The concept suggests that masculinity is not a homogenous bloc, but has an internal hierarchy of its own. In this hierarchy one form of masculinity is held as the ideal, while others are devalorized as being inadequate or insufficient. The hierarchy consists of three layers: hegemonic, complicit, and subordinate. The hegemonic is the suggested ideal, the complicit masculinity is embodied/ performed by those who may not have hegemonic masculinity themselves but aspire to it or support its hegemonic power. Subordinate masculinity belongs to those who are unable to or choose not to aspire to hegemonic masculinity.

2. The sculptures, on painted and gilded wood, can be seen at the Bayerisches National Museum, Munich and Staatliche Museen Preußischer Kulturbesitz, Berlin and reproduced in *Sculpture*.

3. "There were aspects of the Vedanta Society of Souther California that repelled him strongly — "the specifically Indian aspects of the Rāmakrishna cult." He protested, "Why did the rituals in the shrine have to be Hindu rituals? Why did several of the women devotees like to wear sarees in the shrine-room? Why were the prayers in Sanskrit? Why did we so often have curry at meals?" in *An Approach to Vedanta*, p. 32. He approved of the puja on Vivekānanda's birth anniversary. He recorded in his diary, "And I hate the thought of all pujas. With one exception: on the morning of Vivekānanda's birthday, Sister personally serves him his coffee in the shrine room — two cups — and a cigarette, which she lights and leaves burning on an ashtray." *Diaries: Volume One, 1939–1960*, p. 348.

4. Unrecorded conversation. 23 January 2013.

References

Blackman, Lisa (2008). *The Body: The Key Concepts*. Oxford: Berg.

Carrigan, T. R., R. W. Connell, and J. Lee (1985). "Towards a New Sociology of Masculinity." *Theory and Society*, 14:5, 551–604.

Chatterjee, Niladri R (2008). "'Peace': Vivekānanda's Subversion of English." *JSL: Journal of the School of Language, Literature and Culture Studies* (New Delhi: Jawaharlal Nehru University) New Series: 10 (Autumn 2008): 38–46.

Foucault, Michel (2008). *History of Sexuality, Vol. I (The Will to Knowledge)*. Trans. Robert Hurley. Australia: Penguin.

Higgins, Patrick (Ed.) (1993). *A Queer Reader*. London: Fourth Estate.

Isherwood, Christopher (1963). *An Approach to Vedanta*. California, Vedanta Press.

_____ (1984). *A Meeting by the River*. Great Britain: Methuen.

_____ (1997). *Diaries: Volume One, 1939–1960*. Ed. Katherine Bucknell. U.S.: Harper Collins.

Jespersen, Otto (1984). *Growth and Structure of the English Language*. New Delhi: Oxford University Press.

Sculpture (2004). Kent: Grange Books.

Vishwanathan, Gauri (1990). *Masks of Conquest: Literary Study and British Rule in India*. London: Faber and Faber.

Of *Girmitiyas* and Mimic Men
Alternative Masculinity in
V. S. Naipaul's *A House for Mr. Biswas*
VISHNUPRIYA SENGUPTA

Father and Son

In the essay *East Indian*, Vidiadhar Surajprasad Naipaul writes:

...A hundred years ago the West Indies must have seemed like the end of the world. Yet so many left, taking everything — beds, brass vessels, musical instruments, images, holy books, sandalwood sticks, astrological almanacs. It was less an uprooting than it appears. They were taking India with them. With their blinkered view of the world they were able to re-create eastern Uttar Pradesh or Bihar wherever they went. They had been able to ignore the vastness of India; so now they ignored the strangeness in which they had been set. To leave India's sacred soil, to cross the "black water," was considered an act of self-defilement. So completely did these migrants re-create India in Trinidad that they imposed a similar restriction on those who wished to leave Trinidad [Naipaul, 1972, p. 35].

It is this essence, which imbues the act of recreating India in Trinidad, that Naipaul captures in *A House for Mr. Biswas*. Set in Trinidad, the novel explores the "place of origin" myth that underlies the diasporic consciousness intertwined as it is with the fortunes of its protagonist, Mohun Biswas. Modelled on Naipaul's own father Seepersad Naipaul, Mohun Biswas's alternative masculinity outlines the tensions, frailties and foibles of an individual trapped in a claustrophobic ghettoized society through a series of powerful and evocative metaphors. Non-hegemonic alternative masculinity in this context surfaces through Mr. Biswas's double status as both a "girmit"[1] and a "mimic man"[2] resulting in a compelling interplay.

The novel takes off from Seepersad Naipaul's story, *They Named Him Mohun*, which was inspired by Seepersad Naipaul's parents and his birth. Naipaul Senior's story revolves around a pregnant woman who seeks protection from the abuses of her husband, in this case, his stinginess and anger, expressed in words and blows. The child Mohun's birth is inauspicious. Born under "a bad planet" and "in the wrong way," and "with six fingers on each hand," he is declared by the midwife a child "bound to eat its mother and father" (Naipaul, rpt. 1992, p. 19). On the pundit's advice, his grandmother performs a ritual to mitigate these forebodings and holds a celebration of Mohun's birth. The story contains realistic details — the husband's meanness, and pregnant wife's seven-mile journey on foot to her mother's house. Seepersad Naipaul did not reveal any further but his son used the material for the opening section of *A House for Mr. Biswas*. In course of fleshing out the father figure of Mohun Biswas, Naipaul compensated for his father's resistance to expressing the full measure of his hatred for his own father.

Mohun Biswas fulfills the prophecies that attended his birth when, inadvertently but effectively, he is instrumental in his father's death. On a broader level, the story of Mr. Biswas's existence from birth to death, structured by his search for a house, represents — in the form of an individual life — the historical process leading up to Trinidadian importance in terms of the *girmit* ideology as well as a form of mimicry.

Oscar Wilde in *The Picture of Dorian Gray* had written, "Children begin by loving their parents, and end by judging them. They never forgive them." Naipaul, on his part, wrote this book about them. Versions of Seepersad Naipaul's struggle for autonomy in an inhospitable setting are also woven into the plots of several of Naipaul's later novels, including *Half a Life*. The facts that emerge chiefly from these sources describe a man who was paradoxical in many respects. And yet, he was consistent in defying the barriers of his personal and social history in order to make himself a writer and finally to live in his own home. His stories recording the life of the Hindu community in Trinidad in the first fifty years of the century are, therefore, are a vital portion of Naipaul's heritage. Unwilling to assimilate with the local West Indian community, this community chalked out an alternative path that disallowed contamination by external influences.

Naipaul admits in an interview with Tarun Tejpal:

> My father was a writer. He wrote stories, a journalist who wrote stories. These things were very important to me, the writing. And my father's attitude was one of examining our Hindu background in the stories. He found it a very cruel background, and I understood from his stories that it was a very cruel world. So I grew up with this idea that it was important to look inwards and not always define an external enemy, and I still believe that [Tejpal, 2001].

It is with this belief in mind that Naipaul depicts the plight of the Hindu East Indians. He modelled the frenzied pace of activities in the Hanuman House — the traditionalist Tulsi family home — on his mother's side of the family. Dispossessed, the residents of Hanuman House (named after a Lord

Ram loyalist from Hindu mythology who wards off all evil) struggle to maintain the social patterns of their original cultures, though not always with success. The remnants of their inherited culture prevent the development of even a rudimentary sense of identification with their new homeland and prompt them to lead a ghettoized existence, characteristic of a *Girmitiya*.[3]

"Trunk Load of Memories"

Suspicious of the colonial masters and the indigenous race, and sensing a threat that arose from their own inherent structural inadequacies as a fragment, the Indians in the West Indies felt a need to be unified. They called themselves *girmitiyas*, a Hindi neologism, according to Vijay Mishra, coined from the term for the "agreement" that the indentured laborers had to sign. (Mishra, 1992, p. 1)

This parochial, almost xenophobic, coalescence separated them from both colonizers and the natives of the islands. Out of sync with the new world of Trinidad, they lead a cocooned life hardly ever looking outside their own cloistered existence for sustenance. It is only when Mr. Biswas marries Shama, a daughter of this house, that there is a disturbance in the equilibrium.

Mr. Biswas — contrary to the attributes of hegemonic masculinity that include aggression, power, competitiveness — is etched as a man aware of the void of his own future and the obscurity of his origin. Despite his limitations, he desperately seeks to carve a niche for himself. That is where his conventional masculinity governed by his male ego crosses paths with his alternative masculine traits, making him distinctive, bordering on the tragic. He surrenders to the dictates of the matriarch Mrs. Tulsi — at least on the face of it, but demonstrates a rare resistance beneath the surface. Time and again, he is observed sitting before the typewriter attempting to produce a work of fiction.

> Mr. Biswas ... inserted a sheet of *Sentinel* paper, typed his name and address at the top righthand corner ... and wrote:
> Escape
> by M. Biwas
> At the age of thirty-three, when he was already the father of four children...
> None of these stories was finished, and their theme was always the same. The hero, trapped into marriage, burdened with a family, his youth gone, meets a young girl. She is slim, almost thin, and dressed in white. She is fresh, tender, unkissed; ... [Naipaul, 1992, p. 344].

It appears that this girl symbolizes the escape route that Mr. Biswas longs to find, but to no avail. "Trapped" as he is in the claustrophobic "traditionalist" milieu of the Tulsi household, there is no escape; the stories thus always hit a dead end at this juncture. But though Mr. Biswas finds his world engulfing and repulsive, and a deterrent to ambition, the faith in life with which the author endows him, his obstinate knowledge "that below it all there was an excitement which was hidden but waiting to be grasped" (Naipaul, 1992, p. 341) is greater than the fictional character's impulse to escape. For Mr. Biswas, living may have been a preparation, a waiting or anticipation, but for his children it is a waiting before the world opens up for them. Savi, his elder daughter, wins a scholarship and goes abroad. Two years later Anand, the author incarnate, bags a scholarship and "escapes" to England.

The *girmit* ideology that underlines the work meshes with a profound sense of cultural loss, calling attention to the gap between the imagined and real worlds. For Naipaul, the mythological world of the *girmitiya* is a product of the fossilized memories of the old place. It acts as a substitute for the dynamic reality of the real place, whereby history is stilled and time frozen to construct a fantasy world with no real foundation in fact.

Vijay Mishra calls Naipaul — and not without reason — "the founder par excellence of the *girmitiya* discourse" who "gave form and language to the *girmit* ideology" (Panwar, 2003, p. 27). In the novel, the *girmitiya* constructs what Naipaul calls "our island India" which is "an overdetermined mini-replica of the more conservative aspects of homeland, life ritualised in the memory and actions of the dispossessed" (Pointon, 2003, p. 27). The *girmitiya* psychology is governed by the logic of the fragment — a constructed imaginary belief system meant for its own self-authentication, self-generation and legitimation. That's because the Trinidad Indians themselves were essentially a fragment that had been forcefully wrenched from its Centre, India. So they defined themselves in relation to an absent Centre, the homeland they were forced to leave. The new land was a point of transit, a temporary sojourn at the end of which they believed they would return to their places of origin.

But unfortunately, the *girmitiya*, like Naipaul, does not feel at home in any culture other than that of memory. He carries his homeland — a small place, a particular closed locality — in his "gunny sack" or "trunk load of memories" wherever he moves. His *girmitiya* consciousness is informed by a cultural loss, the part consequence of a progressively waning memory of the dream homeland.

A Home for Mr. Biswas

The notion of *home* plays an important role for Mr. Biswas as for most people. It provides a sense of belonging and security, a place where one can decide on acceptable values and forms of behavior. It is not confined merely to a home but may be extended to a wider social space, even a nation. Home also has an opposing territorial connotation of making space through closure: "only those who belong can come in and a house owner can shut the door on outsiders" (Panwar, 2003, p. 28).

Anjali Gera points out in her essay, *Strange Moves: Girmitiya Turns Cosmopolitan*, the *girmitiya* ideology, as given form and language by Naipaul, may be comprehended as a form of *home-building* and *place-making*, and emerges most strongly in *A House for Mr. Biswas.* (Gera, 2003, p. 28) In that, home-building is "the building of a feeling of being at home" based on "four affective building blocks": security, familiarity, community and a sense of possibility while place-making is defined as the reshaping of ethnic groups to construct their neighborhoods to correspond more closely to their needs and values. The place-making process involves three sets of strategies "naming, rituals and institutions." Home-building and place-making are both important for community formation. Place-making is an essential aspect of migrant existence and the memory of old place, however imaginary, helps authenticate, legitimize and self-generate.

Naipaul's portrayal of Hanuman House, the Tulsi family home, as a "white fortress" — with thick "concrete walls," closed "narrow doors" and "windowless" facades that create a "bulky impregnable" appearance — is an appropriate metaphor for a mentality that sought to isolate and insulate the East Indians against the alien culture around them. And, in that sense, is an apt example of a form of place-making and once again is reflective of the *girmit* ideology. It captures the romantic yearnings of the older East Indian immigrants to return to India. The great rambling Tulsi household, ill-defined and yet curiously hierarchical, eclectic in religious practice, yet noisily pious, generous within limits, yet unrelenting in its demands, is a single, comprehensive, brilliantly evoked metaphor for the traditional Indian community. However, despite their harsh life on the periphery of the larger society, these immigrants, like Naipaul's father, would hesitate if actually offered repatriation. Gathered together in the evenings they "continually talked of going back to India, but when the opportunity came, many refused, afraid of the unknown, afraid to leave the familiar temporariness." (Naipaul, rpt. 1992, p. 190)

On the other hand, recognizing Mr. Biswas's need for making a home that rests on the building blocks of security, familiarity, community and a sense of possibility makes for an appropriate instance of home-building. Naipaul, however, is highly critical of the mythologized, claustrophobic orthodox Hindu world in the Tulsi household, reconstructed in Trinidad. Mr. Biswas is impatient with the Tulsi clan for descending to participate in every family gathering and the accompanying rituals. At weddings and funerals, the displaced population attempts to construct a sense of community whose import is lost on the succeeding generations.

Ambitious in an undirected way, Mr. Biswas, as he is referred to throughout, takes up sign painting. A job at Hanuman House, the store-cum-home of the Tulsi family, leads him into the clutches of old Mrs. Tulsi (Mai), a widow, overblessed with daughters whom she marries off with little care except for the proprieties of Hindu caste law. The sons-in-law she acquires in this way provide the overseers and workforce for the family. Once married into the household, Mr. Biswas is immediately aware in an undefined way that by becoming part of the Tulsi household, he has sacrificed his liberty and his future. Yet, he is also seduced by the security and certainty which this surrender brings as reward. He indulges in small acts of defiance that have him labeled the troublemaker and disturber of peace and demonstrate his resistance to complete subservience.

Hanuman House reveals itself not as a coherent reconstruction of the clan, but as a slave society erected by Mrs. Tulsi and Seth who need workers to rebuild their tottering empires. They exploit the homelessness and poverty of their fellow–Hindus, and reconstruct a mockery of the clan which functions only because they have so completely grasped the psychology of a slave system. Like the West Indies, Hanuman House comprises a vast number of disparate families, gratuitously brought together by the economic need of a "high-caste" minority. To accept Hanuman House is to acquiesce to one's slavery.

Understandably then, we have Mr. Biswas — the colonized in this case — openly rebelling against the matriarchal Tulsi household — the colonizer. He never gives up his struggle against his own internalization of the historical forces that threaten his autonomy. He fights to maintain his independence, swinging between anger, emotional blackmail, his self-recrimination against his own ingratitude and obvious inability to survive alone. He may be part of the Trinidadian Indian community but he constantly questions its customs and values. When he is working at a variety of menial jobs at the Tulsis, he defies their authority, exposes their pretensions, their arrogance sometimes with "vile abuse" and at others, with sarcasm. Unlike the other sons-in-law, he makes it clear that he will never surrender to the Tulsis. Among his most effective defenses against them is his tacit evidence of his inner life, his retreat to his bed with his cigarettes, his Epictetus, and his Marcus Aurelius.

Naipaul, it is also evident, has never dealt seriously with figures of non–Indian origin. That stems from the fact that Naipaul has openly rejected the Caribbean islands, a fact that blatantly surfaced in his Nobel Prize lecture in 2001, when all that he acknowledged was his debt to "England, my home" and "India, home of my ancestors."

As in some of his other works including *A Way in the World,* Naipaul time and again seeks to reaffirm that there has been no proper documentation of the history of the Caribbean islands prior to the arrival of the European settlers; the British in particular with reference to Trinidad and Tobago. He reasons that this is because there has been no history worth the recording before Trinidad became a British colony. In fact he goes a step further to exclude such "simple society" from the discourse of history that, in his opinion, is the rational record of national achievement. For him, there is only the history of Europeans in Trinidad.

His explicit argument that nothing significant happens in "simple societies" so there is nothing to narrate and therefore there is no history buttresses his efforts to mark history as a uniquely Western preserve. Understandably then, Naipaul mounts his most sustained polemics on the interdependent issues of the "simple society," historical form and non-achievement in his Caribbean writings. As he points out:

> Port of Spain was a place where things had happened and nothing showed. Only people remained, and their past had dropped out of all the history books. History was a fairytale about Columbus and a fairytale about the strange customs of the aboriginal Caribs and the Arawaks; it was impossible now to set them in the landscape. History was the Trinidad five-cent stamp ... [Naipaul, 1969 rpt 1972, p. 375].

So while traces of the socio-cultural ambience in which Naipaul was born and brought find apt expression in the *Miguel Street, The Mystic Masseur* and *A House for Mr. Biswas*, there is no room for depicting the struggles, frailties and foibles of figures of non–Indian origin. And if by chance he does deal with figures of non–Indian origin, it is reflective of the parochial disposition of the *girmittiya* which results in a form of antagonism towards those of the native culture.

Consider, for instance, this scene at the Tulsi store:

> A fat Negro woman went to Shama's counter [this is before her marriage to Mr. Biswas] and asked for flesh-colored stockings, which were then enjoying some vogue in rural Trinidad.
>   Shama, still smiling, took down a box and held up a pair of black cotton stockings.
>   "Eh!" The woman's gasp could be heard throughout the shop. "You playing with me? How the hell all-you get so fresh and conceited?" She began to curse ... [Naipaul, 1961 rpt. 1992, 83–84].

So deep is the process of conditioning that Shama unwittingly presumes flesh-colored for a Black buyer would denote the color black. This reflects a truth about life on the color scale, about how the oppressed appropriate the behavior of the oppressor.

The Mimic Man

Such appropriation then paves the way for a sense of mimicry. As the imperial mission was designed to impose civilization — denoting reason and order — on a savage world, a concept of savagery and disorder denoting instinct and untapped energy came to be associated with the colonized. So the first task of these culturally constructed colonizing categories was to express "otherness," an affirmation of binary oppositions. In most cases, the "other" became a grotesque mirror of the self, a negation, an inversion, an antithesis, with the colonized essentially aping the colonizer. It is this "otherness," which produced — through a strategy of disavowal where the trace of what is disavowed is not repressed but repeated as something different — a form of mimicry.

This explains why in the turn from the high ideals of the colonial imagination to its low mimetic literary effects, mimicry emerges as one of the most elusive and effective strategies of colonial power and knowledge. It surfaces as the representation of a difference that is itself a process of disavowal. In Naipaul's works, mimicry comes into play both in Homi Bhabha's sense of it as empowerment arising out of a subversive ambivalence and Jacques Lacan's definition of it as camouflage.

For Bhabha, "Mimicry is ... the sign of a double articulation; a complex strategy of reform, regulation and discipline, which "appropriates" the Other as it visualizes power. The ambivalence at the source of traditional discourses on authority enables a form of subversion founded on that uncertainty that turns the discursive conditions of dominance into grounds of intervention." (Bhabha, 1994, p. 86). *A House for Mr. Biswas*, for instance, is a good example of the subversive force Bhabha attributes to mimicry. The novel is a comment on the dilemmas of colonial dispossession, the need for a "portion of the earth" to call one's own. Built on slavery and indentured labor, and governed by policies of racial division, it is the colonial administration that holds together this "manufactured society" with Tulsi at the helm, calling the shots. The chinks in this manufactured society surface in the form of her son-in-law, Mr. Biswas, hurling a stream of revolutionary ideas: economic independence; caste reform; self-help; and love-marriage against the traditional, static Tulsi values.

Lacan, on his part, asserts:

> Mimicry reveals something in so far as it is distinct from what might be called an *itself* that is behind. The effect of mimicry is camouflage in the strictly technical sense. It is not a question of harmonizing with the background but, against a mottled background, of being mottled — exactly like the technique of camouflage practiced in human warfare [Lacan, 1978, p. 99].

In other words, for Lacan, mimicry is like camouflage, not a harmonization or repression of difference, but a form of resemblance that differs from or defends presence by displaying it in part, metonymically. When Anand goes to England, he transforms the landscape by the sheer oddity of his existence in it. Either/or binaries are converted into situations of both/and, mingling opposites. His alien presence changes the aspect of the place even as he seeks to adapt to it. Rather than a confrontation of extremes, there is an eventual integration on both sides in terms of "being mottled against a mottled background."

Evidently, it is here that mimicry, as defined by Homi Bhabha, comes into play, just as the palpable hybrid nature of the novel is in accordance with Bhabha's definition of hybridity.

> A problematic of colonial representation and individuation that reverses the effects of the colonialist disavowal, so that other "denied" knowledges enter upon the dominant discourse and estrange the basis of its authority — its rules of recognition.... Hybridity intervenes in the exercise of authority not merely to indicate the impossibility of its identity but to represent the unpredictability of its presence.... The display of hybridity — its peculiar "replication" — terrorizes authority with the ruse of recognition, its mimicry, its mockery [Bhabha, 1985, pp. 156–157].

The "denied" knowledges may be considered as a pointer to the unpredictability and revolutionary ideas of Mr. Biswas while the "dominant discourse" connotes the one scripted by Mrs. Tulsi. Mr. Biswas manages to establish areas of independence though he can never completely break away from the household, and must submit to his wife and children remaining tied to the Tulsi ménage. In this struggle, an idea of a house of his own becomes an obsession, a symbol of independence that has always eluded him. Yet Biswas's struggle against the Tulsi values is never complete. He is always, despite himself, seduced into a resentful admiration of its vigor and warmth.

He remains tied to the Tulsi world because, despite his wishes, he remains a sideshoot of those values, aberrant but still rooted in the same stock. In a way, he is a representative figure of a generation caught between the security of the old world and the possibilities of the new, a man trapped in the transitional phase between two worlds. His predicament set against the East and West Indian reality provides for a powerful statement about the human condition.

Later in Woodbrook, Mr. Biswas's aspiration level increases and he begins taking pride in his suits and ties, which he, like the Creole society, accepts as symbols of Westernization, progress and respectability. He lures his children to Port of Spain by the exoticism of European-type food. Hampers, picnics and a seaside holiday are now part of his existence. Meanwhile, Shama devotes her attention to acquiring suits for her husband, dropping names, giving expensive gifts, and simply revels in her lone opportunity to converse with a white woman. The children too accept that the dropping of "Mai" for Mummy and "Bap" for Daddy is a sign of cultural advancement.

The breakup of the Tulsi family, too, is not presented in isolation. It is shown as part of the general and widespread changes in the island brought about by war. The American soldiers and their bases usher a new, fluid economic atmosphere to the islands and a social mobility independent of race, caste or family patronage. Ironically, this is the world Mr. Biswas has advocated; the independent, self-reliant idea he nourishes in his crowded room as he thumbs through his copies of Samuel Smiles and Marcus Aurelius, his talismans against the Tulsi world. The mental nourishment however doesn't bring with it material comforts that Indian farmers he visited on his journalistic assignments displayed.

> In daylight, in a Sentinel motorcar and with a Sentinel photographer, he drove through the open plane to call on Indian farmers to get material for his feature on *Prospects for This Year's Rice Crop.* They, illiterate, not knowing to what he would return that evening, treated him as an incredibly superior human being. And these same men who, like his brothers, had started on the estates and saved and bought land of their own, were building mansions; they were sending their sons to America and Canada to become doctors and dentists. There was money in the island.... And from this money, despite Marcus Aurelius and Epicetetus, despite Samuel Smiles, Mr. Biswas found himself barred [Naipaul, 1961. rpt. 1992, p. 438].

"Just a Man You Know"

Naipaul has invested the figure of Biswas with a symbolic force which transcends social and historical bounds. In several subtle strokes he moulds Biswas into a figure whose dreams embody those of all men struggling to carve an identity and to resist conformity to social habit and custom. The flip side of conventional masculinity brings out Mr. Biswas as an artist (his sign-painting, his abortive short stories), as religious reformer (his theological brushes with Hari), as social rebel (his brushes with authority in all forms) and, perhaps, preeminently, as jester whose comic pathos strikes a chord. In Biswas, Naipaul has succeeded in balancing his mild compassion for the East Indian people and his sense of the grotesque, farcical comedy of their condition. He has created a figure in which comic ineptitude is a badge of humanity, not a sign of cultural primitiveness.

Biswas's failings are presented as the failings of man in all times and places, his problems and dreams are common to all humanity. Thus Biswas can answer his son Anand's query "Who are you?" with the unconscious wisdom of the human clown in all ages: "I am just somebody. Nobody at all. I am just a man you know." (Naipaul, 1961. rpt. 1992, p. 279). And, like man, he recognizes his limitation is his strength and that within these limitations, his own creativity and imagination is a force which mirrors the creative force of God himself. Father and son, constructed from Naipaul's youthful "way of experiencing" evoke both an individual and a historical past.

Modeled on the author's own, Anand's reaction to his father — longing, attachment, fear, rage, reconciliation — are a foil for Mr. Biswas who wrests comedy from frustration and pain. Undernourished and mistreated in the household of his grandmother — often for his father's transgressions — Anand is depicted as gradually conceiving a private sense of self within the contradictions of his own extended family: their pride as prominent Hindus who observe religious rituals but do not practice values they profess, their petty tyrannies, their stinginess, their outright cruelties.

In the novel, as no doubt in reality, his father's alternating submission to and rebellion against that family, his skepticism, his rage and wit, however unsettling, provokes the boy to develop his own multifaceted way of perceiving the world around him. He may come from a tradition-bound family which professes a *girmit* ideology that naively expects its members to remain unscathed by their excursions into an alien environment. But that does not in the least affect him. Rather Anand's journey into the Creole world and then abroad, anticipating enrichment and economic gains, indirectly reflects the author's quest for an identity to his liking. He endures domestic strife and poverty, his father's illness and absences, frequent moves from Hanuman House, the home of his grandmother in Arwacas (the fictional Chaguanas) to Green Vale, to Port of Spain, from there to Shorthills and then back to the city. All these are fictional versions of experiences Naipaul has recalled in later autobiographical surveys.

Evidently it was the writing of *A House for Mr. Biswas*, his "most personal" book that "changed" Naipaul. In reconstructing his father's life through the Trinidadian Indian Mohun Biswas, Naipaul was also tracing the inception of his own process of self-creation. Marked out for misfortune from his birth by omen and circumstance, we begin to sense in him a figure unfortunate in his time and place. His childhood is a series of day dreams, punctuated by sores, illnesses and occasional brief moments of glory when his Brahmin status makes him desirable enough to conduct a ceremony or ritual. But these moments merely serve to underline the unreal nature of caste and custom in his East Indian society.

In various contexts Naipaul has disparaged the clan with its emphasis on caste, a system he denounces. Yet, looking back in his *Prologue to an Autobiography* he acknowledges it could have been a psychological advantage: "for all its physical wretchedness and internal tensions, the life of the clan had given us all a start. It had given us a class certainty, a high sense of self." (Naipaul, 1984, p. 57). That would also explain why Anand, like his creator, under the influence of his traditionalist Hindu upbringing, perceives the Caribbean isles as ignorant, superstitious and dumb.

Both Seepersad and V. S. Naipaul were deprived of a father's presence in early childhood. Both were dependent on the arbitrary benevolence of their extended family. In the novel, this similarity initiates an empathy that slowly develops between Mr. Biswas and Anand. During Mr. Biswas's visits to Arwacas when he is living apart from his family at Green Vale, a sugarcane estate owned by the Tulsis, Anand is generally shy with him, avoiding any physical contact. Yet on one occasion when he defends the boy who has been unjustly punished, Anand seems "unwilling to let him leave. He said nothing, he simply hung around the bicycle, occasionally rubbing up against it." (Naipaul, 1961 rpt. 1992, p. 236) Only the gesture discloses his need and gratitude for his father's protection.

In 1938, Seepersad Naipaul was taken on by the *Guardian* again, this time as a city reporter and Naipaul, along with his father, his mother and five siblings — their own little nucleus within his mother's extended family — moved to Port of Spain to the house owned by his grandmother. "That was when I was introduced to the life of the streets (and the mystery of the Negro carpenter in the servant room, making 'the thing without a name'). That was also when I got to know my father," declares Naipaul in *Finding the Centre* adding:

> I had lived before then (at least in my own memory) in my mother's family house in Chaguanas. I knew I had a father, but I also knew and accepted that — like the fathers of others, of my cousins — he was not present. There was a gift one year of a very small book of English poems; there was a gift another time of a toy set of carpenter's tools. But the man himself remained vague [Naipaul, 1994, p. 34].

Evidently his father's greatness lay in his ability to try, at all costs, to rise above his circumstances. *Girmitiya*, on the one hand, and mimic on the other — the two rather than being a contradiction of terms actually serve to complement each other. It is the *girmit* ideology that prompts Mr. Biswas as much as Naipaul's father to carve a niche in the hegemonic setup, emulating the Westerner's footsteps. And this, in turn, effectuates a subversion whereby the image of the "other" rather than that of the "being" is reflected in the mirror, causing a role-reversal between the Centre (colonizer) and the Margin (colonized). Thus, Biswas's fate defines the limit of possibility Naipaul sees in the West Indian situation, its positive and its negative extremities. After this, for him and for his characters there is nothing left but flight and denial.

As Biswas's life unfolds, we recognize that his dreams and weakness, his hopes and failures are an effective chart of the reach and limits of the human imagination. He does not revolt against established customs because of social and political beliefs, which is why he can no more accommodate the new values than the old. His revolt is against any value system that denies the intrinsic importance of man and the autonomous power of the individual to renew the experience of the race through the experience of his own life. The subversion of hegemonic masculinity, as it were, makes Mr. Biswas all the more endearing. What he stands for is the human right to fail in one's own unique way and because of this, although at the end of his life he dies in possession of only a caricature of his dream of responsibility and freedom, a house foisted on him by deception, the reader remains deeply aware of his heroism and the importance of his struggle and what it represents.

Notes

1. Girmit is an expression that best defines Hindu East Indians who felt a compulsion to lead a ghettoized existence on the Caribbean islands.
2. Mimic man is the "other" who, in course of aping the colonizer, effectuates an inadvertent subversion.
3. *Girmitiya* is a particular kind of migrant, who leaves home and takes up residence in someone else's home in a complex milieu. This milieu is characterized by certain forms of antagonism and a *modus vivendi* constituted between the contextual culture (the indigenous or native culture), the transplanted culture and the imposed colonial culture.

References

Bhabha, Homi (1994). "Of Mimicry and Man: The Ambivalence of Colonial Discourse," *The Location of Culture*. New York: Routledge.

Bhabha, Homi K. (1985). "Signs Taken for Wonders: Questions of Ambivalence and Authority Under a Tree Outside Delhi, May 1817," *Critical Inquiry* 12: 1 (Autumn).

Castles, Stephen, and Alastair Davidson (2003). *Citizenship and Migration: Globalisation and the Politics of Belonging* (London: Macmillan, 2000) p. 130. In Anjali Gera, "Strange Moves: Girmitya Turns Cosmopolitan." In Purabi Panwar (Ed.). *V. S. Naipaul: An Anthology of Recent Criticism*. Delhi: Pencraft International.

Gera, Anjali (2003). "Strange Moves: Girmitya Turns Cosmopolitan." In Purabi Panwar (Ed.). *V. S. Naipaul: An Anthology of Recent Criticism*. Delhi: Pencraft International.

Lacan, Jacques (1978). *The Four Fundamental Concepts of Psycho-analysis*. (Ed.) Jacques-Alain Miller, trans. Alan Sheridan. New York. Cited in Homi K. Bhabha, 1985. "Signs Taken for Wonders: Questions of Ambivalence and Authority Under a Tree Outside Delhi, May 1817," *Critical Inquiry* 12:1.

Mishra, Vijay (1992). "The Girmit Ideology Revisited: Fiji Indian Literature" in Emmanuel S. Nelson, *Reworlding the Literature of the Indian Diaspora*. New York: Greenwood Press.

Naipaul, V. S. 1961. rpt. (1992). *A House for Mr. Biswas*. New Delhi: Penguin Books India (P).

_____ (1984). "Prologue to an Autobiography," *Finding the Centre: Two Narratives*. London: Andre Deutsch.

_____ (1969). rpt. (1973). *The Loss of El Dorado*. Harmondsworth: Penguin Books.

_____ (1972). "East Indian." *The Overcrowded Barracoon and Other Articles*. London: Andre Deutsch.

Pointon, Sally (2003). "Tainting the Colonial: V. S. Naipaul." In Anjali Gera, "Strange Moves: Girmitya Turns Cosmopolitan," Purabi Panwar (Ed.). *V. S. Naipaul: An Anthology of Recent Criticism*. Delhi: Pencraft International.

Tejpal, Tarun J. "V. S. Naipaul's Way in the World" as it appeared in *Random Magazine* http://www.stanford.edu/~amitm/naipaul/tejpal.html. Accessed on July 10, 2001.

Gay Writing and the
Idea of Doubleness

AKHIL KATYAL

The Mourning

When the Kashmiri-American poet Agha Shahid Ali (b. 1949) died in Amherst, Massachusetts, in the winter of 2001, a distant friend of his organized a remembrance gathering on the 40th day after his death, the chehlom, the last day of mourning in the Islamic calendar.[1] Hoshang Merchant (b. 1947), lesser known as a poet than Ali but an abiding enthusiast of his verse, arranged this gathering in Hyderabad, a city where he has been teaching literature and writing poetry for years.[2] It was held at the Vidyanarayan School on January 14, 2002. "When she died," Hoshang said referring to Shahid, "I had a maha sabha ['a huge gathering'] here with my money" (personal interview with Merchant: July, 2010 [sic]). "I called it a 'Celebration of Shahid Ali's Life and Poetry' and invited Munna, the sister-in-law of Shahid's sister Sameetah who is my neighbor from down the street here, as the chief guest" (ibid.). "I served walnut cake in sherry, grape juice and Golconda wine as a nod towards Kashmir, towards the resurrection of Ali's spirit in heaven, and for his poetry" (ibid.).

Hoshang wrote a poem for the occasion called "Death of a Poet: 1.1.2002" as a gesture of remembrance and, I think, as a gesture which claimed a form of friendship with the deceased, as if to say that it were strong enough to personally organize a meeting of remembrance, to write a poem on the poet who had gone, and to effectively aver a posthumous closeness with him, a closeness that he had yearned for but never quite achieved when Shahid had been around. During the gathering Hoshang read Shahid's poem "The Country Without a Post-office," "sobbed rather than read it," he told me, along with his own requiem for Shahid. "There was not a dry eye in the audience," he said. This was the most intimate experience Hoshang had had with Shahid Ali, an intimacy that could not be disputed in Shahid's death, in the unavailability of his response.

Hoshang/Shahid, or, What Is Gay Writing?

Around five years before he died, in mid–1996, Agha Shahid Ali had refused to be a part of a collection of writings that Hoshang was putting together as an editor. It was ultimately to be published in the year 1999 as *Yaraana: Gay Writing from India*, with a strong marketing pitch of being "India's first gay anthology" (Merchant; 1999: x).[3] "I am humbled," Hoshang had written in the July of that year, "to have been entrusted with defining the historic moment for India's homosexuals through their literature, old and new, heroic or pedestrian, lovely and lovelorn or rough and ironic" (*ibid.* xxv).

Hoshang told me that it was not easy at all to put together that collection. Repeatedly he said that "'there were slim-pickings,' 'I picked up anyone and put them in,' 'I was a despo lesbo'" (personal interview). Shahid's refusal had "crushed" him (*ibid.*). He tried to persuade Shahid by continuing the correspondence between Amherst and New York City, where Shahid was based in the late 1990s, and Hyderabad, where he himself lived, but to no avail. The collection went into print without Shahid.

Hoshang remembers Shahid's refusal as a snub, a "perfidy," and "perfidies" he told me, campily, "are never forgiven even if they can be understood" (*ibid.*). The introduction to *Yaraana* carried Hoshang's final, hostile dart — "[t]he problem with India's gay literary elite is that most of them (here I'm talking of Indian writers in English) are still in the closet. Some do not want to be identified as gay..." (Merchant: *ibid.* xvi). "Were you referring to Shahid in particular when you wrote that?" I had asked him, to which he had replied with an unequivocal "yes" (personal interview). "I understood his reasons only later, earlier I thought he was just being mean.... I was just a confused fairy then" (*ibid.*).

This essay uses the moment of Shahid's refusal to Hoshang as an entry point to ask and answer some crucial questions about the concept of "gay writing." It sees "gay writing" as simultaneously an exceptionalist and an anti-exceptionalist project. This simultaeneity implies that even as "gay writing" (or "lesbian writing") is seen as a machine of expression for "certain" people and "certain" bodies, it is always necessarily something which also defies the certainty of these boundaries of who can authentically write it and what can be written as authentic "gay writing." This simultaneity, this constant double play, which replaces authenticity as my major frame of understanding, is worked out precisely by sieving out the various histories and dimensions of "gay writing." It was Hoshang's beautifully capricious persona, one that made doubleness impossible not to consider as fundamental to the project of "gay writing," that led to these theoretical insights.

Why Only Gay Folk Can Write Gay, or, the Exceptionalist Art of Gay Writing

In the year 1996 when Hoshang started asking around for contributions for his forthcoming collection, he told potential contributors that "I'm writing a gay anthology and you must come out as gay" (*ibid.*). With the scope of this demand, and the way it was framed, Shahid's refusal to be included was straightforwardly read as a refusal to "come out"; "[t]hat crazy pussy, she wasn't ready to come out ... he wanted to be the poet laureate of a Taliban state called "Azad Kashmir," Hoshang said, smiling, exaggeratedly, with a studied superficiality with Kashmir's history, but with the sense of being wronged intact.

In an interview Hoshang had given to the writer R. Raj Rao, he talked at length and with some sourness about Shahid's refusal. "Then there were living gays," he said, "bright, luminaries, who refused to state publicly in India that they were gay, while living deliciously gay lives in the West. As you can see, the first enemy is always within. Now that Aga Shahid Ali," he continued, "is dead, a person whose poetry I thought as if he were Shakespeare, I can briefly sketch for you the heart-breaking pleading correspondence I had with a totally evasive man — no," he says, thinking about several possible reasons for Shahid's refusal but finally zoning on his desired role as a "national poet" of a free Kashmir as decisive, "it was not the fear of losing an inheritance, nor a fear of an *outing*, not the fear of paining one's devout parents, nor incriminating one's friends.... No, it was something quite else.... Ali was already courting the Indian nation's displeasure once [vis-à-vis Kashmir]. And he did not want to do it twice over — also *as a gay*" (quoted in R. Raj Rao; 2009: 7, emphasis mine).[4]

"It was one of Shahid's contradictions," Shahid's lifelong close friend Saleem Kidwai told me, in a bookshop in central Lucknow, in a mellower tone, and with a sense of understanding that comes with years of friendship and love, "not giving us permission to publish anything in *Same Sex Love* while he was being published in a gay anthology in America" (personal interview with Saleem Kidwai: July, 2010). Saleem was a contemporary of Shahid in Delhi University in the late 60s and early 70s, where he studied History at St. Stephens College and Shahid studied and then taught English at Hindu College, across the road from Saleem.

Saleem, along with another of his Delhi University friend Ruth Vanita, was to be the editor of *Same-Sex Love in India: Readings from Literature and History* (2000) that was published a year after *Yaraana* and was much bigger in its scope and intention, a more enduring collection, it would seem, including material about same-sex desire from ancient and medieval India and from its Sanskritic and the Perso-Urdu traditions. For its last section on the "Modern Indian Materials," which included works of writers like Rajendra Yadav and Suryakant Tripathi Nirala, Vikram Seth and Hoshang Merchant, Saleem had corresponded with his old friend Shahid and asked for his poetry. But Shahid was being difficult, as only friends can be.

Saleem remembers asking him — "why have you not been answering my letters, why are you not giving me permission" (*ibid.*). Shahid had replied with how he "could not stand Hoshang" who had been "pestering him" and "wanted something, anything" for his volume (*ibid.*). "Are you equating me with Hoshang," Saleem had asked, "no no," Shahid had replied, Saleem remembers in his words, "I don't want to be outed in India, for the sake of my father…. Kashmir is another world … because it will hurt his image."

Shahid's father was Agha Ashraf Ali, in his 80s now, who was the Jammu and Kashmir Inspector of Schools, "a teacher of teachers" (Ashraf Ali, quoted in Lepaska) in his own words, in the 1950s and the Director of Education for all of Jammu and Kashmir by 1971. Taught when he was twenty by Dr. Zakir Hussain, the future president of independent India, influenced by the Kashmiri leader Sheikh Abdullah's politics when he was older and educated in England and seduced by the philosophy of Martin Buber, Ashraf Ali belonged to one of the more important political families in Kashmir with a wide net of influence in its education and bureaucracy. "It's still such a feudal system there," Shahid had once told his friend and writer Amitav Ghosh, talking about Kashmir where he had wanted to go to die in his last days of illness on the East Coast, "and there will be so much support — and my father is there too" (quoted in Ghosh; 2002: 15). It was this net that Shahid did not want to overtly disturb, the net held in place by the figure of his father and his friends, by writing in books about "same-sex love" or of "gay writing," things which his father's world did not realize in the same way, or in the same terms.

It was a step that looked like a "fear of a witch-hunt" to the acquaintance and fellow poet, Hoshang (1999: xvi), like an irreducible "contradiction" to the friend, Saleem (2010 *ibid.*) and like a wish for preserving one of his many worlds, to Shahid himself ("I don't want to…").[5] The step was undoubtedly based on the idea, a strong and not unusual assumption that is implicit in the very origin and the development of the genre of "gay writing," that to write for its anthologies is to evidently identify oneself as "gay," an assumption that Shahid reasonably shared with Hoshang, for all their differences. That to be included in such a collection is also to be marked. Hoshang's call to come write to his contributors was also, by his own admission, a call to come out. Saleem's *Same-Sex Love*, unattached as it was to any direct identifying marker unlike *Yaraana* which had "gay" on its cover, was a better bet in this respect. It included, in its "modern" section, the Bengali writer Bankim Chandra Chatterjee, the Urdu writer Ismat Chughtai and the Hindi writer Rajendra Yadav, writers who have been known to produce situations of same-sex desire in their stories, but not majorly in their biographies. But Shahid had desisted, it seems, even from the very proximity of association and the distinct possibility of that news reaching his father's Kashmiri circles. With Hoshang, the game had always been simpler, so the refusal had been blunter. "What qualifies one to write for a gay anthology," I had asked Hoshang, during the two day interview at his house in Hyderabad. His immediate answer was "you need to be a gay person writing about gay experiences" (personal interview: *ibid.*).

Who can write "lesbian writing" or "gay writing"? With whom lies the wherewithal of writing a "lesbian story"? Who cannot write a "gay poem"? These questions are necessarily as old as the categories themselves and have been answered, mostly, without much uncertainty. When we call a piece of writing a "lesbian story," what is the final clincher for us in making that call — is it the content and themes of that story, its form and language, the situations and relationships that come about within them, is it the sexuality as experienced by the specific body of the story writer, or some combination of these? Where does the buck finally stop in deciding whether a story qualifies or not as a "gay story"? What is the factor that matters in making this decision or that which matters the most? This essay would argue that this factor is necessarily a floating object.

It seems that "lesbian writing" (or "gay writing") has sourced itself so strongly from the particularized body of the writer that any other way of creating "lesbian writing" seemed for long conceptually quite impossible. Only certain people, only certain kinds of bodies could write that story. It was a one to one connection between the kind of writer and the kind of writing. "If you're straight," Hoshang told me, "and you write about gay experience, that is mere titillation," not quite writing in his scheme of things, or not yet (*ibid.*). "Your experience in London with women," he told me, "does not make you bisexual, it's mere titillation" (*ibid.*). "Lesbian writing" or "gay writing" is mostly conceived as copyrighted on to lesbian and gay bodies; it is their sole preserve, possible only within them. This copyright condition shares its moment of incipience with that form of writing itself.

In the late 1920s, when Radclyffe Hall (b. 1880) was thinking about writing *The Well of Loneliness* (pub. 1928), nowadays usually recalled as a "lesbian classic," she had gone to her life-long friend and lover Lady Una Troubridge to talk about what she was going to do, and what her fears and excitements were at that moment. Una had later recorded their conversation in her diary:

> ...It was after the success of Adam's Breed that John came to me one day with unusual gravity and asked for my decision in a serious matter: she had long wanted to write a book on sexual inversion, a novel that would be accessible to the general public who did not have access to technical treatises.... It was her absolute conviction

that such a book could only be written by a sexual invert, who alone could be qualified by personal knowledge and experience to speak on behalf of a misunderstood and misjudged minority [Troubridge, quoted in Knopp; 1992: 114, emphasis mine].

The exceptionalism of "lesbian writing," the idea that only some unique people can write it, has for long had a political valence. It was conceived as a project to be taken up, to compensate for all the writing that "others" have done for "us," all the representing that "they" have gone on doing, where "we" have been ridiculed, misjudged and caricatured. It was implicit that others had either a lack of will or certainly a lack of imagination to even comprehend the experience of living out as a "lesbian" and then to put it into a fuller sort of writing. "[P]ersonal knowledge and experience," Hall mentioned to Una, are the hallmarks that qualify one to write such stories. But, more importantly, we should ask, where is this "personal knowledge and experience" grafted? Is it easy for this knowledge and experience to be capable in different kinds of people? What is the place that holds this knowledge and experience and works it out? "[O]nly" the body of the "sexual invert" (*ibid.*). "Lesbian writing" is seen always as emerging from a signature body, a body that the late nineteenth century sexologists, with their extensive "technical treatises," had given their hearts and minds to popularize, to make it the fundamental way of seeing people. Hall's heroine in the novel, Stephen Gordon, literally discovered herself in one of those treatises, the works of the Austro-German sexologist and psychiatrist Richard von Krafft-Ebing (d. 1902).

Around the late 1990s, when Ashwini Sukhthankar, in her early twenties, was putting together the "first" collection of "lesbian writing from India" called *Facing the Mirror*, commissioned by the same publisher as *Yaraana* and published in the same year, she had to get some pieces translated into English from the regional Indian languages. She arranged for a specific team to do this job. "Some pieces were translated ... by other lesbian — and bisexual-identified women, of course: a translator has to be wholly faithful to her author's tongue, the nuance and the music of it, and we could not expect such fidelity from someone with a different erotic awareness" (Sukhthankar; 1999: xxi; emphasis mine). She who does not identify as "lesbian" or "bisexual" was seen as fundamentally incapable of the translator's fidelity, "of course."

Where does the confidence of Ashwini's "of course" emerge? What hedges in "lesbian" emotion, its nuance and music, and makes it untranslatable by others? What is the premise of this distrust, this fundamental lack of expectation and the skepticism for the translator of "a different erotic awareness"? The anthologizing of "lesbian writing" changes, to an extent, the very terms whereby the translators are chosen, now not wholly depending on their familiarity with the two languages involved, or here, even with the subject of eroticism, but another sort of familiarity, one that is routed through the translator's particular body, through a specific kind of "erotic awareness." The terms of inclusion for the translator are the terms of her body.

This is unsurprising. Sukhthankar, a student of comparative literature at Harvard, figures in a dense lineage of feminist, lesbian theorists, editors and writers who have begun their search for "lesbian writing" with the body of the writer, and come only later, to the shape, quality and the content of that writing. They have placed writing in the body; "[w]rite your self, Your body must be heard" (Cixous; 1976: 880). They have seen and struggled to establish an essential and implicit connection between the two, where the body furnishes or yields the writing, is inextricable from the content. "[W]riting," Sukhthankar asserts, in the line before she talks about the translation, "signifies the gritty imperfect media through which the body, with its yearning and its suffering, spoke out; the process though which our lives, put into the tangibility of words, could be made public" (Sukhthankar *ibid.*, emphasis mine). The first point of departure, for "lesbian writing," its original fountain-head is the very tangible body of the writer. Without it, Sukhthankar seems to say, the writing is not "wholly faithful," what Hoshang, in cruder terms, had called "titillation." Without it, it seems to be a lesser form of writing, pleasurable yes but not valid enough. Shahid had refused, it is probable, because, for any one to see his works in a "gay anthology," especially for his father's circles in Kashmir, would make them not only parse his writing, but more crucially, automatically parse his body itself, make decisions on its behalf, carry over the interpretations from their reading onto his body. That's what "gay writing" does to the body of the writer by locating it as its final source and inspiration, by making the body the source of all literary imagination and the final grail of all interpretation. The very act of writing it is an exercise in exceptionalism, it is saying something unique about your own body, about your own "erotic awareness."

Identity based struggles in the 1960s and 70s in Europe and the United States have revolved around the body and made it the exceptional factor in representation, and the main qualifier of who can do the critical task of representing at hand. The specific forms that have done this writing and showing, for women, blacks and lesbians and gay men, have always zoned in on the body — the portrait in photography, the talking-heads in documentaries and the personal narratives in writing. The feminist manifestos that came out in the 1970s and called loudly for launching the genre of "women's writing" in good earnest located women's bodies, in particular, as their unequivocal source and trigger. The bodies have to be mined for writing, so certain bodies become capable of that writing, and others implicitly do not. It was not framed mainly as a question of political imagination but instead as that of bodily experience — body as experiencing desire, body as experiencing assault. Not on what you think but instead on what you are, viscerally, bodily. In fact the body was seen as the basic marker of experience. French feminist activist and writer Helene Cixous' watershed essay "The Laugh of the Medusa" appeared bang in the centre of the 1970s in the journal *Signs* and asked the women "to write. An act which would not only 'realize' the decensored relation of woman to her sexuality, to her womanly being ... it will give her back her goods," she claimed, "her pleasures, her immense bodily territories which have been kept under seal" (Cixous: *ibid.*). All of Cixous's metaphors recruit the body as the wellspring of writing. To make "her shattering entry into history" the woman must lay bare, let her flesh speak true, write in the "white ink" of her "good mother's milk" (*ibid.* 880–1). The visceral metaphors condense into what seems like a common denominator of *ecriture feminine*: "a woman's body, with its thousand and one thresholds of ardor — once, by smashing yokes and censors, she lets it articulate the profusion of meanings that run through it..." (*ibid.* 885).

In the same decade as Cixous's essay, the major political conceit, the main strategy that dominated the 1970s Gay Liberation in Europe and the United States was something that depended on the complete visibility of the individual body: coming out. One of its major and first slogans directly choreographed the movement of this body: "Out of the closets! Onto the streets!" The name of the Italian gay liberation movement, Fuori, means Out; in its newspaper it declared: "What are we asking of you? To come out!" (Richmond and Noguera 1973: 154).... Carl Whitman's "Gay Manifesto," first published in the San Francisco Free Press at the end of 1969, begins its list of "imperatives of gay liberation" with "Free ourselves; come out everywhere" (1972: 341) (Dyer; 2003: 232). Hoshang Merchant was the inheritor of this atmosphere of the 1970s post–Stonewall America. During this decade he finished his masters at Occidental College in Los Angeles and then went on to study for his Ph.D. on Anais Nin at the University of Purdue in West Lafayette, Indiana. His days at Purdue were the early days of the post–Stonewall coming out form of politics, a form that was held to be urgent, very exciting and politically useful. Hoshang cites this moment usually in his introductions at panels, on book covers and in poetry meetings: "[h]e helped establish the Gay Liberation at Purdue." His book was the logical culmination of this form of politics that he had soaked up in his years in the States and Europe, a form of politics that sees "gay writing" as the business only of "gay bodies" who automatically come out when they publish in "gay anthologies." During our conversations over two days about "gay writing," the only book that Hoshang ever picked up to quote to me, out of the clumsy pile of books in his living room, was the one edited by David Bergman. It was called "The Violet Quill Reader: The Emergence of Gay Writing After Stonewall" (pub. 1994).

Why Only Gay People Don't Write Gay: The Anti-Exceptionalist Art of Gay Writing

My conversation with Hoshang lasted over three days. It took place mainly in his living room at his seventh floor one BHK in an apartment building called "Garden Towers" in the Masab Tank area in Hyderabad. The living room itself was quite open and spare, with a settee, a sitting space put together with a dari and some pillows, and shelves and piles of books in two corners. The house was airy and had signs of being lived in for long. Whereas I mostly sat on the carpet or on the small moda (cane stool) in the living room, Hoshang (never in one place) alternated between being sprawled on the settee in his thin lungi, or running in and out of the small kitchen to get me something to eat, while he loudly insisted that I eat something or at least have apple or orange juice every two hours, or sometimes getting me different kinds of Hoshang memorabilia — snippets from his six decade life in three continents — from his bedroom which I could see from where I sat. All the doors of the living room, including the one which opened on to the shared floor area outside and the one on to the balcony were in the permanent state of openness, so we could hear the sounds of the neighbors when they got out, or even see them, and the sounds of city pouring in from the seventh floor living room balcony from where you could see, Hoshang pointed them out, the Char Minar ("Mosque of the Four Minarets," built 1591) and the Mecca Masjid and from the bedroom balcony, the staccato heights of the medieval Golconda Fort itself.

When we were not in his house, he was showing me the city, like its patron saint, taking me to the Friday night dargah (Sufi shrine) music gatherings, introducing me to the head priest of the dargah who was also an antique collector, in a high-kitsch living room with more than ten chandeliers, meeting my friends from the HCU where he taught, feeding me at different old city restaurants, refusing to let me pay, and taking an auto ride around the fort while it rained heavily. All this while, the conversation was on, about him, about Shahid, about his and my sex life and about Hyderabad. In the titular poem in his collection "Hotel Golkonda," Hoshang writes "I was reprimanded always for talking too much" (Merchant; 1992). Hoshang was a friend, a flirt and a grandfather, seamlessly, and I could see that he enjoyed the former roles, performed them to an excess, brashly, in high camp with its staple, unpredictable moments of searing honesty, but sometimes, not infrequently, resigned to the hexagenarian sobriety of the latter. These changes of attitudes, that were implicit in the length of our conversations and in his persona, also inflected his idea of "gay writing" and diversified the scope of the category of the "gay writer" and of the very act of anthologizing.

One of the first stories to become progressively more layered was the story of how the anthology was put together. Hoshang knew that there was a wide assortment of potential contributors for his volume if he only threw his net wide enough. This meant having a very flexible working idea of what goes into a "gay anthology" rather than the more stingy gay-writer-writing-about-gay-experiences formula that Hoshang had advanced to me more than once.

When Hoshang had gotten in touch with the Urdu/Punjabi writer Gyansingh Shatir (b. 1935) he changed his call, altered it considerably to not put him off. "I did not tell them gay-shay," Hoshang said with a distinct sense of cunning, "I told them dosti ['friendship'], uske baare mein hai ['it is about that']" and then "once they gave their consent, phir usko chakka banaya ['then I made him a eunuch'] [claps his hands]" (personal interview *ibid.*). Shatir's six-page story "Never take candy from a stranger!" had little to do, if at all, with friendship. It is written in the autobiographical mode and is about the pleasurable experiences of a fair young boy in a Punjab village whose beauty, classically enough, is his boon and his bane, leading to a brutal climactic episode of assault by an older man. The story spins around on the saying in Shatir's village: "God must not bless anyone with fair colour/It is like inviting the enmity of the whole town." (Shatir; 1999: 152) and ends with a numbed protagonist who is unable to take gifts from "anybody," even his "dear friends" (*ibid.* 157).

Hoshang knew he was playing with categories when he was editing this collection, enjoying outwitting the shatirs in the business (Urdu "shatir" literally means "chess-player" but generally implies "the cunning one") who would fall for one kind of frame, one kind of call for contributions but not for another. Different writers for this one "gay anthology" posed different exigent situations. The premise of the call sent to Shahid underwent a transformation by the time it was extended to Shatir, from being based heavily on the sexual identity of the writer, on experience ratified by his body, it came to be based mainly on the content of "friendship" that the writer writes about. The label "gay" itself metamorphosed into its more flippant version in Hoshang's head —*gay-shay*, using a common Hindi linguistic maneuver whereby words are informalized, made casual by being accompanied by their assonants (*chai-shai, plan-shlan*). Anthologizing the collection was an exercise in such fundamental revisions of what it meant to write "gay" and what it meant to use or discard this cachet of the "gay writer."

Even the iconic manifestoes of identity-based writing are not immune to such basic revisions of what it means to be "woman," "gay," "dalit" or "black." Helene Cixous, who had found all writing by women as rooted in their bodies ("[w]omen must write through their bodies"), lets her essay surprise the readers by betraying this logic quite often enough for it to be considered a consistent parallel track in the work (Cixous; ibid: 886). This happens when she first faces the problem as to "[w]hich works, then, might be called feminine" head on (878). Whereas she defers the question, as to "what is pervasively feminine" in these texts, a question that she picks up later but only skittishly, she see an immense poverty of real "feminine" writing in her home country France. "[T]he only inscriptions of femininity that I have seen," she says, "are by Colette, Marguerite Duras [the ellipsis is Cixous's] ... and Jean Genet" (879).[6] There is literally an odd-man-out in Cixous' list, a man who is incapable of living out of a woman's body but is nevertheless capable of making a "feminine" text.

How is this possible? This is the precise doubleness of "women's writing" that is shot through Cixous's essay and that expands its catchment area of writers to beyond those who are female bodied. Here Cixous sees femininity, not as residing in one's body, but instead in one's politics. This is a major revision of criterion of who gets into the fold. A "feminine" text is not a text written by women. In fact Cixous "deducts" from her list that "species of female writers" which is an "immense majority" and "whose workmanship is in no way different from male writing" (878). "Feminine" or "masculine" here are not a thing of the body, they are placeholders for political viewpoints. The "feminine" text is a text that "cannot fail to be more than subversive," it is an essay that sees "more closely the inanity of [all] 'propriety'" and it is in the hands of those writers, female or male or otherwise, "who would go to any lengths to slip something at odds with tradition" (888, 879). The "masculine" text, on the other hand, is tradition-bound and status-quoesque.

In this scheme of things, the "feminine" text skirts the route of the writer's body and finally comes to sit in the writer's worldview. The condition of women's writing, being "from and toward women," offered by Cixous herself, is kept at bay to elaborate another simultaneous ways of seeing and scripting "women's writing" (881). When Cixous tries to persuade her readers that the mythical "dark continent" of "womanhood" is actually not that dark or impervious at all, she tells them of a short Dantesque trip she took — "...the continent is not impenetrably dark. I've been there often. I was overjoyed one day to run into Jean Genet. It was in Pompes funèbres. He had come there led by his Jean. There are some men (all too few) who aren't afraid of femininity" (885).

When, in December, 1998 in Bombay, Ashwini Sukhthankar started taking stock of all the contributions that she had received for her collection on "lesbian writing in India," she paused before she went ahead and made the political choice of clubbing them all together as "lesbian writing." This moment of pause became the introduction to her edited collection published later next year by Penguin India. "We are all lesbians," Ashwini claimed for each of her contributors, "...but what that means is not necessarily obvious" (1999: xxvii).

Here the word slipped out of her editorial control, and out of her political strategy, and became specific for each instance of contribution to the book. "[F]or some," she relented, "it signifies purely the erotic," for some "lesbianism is in part a deliberate stance adopted in opposition to patriarchy," for some it "indicates a totality of women-centered lives, which we lead for and with each other," for some, "lesbian" is taken up and dropped casually, some grow into and some out of it, whereas some "just want to be" it, rather than "attend conferences about it" (xxvii–xxix). Some refused to identify themselves as "lesbian" preferring home-grown labels like "samyonik" (Sanskrit "sam" is "union," "yoni" is "vagina") or saheli ("female friend"). Others had no truck with the term at all.

This had become amply clear to Hoshang when he had set about finding a "gay poem" (single quotations in original) in the oeuvre of the Allahabad Urdu poet Firaq Gorakhpuri (1896–1982) (Merhcant: 208). Gorakhpuri, which was the poetic alias of Raghupati Sahay, was a prominent Urdu poet and a teacher of Romantic poetry at the Department of English at the Allahabad University. He was reportedly the Prime-Minister-to-be Jawaharlal Nehru's teacher during his university education in Allahabad. In the late eighties when the anthropologist Lawrence Cohen spent some of his time in Varanasi and stayed in hostel rooms at the Banaras Hindu University, he got into several discussions about the then recently deceased Firaq with the M.A. students there. "Firaq," he noted, "was a complex figure of libertinage who, in these conversations, sometimes called to mind sexual license with women even while standing as the classic figure of the exultant and unrepentant lover of young men" (2002: 151).

On April 15th, 1949, in writing a letter to his life-long friend and inconsistent beloved Saghar Nizami (1905–1983), the Urdu poet Josh Malihabadi (1896–1982), who self-avowedly fell in love 18 times, twice with men, declared that he had "written a thousand times that I am dying to see you.... Serious matters over, let's indulge in some vulgarity" (quoted in Kidwai; 2000: 279). He begins by wondering whether a female prostitute who would mount a man would be called a *gandu* (bugger), then refers to a Rampur poet Aslam Khan who "has a young poet staying with him. He has sent me an article in his praise for publication. The poor dove takes pains so that the crow gets to eat the eggs!" (*ibid.*). It is in the middle of this playful mood, right after the reference to Khan's plan to get into the young poet's bed, that Josh refers to his friend Firaq Gorakhpuri of Allahabad—"Firaqwa is having a great time these days, and me, I'm starving" (*ibid.*). He follows that quickly with "I thought of you last night and an earthquake erupted in the crotch of my trousers" (*ibid.*).

In introducing Sahay, Merchant was building on this legend of Firaq and wrote that "it was an open secret that Firaq was a homosexual" (*ibid.*). He added though "[i]t was also a well-known fact that he never wrote a gay line" (*ibid.*). Here again, the fundamental criteria of what is "gay writing" and who can write it perform some acrobatics. A "gay line" does not automatically flow out of "a homosexual." All the "personal knowledge and experience" (Radclyffe Hall's words) that comes with "being a homosexual" cannot be simply read back from the writings. Here, whereas Hoshang sees "homosexual" to be a bodily condition, he does not see a "gay line" as implicit in this condition, the latter comes, rather, with adopting a particular political viewpoint which Firaq never shared with Hoshang — that of sexual identity and coming-out.

Notes

1. Agha Shahid Ali (1949–2001) was a Kashmiri-American poet and taught in several creative writing departments across the United States. Ali was awarded Guggenheim and Ingram-Merril Fellowships and a Pushcart Prize, and his collection *Rooms Are Never Finished* was a finalist for the National Book Award in 2001. The collected poems of Shahid Ali have appeared as *The Veiled Suite* brought out by Norton in 2009.

2. Hoshang Merchant (b. 1947) is a poet and a professor of English based in Hyderabad in Andhra Pradesh, India. He has written more than thirteen books of poetry, most of them published with Writers Workshop in Calcutta. He is the editor of *Yaraana: Gay Writing from India* (Penguin Books: 1999).

3. *Yaraana* is the Urdu and Hindi word for friendship in general, and male friendship in particular. The *yaar* is the male friend.

4. In his obituary for his friend Shahid Ali, the author Amitav Ghosh retells an episode when he talked about his possible role as a national poet for Kashmir: "I once remarked to Shahid," he writes, "that he was the closest that Kashmir had to a national poet. He shot back: 'A national poet, maybe. But not a nationalist poet; please not that.' If anything, Kashmir's current plight," Ghosh continued, "represented for him the failure of the emancipatory promise of nationhood and the extinction of the pluralistic ideal that had been so dear to intellectuals of his [Shahid's] father's generation" (Ghosh; 2002: 14).

5. In the teeth of Shahid's continuing refusal to be in his volume, Hoshang had sent him a long letter that listed, he told me, "eight possible reasons according to me why the queen refused to be in my book" (personal interview, 2010). These reasons, some more serious than others, included, Hoshang recalls, "security of job, the sanctity of his father's circles, his inheritance, his fame as a poet, his wanting to remain a mainstream American poet and not a marginalized one, a future marriage, his image in Kashmir etc." (*ibid.*) Shahid wrote back a letter saying, Hoshang recounts, "it's none of these, I'll tell you when I'm in Hyderabad.... He never came, he was mad, such illusions of grandeur but I have known in my time Palestinian queens in Germany who wouldn't say it because they would lose their scholarship" (*ibid.*).

6. Jean Genet (1910–86) was a major French novelist, playwright, poet, film-maker and political activist. His major works include the novels *Querelle of Brest*, *The Thief's Journal*, and *Our Lady of the Flowers*, and the plays *The Balcony*, *The Blacks*, *The Maids* and *The Screens*.

Bibliography

Cixous, Helene (Summer 1976). "The Laugh of the Medusa." In *Signs*, trans. Keith Cohen and Paula Cohen, Vol. 1, No. 4, pp. 875–893.

Cohen, Lawrence (2002). "What Mrs. Besahara Saw: Reflections on the Gay Goonda." In Ruth Vanita (Ed.) *Queering India: Same-Sex Love and Eroticism in Indian Culture and Society*. New York and London: Routledge, pg. 149–160.

Lepeska, David (2010). "The Life and Times of Agha Ashraf Ali." In *Kashmir Observer*, http://www.kashmirobserver.net/index.php?option=com_content&view=article&id=2201&josc clean=1&comment_id=4341&Itemid=44, accessed 5th January, 2011.

Merchant, Hoshang (1999). "Introduction." In self ed. *Yaraana: Gay Writing from India*, Delhi: Penguin Books India, pg. xi–xxv.

_____ (2006). "Agha Shahid Ali's Kashmir and the Gay Nation." In Brinda Bose and Subhabrata Bhattacharya (Ed.) *The Phobic and the Erotic: The Politics of Sexualities in Contemporary India*: Calcutta: Seagull Books, pg. 465–70.

_____ (1992). *Hotel Golkonda*. Calcutta: Writers Workshop.

_____ (2009). "Hoshang Merchant." Interview with R. Raj Rao in Raj R. Rao and Dibyajyoti Sarma (Ed.). *Whistling in the Dark: Twenty-One Queer Interviews*," New Delhi: Sage, pp. 1–18.

Shatir, Gyansingh (1999). "Never Take Candy from a Stranger." Trans. from Urdu by the author and Hoshang merchant, in "Hoshang Merchant" (Ed.) *Yaraana: Gay Writing from India*. Delhi: Penguin Books India, pp. 152–57.

Sukhthankar, Ashiwini (1999). "Introduction" in self ed. *Facing the Mirror: Lesbian Writing from India*. Delhi: Penguin Books India, pg. xiii–xli.

Knopp, Sherron (1992). "If I Saw You Would You Kiss Me?": Sapphism and the Subversiveness of Virginia Woolf's Orlando." In Joseph Bristow (Ed.), *Sexual Sameness: Textual Differences in Lesbian and Gay Writing*. London: Routledge, pp. 111–127.

PERSONALLY CONDUCTED INTERVIEWS

Merchant, Hoshang. July, 2010, Hyderabad.

Negotiations of Masculinity in Ritwik Ghatak's Partition Trilogy

Tanmayee Banerjee

The patriarchal paradigm suffered a restructuring in the immigrant families which migrated to West Bengal (India) from East Pakistan (now Bangladesh) after the 1947 partition of Bengal following the independence of India. "In the post-partition turmoil, daughters started to be gradually looked upon as sons — this was a new phenomenon.... This dependence on daughters was a shift from the traditional patriarchal mindset." (Chakravarty, 2005: 92) This new phenomenon of the immigrant women being entrusted the responsibilities of men in the new circumstances was a significant socio-cultural change that took place in the refugee community. The female members took over the central role in the families as bread-earners. "They became the shock-absorber, sheltering the younger siblings from the harsh realities of life. As a result, they often decided not to marry and have a family of their own." (Chaudhuri, 2009: 26) The obvious corollary to this particular phenomenon was the re-positioning of the male members in the family — from the center to the orbit; from the position of the controller to the position of being controlled; from the role of the protector to the vulnerable state of requiring protection. This dichotomy of emancipation/exploitation in the lives of the first-generation *Bangal* women has proved to be a favorite subject of investigation amongst scholars. On the other hand, what remains largely unexplored

is the extent to which migrant men (successfully or unsuccessfully) renegotiate the hegemonic masculine identifications, practices and sensibilities embedded in their "old" gender relations; and further, if their pre-migration masculine identifications and practices change, remain unchanged, or are strengthened. In short, there is very little evidence to indicate what happens to their sense of hegemonic masculinity and whether it is eroded or fortified by their active engagement in migration and resettlement [Donaldson, 2009: 210].

The ambiguous position of men in the immigrant families has remained largely unappreciated so far. And this is what is going to be the primary subject of investigation in this essay.

Through the course of the present discussion, I shall reflect on Ritwik Ghatak's trilogy, *Meghe Dhaka Tara* (*The Cloud-Capped Star*), *Komal Gandhar* (*E-Flat*) and *Subarnarekha*,[1] which addresses the dynamics of partition. The films show, through form and content, how gender equations get problematized in the post-partition immigrant families. Through an analytical discussion of these films I will show the widening chasm between the sense of hegemonic masculinity and the real achievements of the male members of the immigrant families, and its consequences. According to Howson, "hegemonic masculinity expresses contextually what men 'should' do and what men 'should' be, but it is not necessarily what men 'really' do or what men 'really' are" (Donaldson, 2009: 23). And it is this gap between expected roles and that actually achieved in reality, that puts hegemonic masculinity in crisis — wider the gap, the more acute the crisis. In the context of the films under investigation, we find that the male members of the immigrant families have to negotiate with the gender roles they are expected to play within the post-partition unsettled order of the society — in the first film through financial dependence of the male members on the sole earning female member of the family; in the second film through men's dependence on the women for emotional and practical support; and in the third film through reduction of men to the state of utter helplessness and their absolute failure to provide, protect and preserve.

But before delving into the main discussion, I shall make a brief account of the partition for the readers to get a better grasp of the situation in which the concerned narratives are placed. The independence of India from British colonial rule in 1947 was synchronous with the ripping apart of British India into two nations — India and Pakistan. Religion being the primary rationale behind the partition, the new nation of Pakistan was created for the Muslim population of British India. But the uneven distribution of Muslim population in colonial India resulted in an uneven partition. Bengal and Punjab were the largest provinces in British India in which Muslims were a majority. Thus the newly formed Muslim nation of Pakistan had two territories — West Pakistan (formed out of the province of Punjab) and East Pakistan (formed out of the province of Bengal). These political territories of Pakistan were separated from each other by more than a thousand miles of the huge landmass of India in between them. Following this partition took place the migration of more than twelve million people — the Muslims resident in India moved to Pakistan and the Hindus already settled in the newly formed Pakistan migrated to India. Bengal and Punjab being the major provinces, which shared borders with

East and West Pakistan respectively, the migration took place largely to and from these two locations. However, "[t]he exodus of the Hindus from East to West Bengal was massive. By contrast, the numbers of Muslims who left West Bengal for eastern Pakistan after partition were relatively small." (Chatterji, 2007: 3) Ripped apart from the province of Bengal, East Pakistan was also referred to as East Bengal, while the part of Bengal which remained within Indian political territory was (and is still) referred to as West Bengal. Eventually, East Pakistan/East Bengal severed its ties from Pakistan after its victory in the *Muktijuddho* (Bangladesh Liberation War) of 1971 and it presently exists as Bangladesh, an independent nation state. In this essay I will refer to this pre–Bangladesh Pakistan-held-territory as East Bengal and the immigrants as *Bangals* (the term was then used synonymously with the term "refugee"), as they have been popularly referred to by *Bangalees* since the wake of partition till date. In the present discussion I will focus specifically on the effect of partition and migration on the *Bangal* families who immigrated to West Bengal.

So far as the migrants are concerned, the partition changed the attitude towards life significantly. uprooted and dislocated from their native land and in many cases their properties confiscated in the frenzy of the situation, these dislocated and dispossessed people had no other choice but to seek shelter in a different place and in a different environment as refugees. To make space for oneself amongst the unknown others is always frustrating, and thus began their struggle for existence. The socio-cultural paradigm suffered significant restructuring in the *Bangal*/refugee community which engendered a new discourse, that of partition and its aftermath. Amongst the intellectuals in West Bengal during the post-independence phase, who contributed significantly to this discourse of partition, the name of Ritiwik Kumar Ghatak (1925–1976) is of paramount importance. Though Ritwik left an indelible impression in the history of Indian theatre, his contribution to the world of cinema outweighs his every other artistic endeavor; so much so, that it will not be an exaggeration to say that he founded a new school of Indian cinema. Ritwik was a victim of the partition himself, which was "etched deeply into his emotions" according to Ashish Rajadhyaksha. He considers Ritwik's preoccupation with the issue of partition an "obsession expressed repeatedly in his films." (Rajadhyaksha, 1982: 13) The angst of the *Bangals* struggling for the basic necessities of life; their suffering from a continual identity crisis and their efforts of re-appropriating their identity within the immediate circumstances; and the re-evaluating and modifying of their socio-cultural values — all these appear as the major problematic in Ritwik's cinema — particularly in his partition trilogy. As mentioned above, I will make an analytical study of the trilogy from the perspective of the negotiations of masculinity in crisis in the *Bangal*/refugee families.

"Masculinities are challenged, problematic, variable, changing, shifting, fluid, fractured, contextualized, contested, complicated, plural, different, diverse, heterogeneous, self-constructing and always emerging." (Donaldson, 2009: 215) Donaldson and Howson rightly observe that men who migrate from their native place do not cast off their sense of manliness as they settle in their new homeland. The immigrant men have to "renegotiate their gender identity," according to Bob Pease, "as they relate their own cultural understanding of masculinity to the meanings and practices in the dominant culture." (Donaldson, 2009: 79) However varied or contextualized the notion of masculinity might be, or in whichever way they negotiate with the dominant culture, the key role that men are expected to play in the family are that of breadwinners or providers. Donaldson and Howson state that these are the two invariable gender roles which give them "their sense of self and masculinity regardless of nationality, education, family background and experience." (Donaldson, 2009: 212) In *Meghe Dhaka Tara*, the first film of Ritwik's partition trilogy, the sense of hegemonic masculinity is in severe crisis, leading to the major crisis in the plot.

Meghe Dhaka Tara (1960), based on Shaktipada Rajguru's novel *Chenamukh* (The Familiar Face) is "Ghatak's most crucial film" according to Rajadhyaksha. (Rajadhyaksha, 1982: 51) It is primarily the story of a struggling refugee girl, Neeta, who happens to be the tragic "hero" of the film. I prefer to present Neeta as the hero as she appears as the "warrior," "defender," and "protector" in the narrative — the roles that are ascribed to a hero on the basis of the etymology of the word itself. "Heroine" is someone who happens to be the principal female character and the character of Neeta (played by Supriya Chowdhury) is much more than that. The position of male characters in a narrative dominated by a non-male hero becomes ambivalent. "Supriya Choudhuri as Nita in Ritwik's masterpiece *Meghey Dhaka Tara* has clinched, for millions of viewers all over the world, both a mythical presence and the realistic portrayal of a struggling girl from a refugee family in post–Independence Bengal." (Bagchi, 1990: 47)

As we are discussing the crisis and the subsequent negotiation of masculinity, I decide not to delve into the character of Neeta except where necessary for reference. Apparently the masculinity of the male characters seems to be overshadowed by the looming presence of Neeta throughout the film. The primary male characters in the film are Neeta's elder brother Shankar (played by Anil Chatterjee), her father (played by Bijon Bhattacharya) and her fiancé Sanat (played by Niranjan Roy). Shankar, a struggling Indian Classical vocalist fails in his duties towards the family, the duties that are automatically incumbent upon the eldest son of the family after the father. By taking up the responsibility of supporting her family financially, Neeta stunts the masculinity of Shankar. Shankar's masculinity lies in his indomitable spirit and overarching ambition to become a famous singer. It is not that he wants to shirk from his responsibilities, but for him there arises no question of compromising his prospect of an artistic career with his immediate circumstances of life. He is an aspiring artist. His talent of music is unquestionable and so are the difficulties owing to his impoverished background which are posing natural hurdles for him to overcome and establish himself as a professional singer. We find him saying to Neeta: "Do whatever you want to do and never lend your ear to what people say about it. This should be the motto of life." Whether or not aware of it himself, his failure to earn and provide for the family brings dishonor to his position as a senior male member of the family. His position in the family exacerbated all the more when his younger brother also manages to find a job for himself and starts treating him with disrespect.

Shankar's scratching of his bristly bearded cheeks every now and then creates an extremely perspicacious cinematic effect. His failure to play the conventional gender role in his family hurts his masculinity in the same way as his unshaved beard. Apart from his parents he is also offended by Banshi, the local grocer (played by Jnanesh Mukherjee) who refuses to sell him a razor on credit. The grocer abuses his family for exploiting Neeta for selfish interests and vilifies him for being one of them. The actual premise of allegation is not actually against Shankar's incapacity to earn, but his financial dependence on his younger sister. The fact which raises the basic point of contention is that he depends on the earnings of his younger sister for every single necessity of his life; whereas it was his duty as the elder brother to protect and provide for her. It initially appears that Shankar is so overwhelmingly engrossed in his music and his dream of becoming a great musician that he is quite insouciant about the affairs of the family and apathetic to the struggle of Neeta who is trying her best to keep the family together. But in a dialogue with Neeta his sense of guilt and helplessness gets revealed.

> SHANKAR: Your whole future, your marriage is at stake. People are turning really nasty.
> NEETA: Does it hurt your manhood?
> SHANKAR: Don't talk like an idiot.
> NEETA: Don't you have an ego?
> SHANKAR: No. I have something much bigger than ego, my devotion to music. I am exploiting you at the moment, and deep down in my heart it really hurts me.

It will not be wrong to say that Shankar's entity of an artist subsumes his masculine entity. According to him, an artist has a unique purpose of life and therefore the gender roles which are expected of a man have nothing to do with an artist. He endures the caustic remarks of his parents for not even try-ing to find a job and contribute to the family. This reminds of Donna Peberdy's reference to Roma, a character in the film *Glengarry Glen Ross* (1992), who claims, "'Man' is a threat to undermine and incite." (Peberdy, 2011: 3) This is confirmed and reconfirmed by the continuous charges that are brought against Shankar by his family and the society. "No young man of your age sits at home like you. They take up any job they can find, as vendors, salesmen or whatever"— to this remark of his mother, he points out categorically that he is an "artist." Being an "artist" is to transcend the defined notions of being a "man."

Gradually, as the narrative unfolds, Shankar's situation changes for the better. He returns home after a long absence. Shankar's going away from home for a long period and then returning as a successful singer conforms, in a way, to Horrocks' claim that "[t]he male has to distance himself from female-ness and femininity, in order to prove that he is a male." (Horrocks, 1994: 33) Shankar distances himself from the all-encompassing shelter of Neeta and sets out to try his fortune on his own. Finally, he returns as a self-sufficient man — a celebrated singer and famous enough for the newspapers to cover his story — casually dressed as ever, carrying just a small bag, which helps us to understand that now he owns whatever little possession he has. Banshi, the grocer, who had once abused him of his dependence on Neeta is found to welcome him enthusiastically. The neighbors flock towards him for his auto-graph and the local physician gets off his bicycle to congratulate him on his success. The dialogue between Shankar and the doctor is noteworthy:

> DOCTOR: "Shankar, we listened to your music on the national programme. You are the pride of Bengal. Let them see that Bengal produces tigers too. Is it true that you charge 500 rupees for a concert?"
> SHANKAR: "Not really. I do not agree with anything less than 1200 rupees."

It is his ego that finally gets a scope to retort to the earlier reproach of Banshi by explicitly stating his standard remuneration for concerts.

Shankar's journey as a musician, from the early days of preparation to his achieving name and fame as a classical vocalist, has been perfectly traced with the help of music. When he sings the line "dukha daridra dur kijiye, sukh devo sab ko" (cast away the misery and deprivation and bestow happiness upon all) in a slow tempo from the bandish[2] *Karim naam tero* of raga Miya ki Malhar, his plight and desperation find expression through the gravity in the melody of the raga. Shankar, supporting his head on the tanpura and singing with closed eyes, creates an outlet for his agony in the form of his music. In one of the scenes where Shankar is seen practicing by the stream, he sings raga Hamsadhwani in the medium tempo. This marks the way towards, and suggests the preparation for, the final section of a *khayal*[3]–when a bandish is sung in fast tempo, thereby bringing the demonstration of a particular raga to completion. Ritwik uses this last phase when Shankar returns home as an accomplished singer. The joyous mood of Hamsadhwani is used to express the jubilance of success in Shankar. The over-enthusiastic reception by the neighbors elates him all the more and thus, he continues singing the raga in an even faster tempo to round it off.

Sanat, who happened to be a student of Neeta's father previously, is a frustrated young man who is in two minds regarding his future plans. He is a scholar who seems to be unable to decide whether to pursue higher studies or sacrifice his scholarly ingenuity for the sake of a permanent job and a secured future. Sanat and Neeta seem to share a fondness for each other in the beginning. The first time when the director brings them together in a scene, Sanat asks Neeta for some money he would need for academic purposes. On Neeta's helplessness he curses himself: "I have to ask you for everything. It makes me feel so incapacitated." This anguish of failure to support himself and play the role of the "provider" is the root of his angst. While Sanat apprehends a surmounting economic crisis which might befall him if he decides to pursue higher education, Neeta assures all support and cooperation from her side. Her inability to sever her practical ties with the family as the only earning member and settle for a certain future by marrying Sanat was gradually creating an irreconcilable hiatus between them. A happy carefree married life seemed far off, if not impossible altogether. In this state of doldrums and incertitude, Sanat responds to the seductive invitation of Geeta, Neeta's younger sister. His male gaze is caught by the camera in a scene where he keeps staring at Geeta. Events follow in an unanticipated order and he settles on a secure job and a certain future rather than an academic accomplishment and a few years of financial stringency. As opposed to Shankar, who fails to provide for himself and his family, Sanat is not only an earning man, he earns more than enough to satisfy the material demands of his wife. But his masculinity is jeopardized by his failure to live up to the moral standards. He is portrayed as a spineless male who abuses the trust and encouragement of a woman to serve his selfish interests. "This boy has no principle"— this remark made by Shankar about Sanat is enough to explain his character in one line. Thus Shankar and Sanat represent the two failures which are instrumental in qualifying the masculinity in the men — economic and ethical.

Neeta's father meets with an accident and is too seriously wounded to go out to work. The root of his angst too is his failure to provide for his family. He is consumed by the guilt that he fails to fulfill the desires of his children for lack of means. Thus, whatever meager contribution he was making for the sustenance of the family, now have to be compromised with, and the entire financial burden falls upon Neeta. Her father is portrayed as a sensible and sensitive character and is profoundly sympathetic to Neeta who seems to be the most favorite of all his children. Despite his sympathies towards his young daughter and his unbeatable craving to work and earn for the family, he is forced by his physical constraints to confine himself at home. He is portrayed as a frail and helpless figure who fails to rectify the wrongs, procure moral justice for Neeta and alter her destiny. He is lonely amidst the loud and vibrant family and his apparent passivity becomes conspicuous within the very happening circumstances. His behavior, rather his behavioral anomalies, can be explained by Nadine Miller's claim that Horrocks refers to: "personal problems such as depression, being withdrawn or unable to relate to people, can only be explained and mitigated satisfactorily when seen as by-products of an oppressive society and its gendered institutions." (Horrocks, 1994: 37) There is no denying the fact that he and his family had been the direct victims of the partition which drove them out of their motherland and forced to settle in a new country. The impact of socio-political oppression upon him is therefore obvious. What Horrocks mentions next is the influence of the gendered institutions of the oppressive society on the psychological ailments of a subject. He is a perfect blend of strength and sensitivity; he is too firm to compromise with the inappropriate affairs of the family and tender enough to take recourse to poetry as his medium of protest. Though his masculinity is not in crisis, it is dysfunctional. He has to negotiate with his paternal duties on account of practical reasons. And it is on account of the incapacitated father and his unemployed eldest son that this family does not fit into the conventional patriarchal model. Their inability to provide for and protect the family denies them the status of the ideal masculine figure in the traditional society. What we gather from this film is that the new phenomenon of the women stepping out of the domestic sphere out of compulsion had inflicted a deep wound in the sense of masculinity of the male members of the respective families. Neeta's father recites the following lines from Yeats' "At Galway Races":

> Sing on: somewhere at some new moon,
> We'll learn that sleeping is not death,
> Hearing the whole earth change its tune...

It will not be erroneous to claim that this old father plays the role of "Vivek," i.e., the conscience (somewhat similar to the role of the chorus in Greek tragedy), a characteristic feature of "Jatra" (the traditional open-air folk-theatre indigenous to Bengal).

Neeta's youngest brother Montu (played by Diju Bhawal) is a sportsman. The first time when he appears on screen, he is seen practicing his punch on a side pillow. He is portrayed as a typical selfish character who leaves his family as soon as he manages to get a job for himself. He exploits Neeta in the beginning and then as he becomes financially independent he shirks from all his responsibilities and moves out of his home to rent a room in the factory quarters. Eventually he meets with an accident in the factory and it is Neeta again who has to take care of his treatment. Towards the end Ghatak uses one shot where Montu's blank look on his pallid face occupies the entire frame. His masculine vigor has been maimed and he seems to have been transformed into a helpless suppliant figure.

Ritwik's involvement with Indian People's Theatre Association (IPTA) was directly reflected in *Komal Gandhar* (*E-Flat*). This second film of his partition trilogy written and directed by Ritwik was released in 1961. Though the plot evolves on the rivalry of two separate theatre troupes Nirikshan and Dakshinapath, it is the growing fondness of Anusuya (played by Supriya Chowdhury) and Bhrigu (played by Abinash Banerjee) for each other, which runs parallel to the central narrative and contributes to the development of the plot. In spite of the fact that Anusuya and Bhrigu belong to each of the rival groups, there are two principal factors which are common in both of them and become instrumental in bringing them close to one another—first, their uncompromising passion for theatre and second, the trauma of partition which neither of them has been able to overcome. In this film the most prominent male figure is that of Bhrigu. It happened to be one single troupe previously which has split into two when the narrative begins. The reason behind their splitting was Bhrigu's dictatorial attitude towards the members of the group. While Bhrigu says the final word in his group, Shanta (played by Gita Dey) leads the other group. Bhrigu leads with his knowledge of theatre and Shanta with her financial strength, both of which are non-negotiable for each other—and this is what creates the split. Later Bhrigu accepts the proposal of joint productions only because Anusuya begins to mediate between the two groups. But his circumstances make him heavily dependent on the two women—while he has to depend largely on Shanta's economic resources for the production, he gradually gets dependent on Anusuya emotionally. Though Bhrigu takes over as the director of the joint productions, he is finally controlled by Shanta, who regulates the finances and maintains the logistics on which the group runs. Thus the final production depends largely on her and we find that she takes full advantage of her position. One being the director of the productions and the other being the financer, there develops a clash of ego between Shanta and Bhrigu which gradually becomes irreconcilable. It attains the height of severity, so much so that Shanta, with the help of her associates, sabotage their final production out of revenge. The ultimate ruination of Bhrigu's long-desired production on account of Shanta's ego establishes the defeat of male ego on part of Bhrigu. After the joint production proves to be a disaster, Bhrigu's feelings of utter despair and dejection is given a conspicuous visual representation with the paint on his face which enhances his helpless and sorrowful state of mind. The paint, resembling a mask, actually unmasks Bhrigu's vulnerability in his immediate circumstances.

Bhrigu is portrayed as an extremely implacable and unrelenting taskmaster. The toughness of his demeanor sometimes adds a shade of inhumanity in his character. He is morally upright, passionate in his work, unostentatiously caring towards his colleagues and guardedly silent about his wounded heart. Horrocks agrees on the iconography of the western hero with Jane Tompkins on the point that the western hero is "cut off" from society and family, suffers stoically and is emotionally severely restricted. (Horrocks, 1994: 42) If we analyze the character of Bhrigu in this light, we are bound to find in his dispositions a natural tendency to shirk from the company of women. At the beginning he feels uncomfortable in the company of Anusuya as he does not want to give in to his fondness for her. But so far as the severance from the society is concerned, we notice a difference. Bhrigu is not at all apathetic to socio-political issues. His ardent passion for theatre is just a manifestation of his helplessness amidst his immediate circumstances and his eagerness to offer some service to the common people in general which he cannot offer in any form other than through his plays. During the initial stages of his interaction with Anusuya and gradually through the exposition of the narrative, Bhrigu's dispositions conform exactly to Jane Tompkins's observation that Horrocks quotes:

> The ethic of self-denial — denial of the needs of the flesh for warmth and comfort, succor, ease and pleasure; and denial of the needs of the spirit for companionship, affection, love, dependency, exchange — turns the hero to stone in the end [Horrocks, 1994: 42].

As Anusuya tries to get access to the emotional space of Bhrigu through his strongly guarded persona, the latter begins to respond. But throughout the narrative the rigor of self-denial keeps him restrained from yielding to his emotions. Deep in his heart he develops an intimacy with Anusuya but he tries his best not to express his emotions. If prioritizing achievement, according to Levant's parameters of hegemonic American masculinity (Levant, 1992: 380), can be appropriated to that of the Bengali masculinity, then Bhrigu (just like Shankar in *Megh Dhaka Tara*) undoubtedly possesses masculine elements in him. The characters of Bhrigu and Shankar, in general, are very different from one another and they share no common trait other than their artistic passions. In spite of that both have to negotiate their masculinities and both manifest their masculinities in different ways. They belong to the same culture and same sub-culture to be specific, but the manifestations of their individual masculinities are conspicuously different. It is here that the very notion of gender attitudes and gender roles get problematized in the narratives of Ritwik.

Through the crests and troughs of the practical day to day situations, Bhrigu gradually gets closer to Anusuya. It is solely his artistic endeavors which form an outlet for the pent up anguish that he still harbored in the deep recesses of his mind — the anguish which was an effect of the ordeal of partition that he had to suffer. As the narrative unfolds we get to know that Anusuya has been waiting for her fiancé for years. While she shares her disappointments with Bhrigu she mentions that it was just once that she had met her fiancé and their relationship had grown only through their epistolary correspondences over the years. It is because her fiancé has been residing in France since their first interaction. There is an allusion to William Shakespeare's comedy *The Tempest* as she reveals that Ferdinand and Miranda were the names by which they referred to each other by. This romantic relationship which had no other basis than the overseas exchange of a series of letters actually suffered from practical substantiality. We do not get to see "Ferdinand" as he never appears on screen. He remains as a name, the holder of which has to be imagined. He is the hero of Anusuya's life who remains unrevealed to everybody except herself. But Anusuya's search of a "man" — a "man" who was dreamed of by her mother in her personal diary, comes to an end when she gets to know Bhrigu.

> My mother used to look for something in every boy right from the days of the revolutionary movement. She wanted to rear me up like herself. She used to say, "our country is being ravaged by evil forces every now and then. So we should bring up heroes, and only women can foster them. You are my mother's son Bhrigu."

Earlier, Anusuya mentioned to Jaya (a young female actor in the troupe played by Chitra Sen) that she noticed exactly the same flame in the eyes of Bhrigu which she always saw in her mother. The very idea that a woman plays a decisive role in the making of a hero is reconfirmed by the mass leader (played by Jnanesh Mukherjee): "It is because women like you are still born in Bengal that men like us survive. We need you, always." The hero or the leader, whoever proves his masculine power in the society, owes his enthusiasm and stamina to some woman or the other.

Subarnarekha, the third film of the trilogy which was released in 1962, was also written by Ritwik jointly with Radheshyam Jhunjhunwala. It is primarily the story of a brother Ishwar Chakraborty (played by Abhi Bhattacharya) and his younger sister Seeta (child Seeta played by Indrani Chakraborty and young Seeta played by Madhabi Mukherjee). The narrative begins in January 1948. Ishwar belongs to the group of refugees who have migrated to West Bengal and are striving to make a shelter for themselves. In the beginning he is portrayed as a socially responsible young man who, along with his compatriots, set up a school for the refugee children in the colony. A voice cries out, "The young men should not sleep at night. You will need to guard the people." As a young man Ishwar is also expected to play the role of a protector of this vulnerable group of people who were passing each moment in the fear of eviction. He is a bachelor whose only dependent is his sister who is as young as could be his daughter had he been married. In due course he is forced to take the responsibility of a little boy Abhiram (played by Sachindra Bhattacharya), almost the same age as his sister. Abhiram is separated from his mother amidst the ruckus of eviction of the refugees from the forfeited land and their rehabilitation in some other location.

Ishwar's name holds a lot of significance in the plot. "Ishwar" in Sanskrit means God. Thus it is expected that his circumstances will demand him to command and control the situations of life. Ishwar is much elder to Seeta and therefore his role in Seeta's life is almost that of a father rather than an elder brother. He is an educated gentleman who has migrated to West Bengal with his little sister and is desperately seeking a job. He bumps into his old friend one day who happens to be an industrialist. Aware of Ishwar's virtues and his moral uprightness, his friend offers him a job in a suburban town where Ishwar is given a prestigious designation. Securing the prospect of Seeta was the only purpose behind Ishwar's accepting this lucrative offer. It is here that he has to compromise with the public role that he was supposed to play. His friend Haraprasad calls him a "deserter" when he comes to know of his decision. According to Haraprasad, Ishwar had negotiated with his solidarity and social responsibility, which were essential virtues for the refugees that helped them to face and fight their predicament.

As the guardian of Seeta, playing almost the role of father to her, Ishwar does succeed to play his gender role by bringing her up and trying to ensure her a good life. Being a confirmed bachelor, he represents the ideal masculine figure. Celibacy, which helps a man to retain his vitality, is a highly prized idea in Indian tradition and its practice has been encouraged through generations. Thus Ishwar, a celibate, who plays the role of the protector and provider for Seeta and Abhiram, represents the ideal man. Not only Seeta, even Abhiram is ensured proper education by Ishwar. He sends the boy to a boarding school where he completes his school education with good results. Ishwar makes arrangements to send Abhiram to Germany to study engineering. It is at this point that the narrative reaches its climax. Abhiram, whose parentage was unknown to everyone till now, publicly claims a dying woman on the railway station to be his mother. Everyone in the small suburban town comes to know about the low caste origin of Abhiram as the dying woman was known to be a "bagdi" belonging to the "scheduled caste" in India. Now Ishwar's prospect in his job becomes uncertain. His employer, who happened to be a stickler for castes would not encourage any of his responsible employees to keep a member of a low-caste in his family. Learning about Abhiram's origin, the owner of the mill postpones the agreement which he was planning to have with Ishwar concerning the latter's promotion to the position of a director of the company. Moreover, Ishwar comes to know about the love-affair that was going on between Abhiram and Seeta. As a result he becomes desperate to send Abhiram off to Calcutta, if not Germany, and takes immediate effort to get Seeta married to someone from a respectable background.

Peberdy refers to Roma, a character in *Glengarry Glen Ross* (1992), who defines masculinity "in terms of honour, male unity and a strong work ethic." (Peberdy, 2011: 3) Here we find Ishwar compromising his sense of morality, ethics and justice once again with his professional ambitions and social respectability. He had once negotiated with his sense of solidarity with his compatriots at the beginning of his career, and now he is compelled to negotiate his sense of moral justice to keep his public honor unblemished. His body language in response to Seeta's shrewd remark, "Dadamoni, whatever you are doing is wrong," proves that he is very well aware of his unscrupulous handling of the entire situation. Still he makes every effort to bring the situation under his control. He goes so far as to abuse his sister physically and wishing her death rather than face dishonor and see his prospect getting ruined. After playing the role of an indulgent and protective guardian Ishwar now turns into an insensitive and dominating man who proves too tough to be affected by petty sentimentalities. The fatherly instincts in Ishwar which overpowered his sense of social responsibility now seem to give in to the temptation of a higher designation in his profession and a richer prospect. Here we come face to face with the selfish Ishwar.

Seeta's eloping with Abhiram on the day of her marriage comes as a great shock for Ishwar. He gets mentally deranged to some extent and one day he attempts suicide. Exactly then Haraprasad, his old friend appears. Haraprasad, stooping with his frail constitution, is a stark contrast against tall and robust Ishwar. He has always been socially and politically active, so much so that he had to compromise with the well-being of his family. His personal life suffered due to his life-long commitment to the welfare of the refugees. His failure to provide for his family ultimately compelled his wife to commit suicide. To Haraprasad's wife Ishwar was an ideal father-figure. Before committing suicide she wrote a letter addressed to Ishwar in which she pleaded him to take care of her children as she was aware of their father's incapacity to look after his own family. But Haraprasad's children did not reach Ishwar as they were taken away by their father who did not want them to be brought up by a "deserter," by someone who does not keep his commitments to the society and compromises with principles. Thus the universal gender roles that man is traditionally supposed to play in the private and public spheres are split between Ishwar and Haraprasad in *Subarnarekha*. But both of them fail to play their respective roles successfully. Ishwar fails to ensure a secured future for Seeta and Haraprasad ends up in a wretched state frustrated by his failure to fulfill his dreams of social regeneration.

The sudden appearance of Haraprasad prepares the narrative for the final climax of the film. He asks Ishwar to take him to Calcutta — the city of fun, of "disgusting fun." He reminds Ishwar that the latter had led a celibate life throughout and therefore it is high time that he must taste the carnal pleasures that life has to offer, as gratification is the only way to salvation. Ritwik uses an extraordinary shot to render a visual presentation to the letting loose of their desires. A sharp cut to the horses being let loose on the track signifies the unfettering of the shackles of ideals and morality in Ishwar and Haraprasad and also the letting loose of their repressed male instincts. They indulge in all those enjoyments which were predominantly typical of the male members of the society in 1960s Bengal. They gamble, they drink till absolute inebriation and Ishwar finally ends up in the clutches of a pimp in order to satisfy his sexual desire.

Towards the end we find Seeta and Abhiram struggling to make both ends meet till at last Abhiram is killed in an accident. Seeta is forced into prostitution and finding drunken Ishwar enter her room on the first night, she commits suicide. Knowing fully well that the murder charge that was brought against him after Seeta's suicide was false, Ishwar claims himself guilty throughout the court proceedings. His guilt was not that of murdering Seeta, he was actually trying to confess a guilt which was more serious and which involved issues much larger than the suicide of a young woman. He thus tried to absolve himself of the sins that he knew he had committed merely for selfish reasons. This attempt of reparation of his tattered masculinity by showing the pluck of confessing his guilt was a manifestation of his masculinity in itself. The film ends with Ishwar beginning a new journey with Seeta's son Binu. On his return to Chhatimpur he finds out that he has been fired by the owner of the mill for claiming himself guilty of his sister's murder. Thus he needs to begin afresh in every sense. Being the only person on earth whom young Binu can depend upon, he now has to begin a new struggle to protect and provide for Binu and prepare him for a better future. Ishwar picks up the luggage and moves on to fight the battle of life all over again. The film ends with the Buddhist maxim playing in the background: "Charaiveti, charaiveti, charaiveti" — after the catharsis, Ishwar again takes up the burden of life on his shoulders and moves on in search of a "new home" for Binu and a new hope for himself.

In the three films by Ritwik Ghatak that I have discussed in this essay, we find representations of the "male angst, or the figure commonly referred to as the 'man in crisis'" (Peberdy, 2011: 4), in various forms. In the discussion of "Performance and Masculinity," Donna Peberdy quite obviously refers to Judith Butler and Tania Modleski's observation:

> masculinity operates according to the cycles of crisis and resolution; ultimately the aim is to restore men and masculinity to their dominant societal position: to reassert patriarchy. If "crisis" occurs when the gendered binaries between masculinity and femininity break down, the threat posed by femininity must be suppressed and the gendered binaries re-established in order for male dominance to be restored (or, at least, the illusion of dominance) [Peberdy, 2011: 28].

The sense of masculinity in each of the male characters discussed so far is in crisis — Shankar, his father Tarankrishna and Sanat in *Meghe Dhaka Tara*, Bhrigu in *Komal Gandhar* and Ishwar and Haraprasad in *Subarnarekha*. There is no denying the fact that all these male characters, their identities and the gender roles they play in the films are evaluated with respect to their relationship to and their bearing with the women who play pivotal roles in all the plots. Neeta's predominant position in her family as the breadwinner; the effect of the inexorable and positive vibe of Anusuya and the conniving scheme of Shanta in the life of Bhrigu; and Seeta as an embodiment of mother and daughter together for Ishwar, pose threats by their femininity in individual ways. In the end neither Neeta nor Seeta survives. Neeta's family gradually revives from the state of penury. Shankar is now an accomplished artist and is more than able to take up every responsibility. His father's health has revived enough to play the role of a perfect grandfather to Geeta's little son. But Neeta dies of tuberculosis far away from home in a sanatorium in Shillong — with an undying spirit and in profound loneliness as ever. Seeta too cannot survive and has to end her life as a victim of circumstances. Though at the expense of Seeta's life, Ishwar finally realizes his guilt and begins all over again to play the role of a provider and protector to his nephew. Bhrigu wins at last. Anusuya refuses to accompany her fiancé to France and returns to Bhrigu. Bhrigu carries on with his theatre in a revived spirit. Shankar, Bhrigu and Ishwar, all reach the point of resolution after the crisis and are ready again to play the expected roles and assert their masculinity.

Notes

1. This film derives its title from the river called Subarnarekha that flows through Jharkhand, West Bengal and Orissa. It literally means "golden lining."
2. A "bandish" is a short poem of four to six lines in general. It is set in tune and rhythm, maintaining the grammar of a specific raga. A "bandish" is supposed to illustrate the principal features of a raga.
3. "Khayal" is a genre of classical singing in North India.

References:

Bagchi, J. (1990). "Women in Calcutta: After Independence." In: *Calcutta, The Living City.* Oxford: Oxford University Press.

Chakravarty, G. (2005). *Coming Out of Partition: Refugee Women of Bengal.* New Delhi: Bluejay Books.

Chatterji, J. (2007). *The Spoils of Partition: Bengal and India, 1947–1967.* Cambridge: Cambridge University Press.

Chaudhuri, H. (2009). "Women Become Breadwinners." In J. Bagchi and S. Dasgupta (Eds.). *The Trauma and the Triumph: Gender and Partition in Eastern India.* Kolkata: Stree, pp. 81–87.

Donaldson, M., R. Hibbins, R. Howson, and B. Pease (Eds.) (2009). *Migrant Men: Critical Studies of Masculinities and the Migration Experience.* Oxon: Routledge.

Horrocks, R. (1994). *Masculinity in Crisis: Myths, Fantasies and Realities.* New York: St. Martin's Press.

Levant, R. (1992). Toward the Reconstruction of Masculinity. *Journal of Family Psychology,* Vol. 5, pp. 379–402.

Peberdy, D. (2011). *Masculinity and Film Performance: Male Angst in Contemporary American Cinema.* New York: Palgrave Macmillan.

Rajadhyaksha, A. (1982). *Ritwik Ghatak: A Return to the Epic.* Bombay: Screen Unit.

Masculinizing the (Post)colonial Subject

The *Amar Chitra Katha* Comic Book

SAYANTAN DASGUPTA

The comic book has long been relegated to the realm of trivia and has not traditionally been given much importance as a productive site of investigation in most academic cultures of the world. This is of course characteristic of a larger and reasonably widespread approach that borders on what may be termed canonocentrism, one which instinctively indulges in an aporia towards what is perceived as "popular." In that sense, the comic book or graphic novel occupies a space somewhat similar in nature to genres such as pornography, nursery rhymes, the thriller, and Bollywood cinema.

Yet, as academic cultures all over the world become less insulated and isolated — often for very different reasons — the comic book, indeed along with all the other genres mentioned with it, has made an entry into academic discourse. It is not that "serious" work on the comic book is a completely new entity — one remembers the invaluable *How to Read Donald Duck: Imperialist Ideology in the Walt Disney Comicbook*, Ariel Dorfman and Armand Mattelart's study of how the Walt Disney comic book was used to disseminate propaganda against the Popular Unity government in Chile and to prepare the ground for a military coup (Dorfman and Mattelart 1984). It is thanks to works like these that academic culture in general has become more open today to incorporating within its body the comic book as object of study.

This is of course tied up with a larger change that can be traced back at least till the late 1950s. The emergence of Culture Studies as a new subject at the University of Birmingham under the influence of the works of scholars like Raymond Williams and Richard Hoggart was predicated precisely upon an expanded, enhanced and liberated notion of what could viably be studied within the walls of academic campuses. Non-canonical texts and genres (such as the comic book) immediately found a route to entering critical discourse as Culture Studies was based on, among other things, the understanding that the "crisis in the humanities"[1] could be combated by erasing the boundaries between "high" culture and "low" culture, and between the canonical and the non-canonical. Today, of course, the comic book and the graphic novel are taught and read at various universities all across the world and quite regularly constitute part of the syllabi of Literature and Culture Studies departments.

Indeed, the comic book often has a lot to offer as far as efforts to understand one's social realities and discursive practices are concerned. Even when it is aimed primarily at a juvenile audience, it cannot help but embody discourses and even discursive conflicts related to historiography, nationalism, religion, gender, class and caste.

The *Amar Chitra Katha* is a pioneering Indian comic book series conceptualized and brought out by Anant Pai. It revolutionized the comic book industry in India and became very popular particularly in the 1980s. The series continues to be in circulation though its heyday is probably over and the *Amar Chitra Katha*, has, in keeping with the demands of our times, also moved on to establish a presence in other visual media, such as television and the internet.[2] Yet it has shaped a whole generation's understanding of Indian history and culture, and merits attention as an object of study in terms of the cultural matrices it embodies, reproduces, and/or interrogates.

The *Amar Chitra Katha* focuses on Indian history, mythology and legends. The *Amar Chitra Katha* publicity slogans and motto are significant — "Give your child a gift he'll treasure for ever — the gift of his own heritage" and "Acquaint your children with the cultural heritage of India." The series predicated itself upon a purported attempt to combat a culture of amnesia that was perceived to have befallen postcolonial India. It evoked the specter of an age where various pressures would gradually result in young India losing its connection with its roots, with the stories, values and ethos that were identified as essentially Indian. By bringing Indian history, mythology and folklore into an accessible and entertaining form, the series claimed to be trying to reversing this amnesia and piloting young Indians back to everything that lay behind their "Indian" identity. Anant Pai himself is on record highlighting this as the main agenda of the *Amar Chitra Katha* comicbook.[3]

This kind of a program, however well-meaning it is, always suffers from the threat of overcompensating for the loss perception by going into a revivalist mode. Unfortunately, this seems true of the *Amar Chitra Katha* brand of historiography, and this has significant repercussions on stereotypes relating to gender and nationalism here, we can argue. In trying to highlight the culture of amnesia as its raison d'etre, the *Amar Chitra Katha* ends up sometimes constructing an essentialist idea of India even as it goes back into the past searching for traces of a glorious Indian history. This, of course, is intimately tied up with and may be read as a direct response to imperialism and its concomitant discourses. One of the pillars of imperialist discourse, and one that has often been used in various geographical contexts across the world, is the tendency to deny the colonized subject a claim to history, tradition and science. And one of the typical responses to that on the part of the colonized has been the painstaking attempt to establish a history (sometimes exaggerated) of its own. That is, indeed, a trap the *Amar Chitra Katha* seems to fall into (Dasgupta 2002). If there is a glorious ancient age for India, and that is to be established as the basis of India's claim to greatness in the modern age, then one needs to establish an intervention that must have led to a "fall" that ultimately results in colonial servitude. In trying to establish this, the *Amar Chitra Katha* falls prey to the light-darkness-light paradigm of history-writing that was part and parcel of the orthodox Western European model of historiography — one that explained away the Middle Ages as "dark," for instance.

It is ironic that the *Amar Chitra Katha* uses the revivalistic model of historiography borrowed from Europe for at no level is the Amar Chitra an apology for colonialism. Indeed, the *Amar Chitra Katha* presents itself as a nationalist venture — one that tries to contribute to the nation-building project that was still very much in the foreground in the pre-globalization India of the 1970s and 1980s. Yet, even as the series publishes a number of titles related to the nationalist struggle and clearly criticizes British rule for the repression it unleashed on Indians, it ends up subscribing to the British/European model of historiography. In the process, it often bases it account of Indian history on works such as Colonel Todd's *Annals and Antiquities of*

Cover image from *Amar Chitra Katha: Rama*

India and ends up producing a complex narrative of Indian history, which at the same time attempts to promote national integration and labels some sections of Indian society as an Other. Thus, the *Amar Chitra Katha* celebrates the legendary Rajput valor by bringing out a number of titles narrating the valorous Rajput resistance against Muslim invaders — on *Hadi Rani, Veer Hammir, Rana Pratap, Padmini, Prithviraj Chauhan*, etc. Again, when it comes to the Mughals, it ends up depicting rulers such as Babur, Akbar and Shah Jahan as heroes and tries to appropriate them within the rubric of Indian national history. This highlights a narrative that is complex and perhaps at some level even contradictory, with carious notions of nationalism colluding and colliding.

Perhaps the *Amar Chitra Katha*'s obsession with tales of valor is not just an attempt to feed the hunger of the juvenile mind for tales of adventure and heroism. The series clearly attempts to construct an iconographic history of India,[4] and there seems a conscious attempt to highlight a tradition of valor, might and physical prowess within the narrative of Indian history that it presents. Imperialist discourse is often seen to construct the colonial Other as effeminate — the Orient has traditionally been cast in that role, and in keeping with traditional stereotypes that are in circulation, this feminization of the Orient has been used to rob it of its claim to agency.[5]

An important part of the struggle for national liberation is fought out in the arena of ideas. Apart from militant struggle, the world of ideas has constituted a site of contest in almost every nationalist struggle. Thus, the attempt to shake off the yoke of colonial rule is seen to manifest itself, among other things, in attempting to contest the stereotypes that colonialism seeks to propagate in order to strengthen itself. One of the possible responses on the part of the colonial subject to the imperialist Orientalist strategies underlined above is to try and refute its implications. If imperialist discourse is to try and imagine the colonial Other as feminine and to divest it of its claim to agency and discrimination thereby underscoring the need for colonial intervention, which is purportedly in the interest of the colonial subject, then one way of responding to this could be for the colonial subject to try and posit oneself in a hypermasculinized idiom. This is a template the *Amar Chitra Katha* series seems to turn to in its attempt to contribute to the Indian nation building project in the postcolonial era.

Colonized people have often resorted to attempts to rediscover and highlight a martial culture in themselves.[6] This strategy seems to be evident in the *Amar Chitra Katha* comic book — in the way it portrays a glorious military past for India and in the way it constructs an iconographic history churning out title after title in remembrance of valorous individuals born of the Indian clime. What we see at work in the Amar Chitra Katha then is an attempted "masculinization" of the Indian psyche by creating a network of icons who symbolize this ideal of machismo, which again is tied up with a perception of what constitutes and characterizes the ideal nation.

The first page of *Prithviraj Chauhan* thus features a mustachioed man (representing Prithviraj Chauhan) astride a horse in close proximity to a leaping tiger. Even as the horse rears, a fearless and proud Prithviraj Chauhan is shown to be shooting a spear down the tiger's gullet. The revivalist nature of the *Amar Chitra Katha* historiography is evident in the textbox below the full-page first panel on the first page — "Much before the advent of the Mughals in India, Delhi was ruled by a brave king, Prithviraj Chauhan." Taking Mughal rule as an index of time, the comic book seems to go out of its way to emphasize that the Mughals were outsiders who *came* to India and to showcase Prithviraj Chauhan's identity as a son of the soil. The text on the inside cover makes the agenda quite clear: "…The following year, Mohammad returned to India and again met the forces of the Rajput king on the same battlefield. This time the Muslim invader inflicted a crushing defeat on the Hindu army. The second battle (between Prithviraj Chauhan and Shahabuddin Ghori) proved to be a turning point in Indian history. It put an end to the Hindu Empire in Northern India forever and established Muslim rule." We see here the clearly defined contours of a nostalgia for some imagined ancient golden age that was symbolized by the likes of Prithviraj Chauhan and which preceded the coming of Islam to India. Perhaps one is then not entirely unjustified here in relating the culture of masculinization enunciated in the *Amar Chitra Katha* series to exclusivist notions of the nation and to nationalist responses to imperialist, Orientalist discourse.

Also striking is the image on the cover of the title. The cover features a proud and fierce-looking Prithviraj Chauhan urging his horse on even as a few other horsemen follow him in the distance. Chauhan brandishes a sword in one hand and clutches the reins of his horse with the other, and clinging to him and sitting on his lap is Samyogita, the woman he has pulled away from her *swayamvara* and is now taking back home with him. It is this hypermasculine image that both characterizes and sustains the idea of India of the golden age that the *Amar Chitra Katha* seeks to perpetuate. And any deviation from the same is to be severely condemned as we see later in the comic book. Any departure from the ideal of the hypermasculine ruler is to be equated with a threat to the security of the country. The notion of the proactive, hypermasculinized, hawkish state — something that has found a hospitable stage in South Asia — is clearly in evidence here.

Thus, the Prithviraj who becomes enraged beyond words on hearing the suggestion that he accept the suzerainty of Jaichand of Kanauj, the Prithviraj who is depicted as lying on the ground, dagger poised to stab the lion who is leaping at him, is praised and held up as the ideal. On the other hand, when he loses to Shahabuddin Ghori on the battlefield, the blame is put on Samyogita, in whose love Prithviraj Chauhan had immersed himself. Familial affection is shown to be a serious threat for the ideal of the masculine man — human emotions such as love and affection are shown to effeminize him and reduce him to the status of a loser in whose hands the country can no longer remain safe and secure. His guru sums this up when he says, "It is a pity that a brave, fearless noble warrior like Prithviraj should care so much for a woman and forget his duties." (*Prithviraj Chauhan* 21).

The ideal of the masculine man who braves all odds and unhesitatingly risks his life for his convictions is a common trope in the *Amar Chitra Katha* series. This applies to titles that relate to the anti–British nationalist struggle as well (such as *Velu Thampi*, *Bagha Jatin*, etc.). It is the same spirit that is celebrated in these titles — the cover of *Velu Thampi*, thus, bears striking resemblance to the first panel of *Prithviraj Chauhan*, highlighting as it does Velu Thampi's physical prowess and bravery, bordering on violence.

Cover Image from *Prithviraj Chauhan* (courtesy Rohit K Dasgupta).

Again, the cover of *Rana Pratap* (No. 24), subtitled "The heroic struggle of a Rajput king against the might of an empire," evokes a similar template as Rana Pratap is shown astride a horse rearing almost ninety degrees right in front of an elephant carrying a Mughal commander even as Rana Pratap balances himself and readies to throw his spear at him. Some way into the comic book, a farmer is brought into Pratap's presence by a guard on charges of farming his land without taking Pratap's permission. When the farmer explains he had taken the Mughal emperor's permission, Pratap says, "I am the king of Chittor and I have not given you permission ... your crop will finally feed the enemy and thus help him" (*Rana Pratap* 9). The textbox then declares, "The following day, the farmer was hanged." The refusal to submit to human emotions that might have ushered in the possibility of clemency in favor of a more "masculine" notion of patriotism is what seems to characterize the hero in titles such as *Rana Pratap* and *Prithviraj Chauhan*. The same conflict is evident again and is resolved similarly later on in the book when

Images from *Rana Pratap*.

Man Singh, the Rajput commander in Akbar's army, comes to visit Rana Pratap. Pratap invites him to have some food but refuses to join him. When Man Singh reminds him of his dharma as host, instead of acceding to the codes of hospitality, Pratap insults him, saying he had bartered his honor off by joining the Mughal forces and he could therefore not join him! (*Rana Pratap* 12–13).

Significantly enough, *Rana Pratap* begins with a three-page eulogy to the valor of the Rajputs of India — "Rajasthan in western India was the home of the valiant Rajputs. Throughout history, they had repeatedly fought for the honor of the country. But the Rajputs of Chittor surpassed all in deeds of bravery and personal sacrifice.... And their women were no less heroic. Chittor's Queen Karma Devi had defeated the powerful hordes of Qutab-ud-din. In the fourteenth century, Queen Padmini and hundreds of Rajput women of Chittor performed sati, an act of self-immolation, to save their honor from the invader, Ala-ud-din Khilji." (*Rana Pratap* 1–3). The last panel on page 3 depicts a group of women marching towards the pyre while a couple of pyres are depicted with women sitting on them devoutly as the flames eat at them. In glorifying "sati" here, the *Amar Chitra Katha* seems to tread a dangerous line and posit a precedent that could have far-reaching repercussions on postcolonial Indian society. It was not too long ago after all that a Roop Kanwar[7] was forced to commit sati and a martyr sought to be made of her.

What is interesting to note here is that the ideal of machismo seems to percolate into the *Amar Chitra Katha*'s construction of the ideal woman as well. Padmini is held up as the epitome of the ideal woman who aptly complements the masculine man, the hero of *Amar Chitra Katha* historiography. Patriarchal discourse imagines the woman's body as an arena in which is invested the honor of the family or community, thereby making her body a site of contest and making rape a tool of underscoring one's masculinity and of challenging the masculinity of the enemy. The ideal woman is then expected to willingly kill herself in advance rather than even entertain the possibility of surviving at the cost of violation, an act that would bring great shame to the community she is seen to represent. This is an ideology that has persisted into the modern, postcolonial age in South Asia as is evident in the phenomenon of so-called "honor killings" all across the subcontinent. This is an ideology that also attained immense prominence at the time of the Partition of 1947, when British India gave way to the two independent states of India and Pakistan. The Partition was accompanied by large-scale and widespread violence, killings and rapes, and women were mostly at the receiving end of the violence, as testified by the stories of writers like Saadat Hasan Manto, Rajinder Singh Bedi and Kishen Chander. If one looks at personal narratives of Partition collected from men and women who experienced and survived Partition,[8] one is struck by the way these discourses have survived down the ages and how they manifest themselves as easily in the *Amar Chitra Katha* comic book as in real-life experiences related to a cataclysmic event like Partition.

The fantasy about the masculinization of the woman is again part and parcel of nationalist historiography in the context of colonial India and the nationalist movement. Writings of icons like Swami Vivekananda bear testimony to this. And this fantasy seems to play out in the pages of the *Amar Chitra Katha* comic book quite prominently in the way the series imagines, constructs and glorifies the figures of Rani Durgavati,[9] Tarabai[10] and Padmini.[11]

Padmini, significantly begins in a vein very similar to the way *Rana Pratap* starts. The first page declares, "Chittor is the soul of Rajasthan. Its history is the saga of Rajput valour." (*Padmini* 1). It is again worth noting that Ratnasen, Padmini's husband, is portrayed as a connoisseur of art and poetry in this title. This is a far cry from the fierce and fearsome Prithviraj Chauhan we encounter in the early part of *Prithviraj Chauhan*. It should come as no surprise then that Ratnasen is no "hero" for the Amar Chitra Katha. Even though he mouths the right words, "A Rajput is never afraid of danger" (*Padmini* 7), he is the one who is taken in by and foolishly succumbs to the false "brotherly" overtures of Ala-ud-Din Khilji and for whom Padmini's life and honor are put on stake. And at the end, when Padmini commits *jauhar* and immolates herself, the Muslim Sultan is shown to be totally at a loss and unable to understand the rationale behind the act — it takes nobility to recognize an act of nobility, and in the *Amar Chitra Katha* narrative of Indian history, it is clear that the Muslim Sultan who is pitted against the Rajput can be no noble person.

The character of Tarabai (No. 48), the Rajput princess, too, is constructed in a similar vein. Her father, Rai Surtan, says, "You are as good as any son. I will train you in all the manly pursuits" (Tarabai 3). And she, on her part, responds enthusiastically with "I can hardly wait to leave, father" when Rai Surtan tells her of his plans to go into battle (*Tarabai* 5) and is only too ready to agree to marry Jaimal of Mewar if he agreed to liberate Thoda, her homeland. And, finally, she commits sati on the last page of the title in an act that symbolizes the ultimate frontier of bravery for contemporary Rajput women for the *Amar Chitra Katha*. These and many other titles in the *Amar Chitra Katha* series go to highlight the fact that the series seems to subscribe to a masculinist notion of history and nation, in the process constructing icons who are imagined in terms of a hypermasculine idiom and who are sought to be presented as essential constituents of the national imaginary.

Notes

1. "The Emergence of Cultural Studies and the Crisis in the Humanities" is, in fact, the name of Stuart Hall's essay tracing the genesis and evolution of the discipline at the University

of Birmingham. See Hall, Stuart. "The Emergence of Cultural Studies and the Crisis of the Humanities." *October* No. 53 (Summer 1990). 11–23.

2. The Amar Chitra Katha has always been open to exploring newer media for dissemination of its texts. In the pre–satellite television age, it tried out the audiobook as one such medium — by the early 1980s, the Amar Chitra Katha had put into circulation a series of Amar Chitra Katha audiocassettes in Hindi and English under the brand name "Amarnad." See Pai, Anant, ed. *Elephanta*. Bombay: India Book House, July 1980. 32.

3. See Pai, Anant. "Comics as a Vehicle of Education and Culture." *Indian Horizons: Telling Tales*. Vol. 44. No. 2. Ed. Amit Dasgupta. New Delhi: ICCR, 1995. 155

4. This seems quite clear from even a cursory browse of the Amar Chitra Katha catalogue — the majority of the titles are biographical in nature and the agenda is clearly to focus on individuals who would serve as icons for modern India.

5. For a detailed analysis of this proposition, see Said, Edward W. Introduction. *Orientalism*. London: Penguin Books, 1995. 1–28.

6. See Dasgupta, Sayantan (Ed.). (2007). *A South Asian Nationalism Reader*. New Delhi: Worldview.

7. Roop Kanwar was burnt to death on her husband's funeral pyre in Deorala village, Rajasthan, on September 4, 1987; the incident was sought to be portrayed as an act of sati.

8. For an analysis of such testimonies, see section on "Honour" in Butalia, Urvashi. *The Other Side of Silence: Voices from the Partition of India*. Delhi: Penguin, 1998. 172–245.

9. Durgavati was the daughter of the Rajput chief of Mahoba, a Rajput kingdom. She is described in the eponymous Amar Chitra Katha comic book as a good horsewoman, a great shot and a brave woman. She carves an alliance with the Gonds and braves all odds to take on the might of Akbar's Mughal empire. When all is lost, she is shown on the last page of *Rani Durgavati* to declare, "I would rather die in honour than live in disgrace," and the final panel of the comic book says, "And like the true Rajputani that she was, the proud Rani stabbed herself."

10. Tarabai was the daughter of Rai Surtan, the Rajput chieftain of Bandor, originally from Thoda. *Tarabai* takes pains to emphasize that she was no less than a man in terms of military prowess, skill and endurance.

11. Padmini was the queen of Chittor and married to Ratnasena, the Rajput king.

References

Dasgupta, Sayantan (2002). "Amar Chitra Katha: Itihas, Bismriti, Gappo o Aro Du-ekti Bishoy." In Sudhir Chakraborty (Ed.) *Dhrubopad*, Vol. 6. Krishnagar, 168–197.

Dorfman, Ariel, and Armand Mattelart (1984). *How to Read Donald Duck: Imperialist Ideology in the Disney Comicbook*. 2d ed. New York: International General.

Hall, Stuart (1990). "The Emergence of Cultural Studies and the Crisis of the Humanities." *October* No. 53 (Summer 1990). 11–23.

Pai, Anant (Ed.) (n.d.). *Tarabai*. Bombay: India Book House.

_____ (Ed.) (June 1981). *Velu Thampi*. Bombay: India Book House.

_____ (Ed.) (June 1980). *Panna and Hadi Rani*. Bombay: India Book House.

_____ (Ed.) (September 1980). *Rani Durgavati*. Bombay: India Book House.

_____ (Ed.) (1980). *Rana Pratap*. Bombay: India Book House.

_____ (Ed.) (July 1980). *Prithviraj Chauhan*. Bombay: India Book House.

_____ (Ed.) (1980). *Padmini*. Bombay: India Book House.

_____ (Ed.) (October 1980). *Veer Hammir*. Bombay: India Book House.

Said, Edward (1995). *Orientalism*. London: Penguin Books.

Rethinking the Circuits
of Male Desire Across
Multiple *Dostanas*

DASHINI JEYATHURAI

Introduction

In "Lyrical Nationalism: Gender, Friendship and Excess in 1970s Indian Cinema," Priya Jha challenges critical works that have simply relegated the *dostana* genre to one of the many formulas that Bollywood both relies upon and succumbs to in the film-making process. Jha's critique is a valid one and I have purposefully devoted much of this essay to close readings of two such films in order to map the richly complicated circuits of male desire that cannot possibly be reduced to simple formulas. In order to do so, it is imperative to question the dominance of Eve Kosofsky Sedgwick's model as *the* one lens with which to read the circulation of male desire that takes place within the deeply homosocial space of the *dostana* genre. The persistence of this sole model in scholarship surrounding this particular genre eclipses the potentially more nuanced readings possible by utilizing the Sedgwickian model *in tandem* with alternative schemas of male desire. A particular schema that is eminently visible in both productions of *Dostana* that I have chosen to trace is the male triangle. Why, in fact, are these third men necessary to these narratives of *dostana*? What roles do they occupy? After all, neither of these men are marketed as playing any role whatsoever based on the advertisements for these films. Both posters for these films are remarkably similar despite the almost three decades between them in their erasure of these third men and the central positioning of a somewhat scantily clad woman between the two men. I wish to posit that these third men, rather than being superfluous plot devices, are lynchpins that maintain the stability and shore up the exclusivity and sanctity of male friendship in the *dostana* genre. Difficult questions follow this formulation. Why third *men*? Despite being markedly less important than the leading female characters in the eyes of movie publicists, can these third men further occlude they who are already perceived to be no more than bolsters for the primary relationship or the "real story" between the two leading male characters?

Dostana *(1980)*

Dostana (1980) opens with a duet in which the leading men return to their alma mater to sing about their flawless friendship at a concert. However, it is the second song with which Vijay Varma (Amitabh Bachchan) serenades Ravi Kapoor (Shatrughan Sinha) that adequately renders the male desires that are actively circulating within *dostana*. At this moment in the film, the heroic friendship has already encountered a significant impasse in the form of Sheetal (Zeenat Aman), a beautiful socialite who finds Vijay's brusque ways entirely irresistible. Unbeknownst to Sheetal or Vijay until well into their romantic relationship, Ravi too has fallen in love with her. Ravi only discovers their romance after the villainous Daga (Prem Chopra) provides him with photographic evidence of the relationship between Sheetal and Vijay. upon this revelation, Ravi is both inconsolable and furious. Daga pounces upon this opportunity to both intercept and disrupt the friendship between Ravi and Vijay. Indeed, Daga wishes to replace Vijay. Daga promises Ravi, "The day we unite there will be no place for Vijay in this world." As a note, all translations are from the English subtitles of these motion pictures unless otherwise stated. The camera moves from the cracked photograph of Ravi and Vijay in warm embrace to the now clasped hands of Ravi and the usurping Daga. Thus, the purity and self-sacrifice characteristic of the friendship between the two heroes with which the film begins is displaced, albeit temporarily, by the whorishness of this new friendship that is motivated by profit and revenge. However, Daga's presence in the narrative as both the third man and the *other* man has been elided in current scholarship surrounding the film. Instead, the scholarship is largely invested in the position of Sheetal as a conduit of desire between Vijay and Ravi. In her essay "Alternative Sexualities in Popular Indian Cinema," Gayatri Gopinath provides a reading of Vijay's woeful serenade:

> The homosocial triangulation that structures *Dostana* is most apparent in a scene in which ... [t]he camera very obviously traces the triangulated desire among [Vijay], [Ravi], and [Sheetal]; what is striking in this scene is that while both men appear somewhat animated and active in different ways, [Sheetal] remains curiously inert, and simply stares blankly at the camera [291].

Yet, an alternative reading of *Mere Dost Kissa Yeh Kya Ho Gaya* yields a different schema than the Sedgwickian model that Gopinath posits. Gopinath is entirely accurate in the way in which she traces the camera's purposeful movement from Ravi to Sheetal to Vijay, however, she neglects the triangulation of desire amongst Vijay, Ravi, and Daga. Had Ravi sung this song, the Sedgwickian model would be in full effect for his sense of betrayal would stem from Vijay choosing Sheetal over their *dostana*. However, it is a betrayed *Vijay* who serenades Ravi after having lost him to Daga:

> My friend, why did this happen?
> My friend, why did this happen?
> I've heard you've become a deceiver...
> I've heard you've become a deceiver...

In "Memories Pierce the Heart: Homoeroticism, Bollywood Style," Raj Rao provides an alternative translation of this song (305). Rao's essay is a particularly significant in that it acknowledges the homoeroticism that transcends the barrier of the screen and percolates within the space of the Indian movie theater Rao describes:

> The bond that Amitabh Bachchan formed with other male actors on the screen, complemented by the presence of an all-male audience that had gathered to watch him, engendered a sort of homoeroticism in the dark of the movie hall.... Take a look at the audience as the movie is showing (as I have frequently done), and you are likely to find young men all over each other, clasping hands, putting arms around shoulders and waists, even a leg on a leg. Few of these men might be consciously gay [303].

Rao discusses Vijay's use of the word "*bewaffa*" which he translates as "unfaithful" rather than "deceiver." Rao's translation registers the homoerotic valence of this song. Strikingly, Daga emerges within the frame of the song immediately after Vijay has sung the word "*bewaffa*." Daga's entrance into the space of the song is simultaneously signaled by a sudden and pointed disharmony in the music wherein the mournfulness of the melody becomes increasingly acute. The music appears to belie both Vijay's and the genre's anxiety when confronted by Daga's intrusion. Ravi, standing by the bar that faces a mirror, raises his glass of alcohol to no one in particular. In fact, Ravi has raised his glass to Daga. The camera cuts smoothly to Daga who drinks to the unspoken toast and then shifts to a visibly shattered Vijay. When Vijay and Ravi are finally within the same screenshot, it is not Sheetal but Daga who stands between the two men both literally and figuratively.

Dostana *(2008)*

This alternative schema to the Sedgwickian model of the circulation of male desire emerges in a more nuanced fashion in *Dostana* (2008). Unlike

Daga in the 1980 production of *Dostana*, Abhimanyu Singh (Bobby Deol), the third male in question, poses no threat to the relationship of the two heroes. Abhi is Neha Melwani's (Priyanka Chopra) third potential love interest and the man she eventually marries. In the denouement of *Dostana*, Abhi is the most active agent in sexualizing the male friendship for the audience onscreen and offscreen. Sameer Kapoor (Abhishek Bachchan) and Kunal Chopra (John Abraham) jump onstage at a glitzy party where Abhi and Neha are in attendance. There the two men proceed to confess that they have deceived Neha and that they are not gay. They simply fell in love with her Miami apartment and lied in order to live there. They attempt to mobilize their audience of white partygoers to urge Neha to forgive them. It is worth noting that the 2008 production of *Dostana* configures Miami as a predominantly, if not completely, white city. Every person of color (and they are few and far between) who appears in the film with the exception of the Indian cast is in a service position ranging from the East Asian beautician to the black bouncers. The whiteness of the world outside India is not entirely abnormal for song-and-dance sequences that are shot overseas where the exoticness of the foreign locale is marked by whiteness. However, the plan backfires when one of the audience members heckles the duo and asks them to give each other a kiss onstage. It is at this opportune moment that Abhi yells, "You want to be forgiven right? Then give a kiss to each other in front of everyone. Come on guys! You like being gay, right? Kiss! Everyone, don't you want them to kiss?" However, the translation, "You like being gay, right?" is lacking. The translation provided by the subtitles of the film fails to sufficiently illuminate Abhi's use of the Hindi word, "shok." His use of the word "shok" insinuates that Sameer and Kunal have experienced a certain pleasure and euphoria during their pretence.

Meanwhile, Neha remains both silent in a pageant-like expression of serenity as Abhi, Sameer and Kunal broker her forgiveness. Unlike scenes past where Sameer and Kunal must perform their understandings of queerness in order to be deemed authentic, now they are chillingly punished for the authenticity and the pleasure they may have derived from their past performances. The audience of partygoers gleefully watch as the two men wrestle with the decision to either kiss each other or to lose Neha's friendship altogether. Throughout the anticipation of this kiss, the camera returns to Abhi as he watches the two men with an unmistakable smirk across his face. Abhi's scopophilic pleasure is palpable as he imagines the abjection they must subject themselves to in order to retain their friendship with Neha. After much dallying and false starts, Kunal finally grabs Sameer and plants a kiss on him. Cameras flash onscreen to document the tableau of these two brown bodies, forcibly queered. The audience roars with excitement. In this moment, Abhi's heterosexual relationship with Neha is sustained by the forced albeit brief queering of their bodies. At the end of this kiss, Abhi whispers to the still silent Neha, "I would never have done this. Not even for you. These guys, they truly are your best friends." What happens next reveals that it is more than simply a punishment which has been meted out. In fact, a marriage contract has been negotiated. Sameer and Kunal leap off the stage, kneel before Abhi, each hold one of his hands and say in unison, "Mr. Abhimanyu Singh, will you please marry our best friend?" Abhi, Sameer and Kunal are physically linked at this moment in the film while Neha stands outside of this triangular schema. Abhi assents looking at both Sameer and Kunal first before raising his eyes to meet Neha's. Earlier in the film when Neha discovers that Sameer and Kunal have been working in concert to ruin her relationship with Abhi, she mistakenly thinks it is because both men desire Abhi. Her mistake foreshadows this moment in the film when Sameer and Kunal actually propose to Abhi. This successful all male proposal replaces the first failed heterosexual proposal in the film where Abhi plans to ask Neha to marry him during the halftime show at a basketball game.

Not only is Abhi the voice that articulates the homoeroticism of this male friendship, he is instrumental in entrenching the boundaries of *dostana* as an all male space. When Kunal uses the word "*dostana*" for the first time in the film, it refers to his friendship with *both* Sameer and Neha. Indeed, the song *Jaane Kyun* during which the three of them carouse through the Miami landscape, marks Neha as being very much a part of this *dostana*. Moved by Kunal's inclusiveness, Neha rushes towards Kunal to embrace him, only to be pushed out of the way by Sameer as he hugs Kunal. Neha then must muscle her way back in exclaiming, "Group hug!" This scene is replicated later in the film when Kunal and Sameer embrace but realize that the embrace is incomplete without Neha. While there is initial resistance to a female entering this male space, the filmic narrative seems to initially imply that there is room for Neha within this *dostana*. However, this alternative configuration of *dostana* as one that potentially includes a woman as more than a conduit is disrupted by Abhi's entrance into the narrative. When Sameer and Kunal encounter him for the first time, Abhi's romantic interest in Neha jettisons her from that originally inclusive configuration of *dostana*. upon Abhi and Neha flirt, Sameer says, "It seems [Neha's] boss wants to toss us out." When Kunal asks Sameer what their plan of action should be to rid themselves of Abhi, Sameer says, "Whatever we do, we'll do it together." Sameer then clasps Kunal's hands. Abhi cements their *dostana*. The clasped males hands, united against Abhi's capacity to usurp their potential places as Neha's lover, supersedes the inclusivity of that original embrace. The entrance of this third male into the film's narrative marks Neha as a woman to be pursued rather than being a part of this *dostana* in far more powerful way than all the tight dresses and heels in Miami.

In the epilogue to the film, Neha asks Sameer and Kunal, "When you both were pretending to be gay, at any point, did anything happen between the two of you?" Sameer and Kunal are aghast at such a question and Neha huffs off at their touchiness about the subject. When Neha leaves the frame of the camera, the two men look at each other before drifting back to their spectacular kiss onstage. Sameer and Kunal remember only the kiss that Abhi forces them to share. The primary reason for that kiss, Neha's forgiveness, has been excised from their memory of the event. Indeed, Abhi catalyzes Neha's permanent expulsion from the *dostana* narrative for the final visual that the film leaves the audience is a framed photograph of Sameer and Kunal with "and they lived happily ever after" written in English across it. Thus, Abhi inadvertently safeguards the "happily ever after" of the *dostana* genre that is reserved for the two leading men.

Gopinath remarks upon a similarly odd, omniscient scripting of the final scene of the 1980 production of *Dostana*. "...indeed, by the end [Sheetal] has disappeared entirely. The movie closes with a shot of the two men embracing and walking hand in hand into the sunset, as the words 'This friendship will live forever!' flash on the screen" (291). Gopinath misquotes these lines for they actually read "Thus friendship lives on forever!" This misquotation is significant because it is not simply the individual friendship that of Vijay and Ravi that lives on forever but the dostana genre that persists. Reading the end of the film solely in relation to Sheetal's disappearance from the narrative is incomplete. Prior to this climactic end, Daga attempts to frame Vijay with the murder of a suspect he has in police custody. However, Ravi agrees to defend Vijay in court at Sheetal's behest. "Behest" woefully fails to convey that Sheetal agrees to meet Ravi's demand that she spend the night with him should he defend Vijay. Sheetal defiantly claims that her willingness to spend a night with Ravi reflects how much she cares for Vijay. By the time she arrives at Ravi's home to fulfill her end of the bargain, he has already read a letter from Vijay addressed to Sheetal asking her to sacrifice their love for Ravi's happiness. It is worth noting that Sheetal had planned to ingest poison after sleeping with Ravi. Her body used to save Vijay was to be voluntarily destroyed once trespassed upon by another man. Furious at Ravi's decision to defend Vijay, Daga kidnaps Ravi and Sheetal in order to lure Vijay into a confrontation. It is Ravi and not Sheetal who is constructed as Daga's primary hostage. Ravi's arms are strung up to two pillars in the main section of the hall while Sheetal is relegated to the corner of the room and the screen. When Vijay arrives to save Ravi and Sheetal, he is disarmed by Daga's men and is strung up alongside Ravi. Daga proceeds to whip Vijay in order to extract information from him but Vijay gives up none. Pained as they are from the torture, Ravi and Vijay taunt Daga refusing to give information or allowing their *dostana* to be used as leverage against one another. As in the 2008 production of *Dostana*, once again, it is the third male who is instrumental in marking Sheetal as both woman and as outside of the *dostana* that Ravi and Vijay share. upon hearing her cry out, Daga leaves the now impenetrable space of *dostana* and walks over to Sheetal, threatening to whip her. Daga rips the back of her *choli* exposing both the straps of her brassiere and the potential threat her frailty poses to the noble solidity of *dostana*.

While Gopinath rightly addresses that Sheetal has all but disappeared by the end of the film, she does not trace who precipitates this disappearance. It is Daga who forces Vijay, Ravi and Sheetal into a space of violence in which he demarcates the susceptibility of Sheetal's body. She is the weak link that must be left behind. Hereafter, when Ravi and Vijay are in hot pursuit of Daga, there is no question of where Sheetal is. We last see her tending to a wounded woman. As Daga attempts to make a getaway in a small plane, Ravi hovers over him in a helicopter while Vijay rides alongside Daga in a van. Hemmed in by the two heroes, Daga moves from being the *other* man polluting their *dostana* to the man whose eventual death marks the renewed purity of Vijay and Ravi's *dostana*. Daga's melodramatic death cues the first song of the film that celebrates the eternity of their *dostana*. Ringing triumphantly in the background are the lyrics, "If you have any doubt of us, you can test us." The original test of their *dostana*, Sheetal, is ousted in this last scene where Daga is marked as the ultimate test. In her reading of this scene, Gopinath neglects to mention that Vijay and Ravi embrace over Daga's dead body forming a morbid triangle of friendship. In fact, Daga's crumpled and lifeless body is immortalized in the final frame of the movie that bears the words, "Thus friendship will live forever!" Daga, vanquished, preserves not only this friendship but *dostana*.

Emasculating the Third Man

Nevertheless, one cannot possibly miss the distinct otherness of these third men that is crucial to codifying male desire and highlighting the supremacy of the *dostana* shared by the two leading men. When Daga holds Ravi hostage, Daga admonishes him in a cruelly playful manner for defending Vijay in court. He says, "You didn't think how upset I would be. You've made a very big mistake." Daga follows this with a slap across Ravi's mouth, cracking his lip open. When Ravi begins to bleed, Daga makes a comforting, cooing noise. This cooing is instantly familiar to a Bollywood audience who would have undoubtedly seen and heard it in films where a mother attempts to comfort a child with a scraped knee. Daga then puckers his lips as he gently dabs Ravi's mouth with a handkerchief while coquettishly saying "Vo ... vo ... vo." This scene is reminiscent of countless others in Bollywood filmic history wherein the hero having single-handedly fought off a horde of bandits, flinches at the slightest touch of the heroine attempting to tend to his injuries. Such moments of physicality typically catalyze the heterosexual romance in Bollywood film. However, in *Dostana*, the insincerity and mockery laden in Daga's overtly feminized gesture reinstantiates the sanctity and robust masculinity of Ravi's relationship with Vijay. Yet, this emasculation of Daga is not without precedent in the film. Indeed, when Daga is providing Ravi with evidence of Vijay's relationship with Sheetal, Daga is bathed in garish pink lighting while he simpers at the possibility of unseating Vijay. The simultaneous emasculation and vilification of Daga's character makes the final moments of the film in which Vijay assaults him deeply disturbing. Beaten, Daga lies on the ground, a pile of cowardice and treachery, while Vijay towers over him exuding clean masculinity. Even in his moment of triumph over Daga, Vijay is too noble to kill a wounded man for he does not wish to take the law into his own hands. However, Daga forces Vijay's hand when he shoots at him with his last remaining pistol and Vijay must defend himself.

In 2008, when Abhi appears before the film's audience for the first time, he is awkwardly and abruptly thrust into the space of queer desire. A flamboyantly gay co-worker of Neha's (who we only see in this one moment of the film) exclaims in English upon seeing Abhi, "He's so hot!" There is nothing particularly unusual about today's Bollywood actor being attractive. However, in comparison to the two leading men in the film, Abhi is the most petite and possesses particularly delicate features. Unlike Abhi, Kunal is frequently semi-naked, exposing his bulky physique. In fact, the film opens with Kunal emerging from the ocean clad in a miniscule pair of yellow swimming briefs, shimmering with virility. The only sign of Abhi's virility is his child from his failed first marriage that ends when his wife abandons him for another man. Meanwhile, Kunal and Sameer appear to floor every woman that they meet. However, the most active emasculation of this third male takes place when Sameer and Kunal proceed to strip Abhi of the qualities that Neha confides she finds the most appealing about him. They take Abhi out of his pristine Armani suit and dress him in multi-colored, striped pants and a flimsy blouse for his date with Neha. The audience is encouraged to consume this vision of Abhi as the camera travels slowly from the bottom of his pants upwards, documenting this garish transformation. Sameer and Kunal appear to take the most pleasure in forcing Abhi to get his chest hair waxed. Here, Abhi's facial expression is captured in a rictus of torment as he screams while Sameer and Kunal guffaw in the background. This particular moment in the film is reminiscent of the macabre embrace that Vijay and Ravi share over a prostrate body.

Perusing the Dostana *Archive*

As Kunal and Sameer are walking in to file their residency permits at the Immigration and Naturalization Services, Sameer says, "Now don't tell me there wasn't anything between Munna and Circuit. I mean, come on. That was by far the most obvious one." This allusion to the dostana that exists between the protagonist Munna and his best friend, Circuit, in the 2003 film Munna Bhai M.B.B.S is casually dropped into this conversation between Kunal and Sameer with no explanation given or necessary. The film anticipates the audience's storehouse of filmic history when it comes to the dostana genre. Importantly, this is the first time that a Bollywood film has commented upon the very genre within which it exists as a space in which male desire percolates. When Kunal attempts to wrangle this allusion back into the space of pure fraternity by saying, "Circuit addresses Munna as brother," Sameer cheekily resists this rhetorical move. Sameer responds, "So? Even I call you brother in public" before giving Kunal a nudge. The self-reflexivity of this film is particularly crucial because it provides the characters with a language with which to configure queerness. In Deepa Mehta's Fire, Sita says to Radha, "There are no words in our language to describe what we are to each other." In her reading of this text against Ismat Chughtai's The Quilt in Impossible Desires: Queer Diasporas and South Asian Public Cultures, Gopinath takes critics to task for pouncing upon this sentence as a marker of utter backwardness. When Kunal and Sam are still barely friends and attempt to dupe Aunty with the claim that they are a couple, she cannot comprehend them nor can they find the words in Hindi to articulate this relationship. The conversation between the two men and Aunty begin with them saying, "We're both girls." When Aunty looks at them with horror, Sameer tries "Kunal and I are together" followed by "Kunal is a special friend of mine." Exasperated, Kunal blurts, "We're gay. He's my boyfriend." In this entire conversation that takes place in the first twenty minutes of the film, the only words that are in English are "gay" and "boyfriend." At this early stage of their friendship with each other, Kunal resorts to this Western formulation of queerness in order to register the fact that neither he nor Sameer would be a legitimate threat to Neha's honor. At this point in their friendship, Kunal and Sameer do not in fact have the words in Hindi to mark themselves as queer. However, moments prior to his reference to Munna Bhai M.B.B.S mentioned earlier, Sameer alludes to yet another founding film of the dostana genre, Sholay. Here, he tells Kunal, "We're two regular Gabbars." In this moment, Sameer actively and consciously queers the character Gabbar Singh from Sholay. Sameer repeatedly peruses the archive of the dostana genre in order to unearth a discourse of queerness that he may opportunistically use to upkeep the artifice of homosexuality.

Outside the Filmic Narrative?

While the narratives of these films end with framed shots of *dostana* preserved *for* males and *by* males, the narrative of *dostana* potentially seeps outside the very space and boundaries of the films themselves. When the cast of the 2008 *Dostana* was being interviewed by the producer of the film, Karan Johar, the initially imperceptible seepage of *dostana* outside the space of the film becomes increasingly visible as the interview progresses. The very title of the movie ceaselessly taps into the Bollywood audience's familiarity with the form of this genre and its founding fathers. Indeed in an industry brokered by dynasties, paternity matters. Abhishek Bachchan is the scion of Amitabh Bachchan's acting empire. Bachchan's empire was built in large part by dostana films. Meanwhile, Karan Johar, the producer of *Dostana*, is the son of Yash Johar, the producer of the 1980 *Dostana*. However, by naming the film *Dostana*, it returns the audience to one of the originating films of the genre.[1] Johar inhabits the role that the third male bears in these films. Johar is instrumental in marking the space of *dostana* as an exclusively male space and repeatedly highlighting the supremacy of that male friendship. At the beginning of the interview, Johar does not simply invite the entire cast to come onstage. Instead, he segments the cast such that it is actress Priyanka Chopra who comes on for the first five minutes by herself, followed by John Abraham *and* Abhishek Bachchan, and finally Bobby Deol. Asked why she was "traumatized" when she had to share the Miami apartment with her two male co-stars, Chopra replied, "Because they completely ignored me. They were so into each other so they totally ignored me." He uses Chopra's lament of being completely disregarded by her co-stars as a neat segue to invite Abraham and Bachchan on stage. "Shall we call them on and ask them why they left you all alone? Shattered? Let's find out why Priyanka Chopra was left all alone on the set and the boys had all the fun." Chopra's tongue-in-cheek complaint can be easily dismissed as nothing more than a case of being the only girl at the boys' party. Yet, this unmistakable pattern where the interviewer repeatedly marks her as outside the circuits of *dostana* persists. In a segment called Truth and Dare, the interviewer poses a series of challenges to each actor. Abraham is asked to look into the eyes of Bachchan and to sing a love song to him while

Bachchan is subsequently asked to propose to Abraham. It was particularly striking that Bachchan saw no need to inhabit his screen character in order to propose to Abraham. He proposed to Abraham rather than to Kunal. In fact, Bachchan makes specific references both to his own wife and to Abraham's girlfriend during this proposal. Bachchan reminds Abraham that while their respective partners are "hot," he would let Abraham "watch the Sports Channel" and would refrain from "shopping spree[s]." While Abraham and Bachchan's respective dares firmly ensconce them in the simultaneously homosocial and homoerotic space of *dostana*, Chopra's dare to sing a song "sexily" to the interviewer excises her from that privileged space. The only moment in which Chopra is briefly drawn into that space is during Bachchan's proposal to Abraham where Bachchan assures him, "If we ever need someone to do our washing and cleaning, we have Priyanka." In the final moments of the interview, when the third male co-star, Bobby Deol is invited on stage, Bachchan confirms that the film is indeed a love triangle as is the case in the 1980 *Dostana*. He says, "There's John, myself and Bobby. Priyanka is just there for the poster to sell a few more tickets." Bachchan even draws attention to the visual uniformity of the three male actors dressed in all-black suits. When the interviewer points out that he too is dressed like them, Bachchan alters his initial formulation of the love triangle to a "love rectangle" that includes Johar. How apropos that the men of *Dostana* find themselves in a love rectangle! With the script and cast of the sequel to the film finalized, there will be 4 men pursuing a new leading lady. The search for a new heroine was exhaustive. Finally, Dharma Productions simply chose to go with the actress who had the most hits from Google searches. They felt that Katrina Kaif's "most hit" status on the Internet makes it apt for her to play the role of the "most hit" girl by the boys in *Dostana 2*. Thus, while the space for *dostana* briefly expands to include Deol and Johar, the elasticity stops short of Chopra and her red dress.

Conclusion

It is worth considering that the increased occlusion of both Neha and Sheetal that Abhi and Daga precipitate may be symptomatic of a shifting cinematic space both onscreen and offscreen. Ashok Row Kavi, the editor-in-chief of *Bombay Dost,* India's "oldest registered gay news magazine," suggests that "the Bollywood hero has been (particularly in the past three decades) the focus of increased homoeroticization ... rather than another filmic character falling in love with the hero, the audience itself is invited to see the macho hero as unattached and therefore available for homoerotic desire" (307). A worthwhile addendum to Kavi's argument is that it is not simply a question of the hero being "unattached," he must be unattached to a woman at the end of the narrative. It is both acceptable and desirable that he remains deeply attached to his male friend. Raj Rao addresses the increased masculinization of the Indian cinema-hall space with the onset of what he calls the "action era" in Bollywood cinema during the 80s. Raj Rao does not make note of this but the onset of this era coincides with the genesis of *dostana* narratives and the actual production of the 1980 *Dostana*. He suggests that women were less interested in films of this genre and chose to indulge in more intimate viewings of their screen idols within the space of the home. "If women wanted to see *Sholay* or *Zanjeer* (and indeed Amitabh Bachchan was the heart-throb of many of them), all they had to do was borrow a video cassette of the film from a neighborhood video library and see it in the privacy of their own homes, far away from the lecherous cat-calls of men in the cinema-hall" (303). Raj Rao's filmic examples are significant in that they point to a misstep in his explanation behind the decrease in women peopling cinema-halls. *Sholay* and *Zanjeer* are two founding films in the dostana genre that coalesce the narrative of friendship with that of the action narrative. Thus, what Raj Rao sees as disinterest in a genre (or two) may have been a disinterest in a less than welcoming cinema-hall that was filled with "the lecherous cat-calls of men." However, Karan Johar's comment regarding Priyanka Chopra's performance in the 2008 *Dostana* is potentially telling. "You walked out in that swimming costume, *not* bikini, and there were cat-calls in cinema-halls across the country." Almost ten years after Raj Rao's article, the most familiar and audible sound in a cinema-hall is a cat-call. The combination of these two factors both onscreen and offscreen is by no means meant to be a conclusive or substantial answer to the questions that these alternative schemas of male desire raise in this essay. However, it does begin to tease the implications of a cinema space that is increasingly masculinized and eroticized and invites us to consider how the homoeroticism of the genre may offer a viable language with which to narrate male queerness.

Notes

1. Abhishek Bachchan and Karan Johar engage in an extended discussion of the titling of this movie during this interview. I have transcribed that particular segment of the interview. **Abhishek Bachchan to Karan Johar:** I remember the day we were sitting in your cabin, and there was Tarun, yourself and we were sitting there and having some lunch and the whole discussion was what do we title this film and everybody was racking their brain for a couple of months and suddenly you said "I've thought of something. What about Dostana?" And I said great. I'm going to call Hiro Aunty and tell her. And I thought yeah fantastic, great, friendship, Tarun loves it ... so I called up Hiro aunty. "We've decided the title of the film." She said, "What is it?" I said it's Dostana and she started crying. And

that's when it dawned on me, wait a second ... we have something to live up to over here, there is this legacy, there is this one great film that has already been made and we shouldn't mess it up. We have to be responsible and so we went in and then did the complete opposite... [Laughter].

References

"Date with Dostana" December 25, 2008. http://www.youtube.com/watch?v=p5Gv9HkeZc0 &feature=fvw.

Dostana. Dir. Raj. Khosla. Prod. Johar Yash. Perf. Bachchan, Amitabh, Shatrughan Sinha, Zeenat Aman, et al. 1980.

Dostana. Dir. Tarun Mansukhani. Prod. Johar Karan. Perf. Bachchan, Abhishek, John Abraham, Priyanka Chopra, et al. Dharma Productions, 2008.

Gopinath, Gayatri (2000). "Queering Bollywood: Alternative Sexualities in Popular Indian Cinema." *Queer Asian Cinema: Shadows in the Shade*. (Ed.) Andrew Grossman. New York: Harrington Park Press, 283–299.

_____ (2005). *Impossible Desires: Queer Diasporas and South Asian Public Cultures*. Durham, NC: Duke University Press.

Jha, Priya (2003). "Lyrical Nationalism: Gender, Friendship, and Excess in 1970s Hindi Cinema." *The Velvet Light Trap* 51: 43–53.

Kavi, Ashok Row (2000). "The Changing Image of the Hero in Hindi Films." *Queer Asian Cinema: Shadows in the Shade*. (Ed.) Andrew Grossman. New York: Harrington Park Press, 307–313.

Munna Bhai M.B.B.S. Dir. Rajkumar Hirani. Prod. Vidhu Vinod Chopra. Perf. Sanjay Dutt, Arshad Warsi, Jimmy Shergill, Sunil Dutt, Gracy Singh. Vinod Chopra Productions, 2003.

Raj Rao, R. (2009). "Memories Pierce the Heart: Homoeroticism, Bollywood-Style." *Queer Asian Cinema: Shadows in the Shade*. (Ed.) Andrew Grossman. New York: Harrington Park Press, 299–307.

Sedgwick, Eve Kosofsky (1985). *Between Men: English Literature and Male Homosocial Desire*. New York: Columbia University Press.

Sholay. Dir. Ramesh Sippy. Prod. G. P. Sippy. Perf. Dharmendra, Amitabh Bachchan, Hema Malini, Sanjeev Kumar. Sippy Films, 1975.

Zanjeer. Dir. Prakash Mehra. Prod. Prakash Mehra. Perf. Amitabh Bachchan, Jaya Bachchan, Pran. Asha Studios, 1973.

About the Contributors

David A. **Ansari** received a master's degree from the London School of Economics. He was also a Fulbright fellow in Dakar, Senegal. He is pursuing a Ph.D. in comparative human development at the University of Chicago, where he also teaches. He was previously a researcher at King's College London.

Tanmayee **Banerjee** is pursuing a Ph.D. at the University of Westminster (UK) and was a lecturer at Bidhan Chandra College (India). She recently presented "Nationalism and Internationalism in Indian English Fiction, 1909–1930" at the Royal Asiatic Society of Great Britain and Northern Ireland as a part of their Student Lecture Series.

Niladri R. **Chatterjee** is head of the Department of English, University of Kalyani (India). He is the co-editor of *Muffled Hearts: Stories of the Disempowered Male* (2005) and has contributed to *The Oxford Dictionary of National Biography* (2004), *The Isherwood Century* (2000) and *The Reader's Companion to Twentieth Century Writers* (1995).

Rohit K. **Dasgupta** is an associate lecturer and Ph.D. candidate at the University of the Arts London and a visiting lecturer at the University of West London. His writing has been published in the journals *Digital Culture and Education* and *Asian Affairs* and the edited collection *Cartographies of Affect: Across Borders in South Asia and the Americas* (2011).

Sayantan **Dasgupta** is an assistant professor in the Department of Comparative Literature, Jadavpur University (India). He is the author of *Indian English Literature: A Study in Historiography* (2006) and *Shyam Selvadurai: Texts and Contexts* (2007). His edited volumes include *A South Asian Nationalism Reader* (2007), *Readings* (2002) and *(Re)views* (2003).

Roshan **das Nair** received a Ph.D. from the University of Nottingham (UK) where he is a senior research tutor. He trained at the National Institute of Mental Health and Neurosciences (India) and is a consultant clinical psychologist with Nottingham University Hospitals NHS Trust. He co-edited *Intersectionality, Sexuality, and Psychological Therapies* (2012).

Aniruddha **Dutta** is an assistant professor in gender, women and sexuality studies at the University of Iowa. His writing has been published in journals including *Gender and History*, *Jindal Global Review*, *Wide Screen* and the edited collections *Law Like Love: Queer Perspectives on Law* (2010) and *Out of Place: Interrogating Silences in Queerness/Raciality* (2008.

K. Moti **Gokulsing** is a former reader in education and senior visiting research fellow at the University of East London. He is the founder and co-editor of the journal *South Asian Popular Culture*. His books include *A Handbook of Indian Cinema* (2013) and *From Aan to Lagaan and Beyond: A Guide to the Study of Indian Cinema* (2012).

Dashini **Jeyathurai** is pursuing a joint Ph.D. in English and women's studies at the University of Michigan, Ann Arbor. Her dissertation examines questions of citizenship and statelessness of Indians in English language Malaysian literature.

Akhil **Katyal** completed a Ph.D. in South Asian studies from the School of Oriental and African Studies (SOAS), University of London. He is based in Delhi where he teaches literature at St. Stephen's College, Delhi University. His bilingual Hindi and English poetry collection is forthcoming with Vani Prakashan.

Mangesh **Kulkarni** teaches in the Department of Politics and Public Administration, University of Pune (India). His research interest is in critical masculinity studies. He is an international advisory editor of the journal *Men and Masculinities*. His latest book is the edited volume *Interdisciplinary Perspectives in Political Theory* (2011).

Kama **Maureemootoo** lives in Canada and holds graduate degrees from the University of Pune and Trent University (Canada) where he completed his thesis *(Re)imagining the Past, (Re)mapping the Nation: Masculinity and the Nationalist Imaginary in the Indian Subcontinent*.

Pranta Pratik **Patnaik** is an assistant professor in the Department of Culture and Media Studies, School of Social Sciences, Central University of Rajasthan (India). He has published widely on visual representations of gender and trafficking.

Vishnupriya **Sengupta** received a Ph.D. from Jadavpur University (India) where she wrote her dissertation on V.S. Naipaul. She was a postdoctoral research fellow at the University degli Studi di Milano and has guest edited a special edition of the *Journal of Caribbean Studies* on V.S. Naipaul.

Sanjay **Srivastava** is a professor of sociology at the Institute of Economic Growth, Delhi. He is the author of *Constructing Post-colonial India: National Character and the Doon School* (1998), co-author of *Asia: Cultural Politics in the Global Age* (2001), and a contributing editor of *Sexual Sites, Seminal Attitudes* (2004).

Index